Mary Berry's Ultimate Cake Book

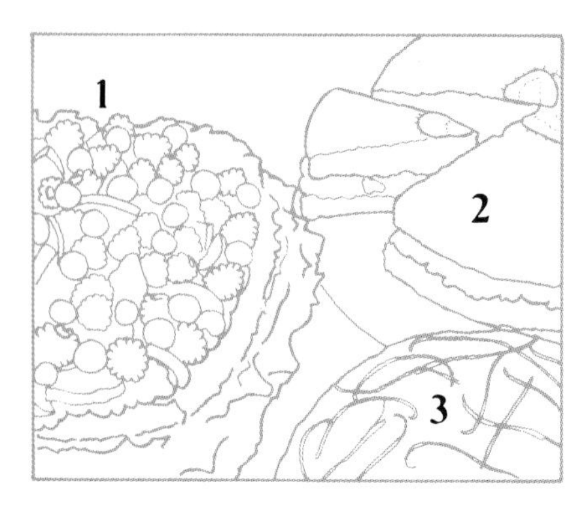

Summer Selection

1 *Pavlova (page 66)*

2 *Wimbledon Cake (page 102)*

3 *Double Orange Cake (page 202)*

Mary Berry's Ultimate Cake Book

Over 200 Classic Recipes

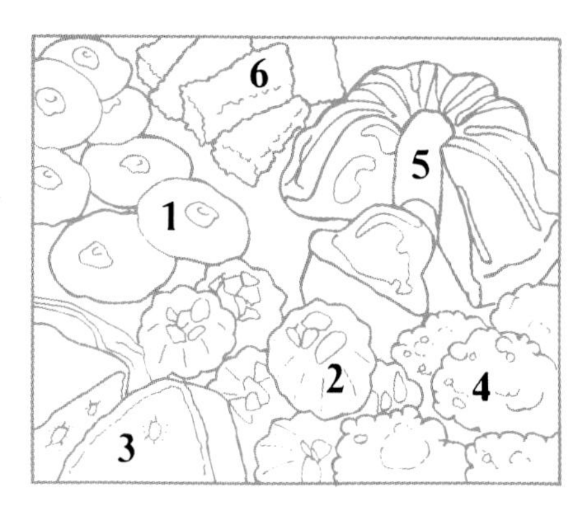

Winter Selection

1 *Melting Moments* (*pages 150–51*)

2 *Coburg Buns* (*page 297*)

3 *English Cherry Cake* (*page 201*)

4 *Traditional Rock Cakes* (*page 217*)

5 *Marbled Chocolate Ring Cake* (*page 37*)

6 *Fast Flapjacks* (*pages 152–3*)

The warmest of thanks are due to Fiona Oyston, who has
helped me enormously with the testing and tasting of all the cakes in this book.
She worked at the Good Housekeeping Institute, where home baking is still very much valued,
and this has been reflected in her meticulous and unstinting professionalism.

This edition first published in 2003 by BBC Books, an imprint of Ebury Publishing
A Random House Group Company

The Random House Group Limited Reg. No. 954009

Addresses for companies within the Random House Group can be found at
www.randomhouse.co.uk

A CIP catalogue record for this book is available from the British Library

Edited by Susan Fleming
Designed by Grahame Dudley
Photographs by Philip Webb
Cakes and biscuits made by Sarah Ramsbottom
Illustrations by Barbara Hampton
Project editor for second edition: Rebecca Hardie

The Random House Group Limited supports The Forest Stewardship Council (FSC®),
the leading international forest certification organisation. All our titles that are printed
on Greenpeace approved FSC® certified paper carry the FSC logo.
Our paper procurement policy can be found at www.rbooks.co.uk/environment

Printed and bound in China by C&C Offset Printing Co., Ltd.
ISBN 978 0 563 48751 7
24

Contents

Introduction

When I first collected together the recipes for my *Ultimate Cake Book*, my aim was to inspire a whole new generation of cooks to discover the delights of home baking. Little did I realise, however, just how enthusiastically the book would be received or that now, almost 10 years on, I would be releasing a revised edition. I am, of course, delighted that so many people have enjoyed using the book and I do hope that many more of you will continue to find it useful.

Cake making is often thought of as a difficult and complex method of cooking. This is because you need to follow the measurements and instructions very precisely. But if you are accurate, stick to the recipe, and you keep some general 'rules' in mind, you should enjoy success every time. To help you get to grips with these rules, I've included a general introductory section in this book which includes comprehensive information on cake-making ingredients, equipment and the different techniques that are used in my recipes. Once you've read this section you'll be truly equipped to get baking. There is a diverse selection of cake recipes – some traditional, some old favourites with a twist, and lots of my own unique recipes – all have been thoroughly tested and appreciated. If there is a potential trouble spot or tricky technique involved, I have suggested tips and ideas to help you cope. Where possible, I have simplified the methods, and the finishes and decorations which can often be awkward, are easy to do, but remain stylish.

The popularity of cake making is constantly growing. More and more cake and cake icing and decorating books are filling our bookshelves, and magazines are available, overflowing with delicious recipes and mouthwatering photographs to tempt us. I don't find this new-found enthusiasm particularly surprising, for home baking has never been easier than it is now: methods and techniques have been simplified; good quality, reliable ingredients are readily available; and most modern kitchens are now equipped with gadgets such as electric food mixers and processors to speed things up. In the old days, cake making used to be a rather more difficult and time-consuming task, involving creaming butter and sugar by hand (taking up to 30 minutes!), meticulously preparing tins, and persuading untrustworthy ovens to produce and maintain the correct temperature. Nowadays, due to the introduction of fan ovens, modern non-stick tins and trays and fancy decorating utensils, virtually none of this is necessary – a cake can be prepared and baked in no time at all, ready for devouring at a special celebration, a picnic or a simple family tea.

The recipes in this book cover every occasion possible where a cake, bake or biscuit might be required. There are sumptuous chocolate cakes for an irresistible treat, lighter alternatives such as cheesecakes and crisp meringues, cakes for special celebrations such as Christmas, weddings and birthdays, Continental specialities, as well as family cakes

and homely scones, small cakes for children's parties or packed lunches, traybakes for selling at your local fête, and melt-in-the-mouth biscuits and cakes which would make ideal gifts.

Whether you're a beginner or an experienced cake-maker, there will be many cakes here that you will enjoy baking time and time again, and which your family and friends will definitely enjoy eating! This is a book to *use,* so have fun baking!

Mary Berry

Cake-making Ingredients

The best quality ingredients are needed to make cakes that taste as fresh and as good as possible.

Fats

Butter and margarine are the usual fats used in cake making, but lard, blended white vegetable fat and oil can also be used.

Butter

It is not always necessary to use butter to obtain the best results, but it must be used where a buttery flavour is all important, for instance in shortbread. I tend to use a salted or lightly salted butter – the unsalted kind is far too expensive! The temperature of butter is crucial to the success of a cake mix. Butter needs to be left at room temperature for at least 30 minutes before using in a creaming method. Even then it is often best to cream the butter alone to soften it further before adding the sugar.

If rubbing in for pastry, say, cut the cold butter into pieces, or grate it into the flour. Use softened butter for the all-in-one method.

Butter can be stored in the freezer.

Soft Baking Margarine

These have improved greatly and now have a good flavour, and cakes made with them have excellent keeping qualities. They are specifically useful for the all-in-one method of cake making.

For all cake making, use either a baking margarine at room temperature, or a spread with a high percentage of fat i.e. 70–72 per cent, straight from the fridge. If making cakes by hand, the fat should be slightly softer than if using a mixer.

Whatever brand you choose, always check the side of the packet for any instructions. It is very easy to pick up a low-fat spread by mistake, and these are not suitable for baking due to their high water content.

Hard or Block Margarine

Block margarines vary in their degree of hardness according to the brand; look for one which has been manufactured specifically for baking purposes. Block margarines are best used in the melting or rubbed-in methods; see *Butter* notes for ways of using. They can also be used when the flavour of the fat doesn't matter too much, when the cake has a strong flavour of its own, such as in a chocolate cake or parkin.

Oils

Cakes made using oil are very easy, and tend to be very moist. Choose a light oil with almost no flavour such as ground-nut or sunflower oil.

Cakes with oil need a little extra raising agent to prevent heaviness, and this can be in the form of baking powder or whisked egg whites.

Flours

Many types of flour are available and the difference between them is largely due to the gluten content and also any added raising agents. Gluten is a protein which becomes elastic and sticky when the flour is moistened. It sets when heated, trapping air in the mixture and giving a light texture.

Whatever kind of flour you buy, do pay attention to the use-by date: after that the flour will not be so good.

Plain and Self-raising Flour

For cake making, a flour with a low gluten content is used as it is more starchy, absorbing fat well, to give a light, soft texture. Ordinary plain and self-raising flours are of this type, and are therefore used for cakes. There are other 'cake flours', but the formulae used in these tend to vary, so you may find them less reliable.

Always sift flour when making cakes. This

is not to remove lumps as most flour is not lumpy, but it lightens the flour by incorporating air.

Wholemeal Flour

Wholemeal or brown flours can also be used in cake making. They give a coarser texture but add a delicious nutty flavour. Brown self-raising flour is now widely available and is the best one to use for wholefood cakes.

Strong Flour

Strong flour has the highest gluten content and is used for bread making and for some pastry. It is not used for cakes.

Other Flours

For various types of cakes, I use different types of flour, among them semolina, cornflour and rice flour: these are good in a shortbread for instance, adding to the crunchy texture. Buckwheat flour has a rather strong flavour, but is delicious in a courgette loaf (see *page 293*); potato flour can be useful, too.

Raising Agents

There are many agents which help make cakes rise, but the chief among them are baking powder, bicarbonate of soda and easy-blend dried yeast.

Baking Powder

This is the raising agent most commonly added in cake making. It consists of an acid (usually cream of tartar) and an alkali (bicarbonate of soda) mixed with a dried starch or flour. When moistened the chemicals react to produce carbon dioxide which expands during baking, making the cake rise.

The baking powders which are on the market today contain a slower-acting raising agent which is more tolerant if mixtures are made up and left before baking. If it is more convenient, make up the cake mixture, then bake it later.

Don't be tempted to add more baking powder than the recipe specifies or the mixture will rise well at first but will then collapse, resulting in a heavy, close-textured cake.

Bicarbonate of Soda (Baking Soda)

This can be used alone as a raising agent in cakes with a strong flavour, such as gingerbread, where the bitter flavour of the soda is masked, and where it can react with the natural acids present in ingredients such as black treacle, lemon juice or buttermilk.

Cream of Tartar

This is not used alone as a raising agent, but is sometimes used with bicarbonate of soda in recipes to replace baking powder.

Easy-blend Dried Yeast

This is the easiest of all the yeasts to use: simply mix it with the flour and then add the liquid. It keeps well, but do not allow it to go beyond the use-by date.

However, if you do use ordinary dried yeast, follow the manufacturer's instructions when adding liquid. I'm afraid you will find this a more lengthy process.

Eggs

Large eggs are used in the recipes unless otherwise specified. If your kitchen is warm, keep the eggs in the fridge, but allow them to come to room temperature before using.

If you keep ducks, you can use their eggs in recipes, depending on size.

While the proven risks of healthy people becoming ill from eating fresh raw eggs is minimal, the elderly, pregnant women, the sick and the very young should not do so just in case.

Sugars and Other Sweeteners

I like to use the more natural sugars in my cake making, such as golden caster and golden granulated – there is so much more flavour – but there is now a huge variety of sugars and sweeteners available which can add different textures and some interesting flavours.

Caster Sugar

This is the sugar used most commonly in cake making but especially for whisked sponge cakes, creamed mixtures and meringues. The small, regular grain ensures that it blends smoothly in mixing to give an even texture.

Granulated Sugar

This has a coarser texture than caster, and is best used for rubbed-in cake mixtures or in melting methods. If used in a creamed mixture it will give a slight grittiness and a speckled appearance to the cake. Neither would the cake have such a good volume.

Icing Sugar

Although usually associated only with cake icings, icing sugar is a vital ingredient for *meringue cuite* where the fine sugar crystals are easily dissolved when whisked with the egg whites. It is not generally used for basic cake mixtures as it produces a poor volume and a hard crust.

It is essential to use icing sugar in cake icings, although we now have the option of buying ready-made royal icing.

Muscovado Sugars

Muscovado sugars are traditionally made from raw cane sugar, and the colour and flavour vary according to molasses content.

Light muscovado is excellent to use in many cakes as it creams well and has a lovely caramely flavour. Brown sugar meringues, using half soft brown sugar and half caster sugar, are particularly delicious.

Dark muscovado sugar easily overpowers other flavours and therefore needs to be used with care. It gives an excellent flavour and colour to gingerbreads and rich fruit cakes.

To prevent muscovado sugars from going hard, put a damp piece of kitchen paper or J-cloth in the bag or jar.

Demerara Sugar

This is traditionally unrefined, but it has a fairly low molasses content, thus is light in colour. It is most suitable for use in cakes made by the melting method where heat and moisture dissolve the large crystals. It can also be used in rubbed-in mixtures but not successfully in creamed mixtures as the large crystals do not break down sufficiently during the mixing. It is also useful for sprinkling on top of cakes and to add crunch to cheesecake bases.

Nibbed Sugar

The nibs were the rough-shaped 'shavings' that fell from the early form of cut cubes. It is useful as a topping for cakes before baking, but you can use crushed sugar cubes or lumps instead.

Golden Syrup and Black Treacle

These are made from selected refinery liquor after the refined sugar has been crystallized. Golden syrup is light and sweet; treacle, which has added cane molasses, is very much darker and stronger.

Condensed Milk

This is used as a sweetener in some recipes. It is canned milk from which half the water content has been removed, and to which sugar has been added. (It makes wonderful toffee and fudge.)

Malt Extract

Made from powdered malt reduced to a syrup, malt extract helps the action of carbon dioxide in bread making, and adds a sweet flavour.

Honey

The world's oldest sweetner, use a clear or runny honey in cake making, as this dissolves more quickly.

Vanilla Sugar

This adds a wonderful flavour to many cakes. Simply store two or three vanilla pods in a jar of caster sugar. After about a couple of weeks, the sugar is imbued with the pungency of the vanilla; as you use the sugar, simply top up the jar with more.

Dairy Produce

This includes milks, creams, yoghurts and cheeses.

Milks

The liquid in many of my recipes is milk, and I just use my ordinary doorstep variety. If you are watching your weight, a lower-fat milk such as semi-skimmed will work just as well.

Buttermilk can be found in good supermarkets. It is pasteurized skimmed milk which has been treated with a culture to produce an acidity ideal for certain breads and scones.

Creams

I never use synthetic creams. I normally use whipping cream for filling cakes – it is healthier and cheaper than double – but double is best if you want to pipe the cream into cake decorations. Whipping cream *will* hold its shape, but not for as long as double. If adding brandy or other flavouring to a cream for whipping, use double. Cream is best whipped from cold.

Single and soured creams also have their uses in cake making. *Crème fraîche* is, literally fresh cream, but it is cream treated with a culture to give it a light acidity. It is lighter than double cream and is available in half-fat and full-fat.

Yoghurt

You can use low- or full-fat natural or plain yoghurt, whichever you please. The full-fat, or Greek-style, yoghurt has the best flavour.

For reasons of both health and economy, I often use half whipped cream and half low-fat natural yoghurt as the filling for a cake. Remember, though, that yoghurt is wetter than cream so if you want a firmer filling use full-fat natural yoghurt.

Soft Cheeses

For cheesecakes, use low-fat or full-fat soft cheese, whichever you like. Curd cheese, with its slightly tart flavour, is useful, too. For healthier, but less tasty, cheesecakes, cottage cheese can sometimes be used if it is made smooth by processing or sieving.

The texture of *fromage frais*, made from skimmed cows' milk and sometimes enriched with cream, can vary from firm, to floppy and pourable. You can use it to great effect in cheesecakes as a substitute for low-fat soft cheese.

Hard Cheeses

Perhaps surprisingly in a cake book, some hard cheeses are used, in savoury scones, cheese straws etc. Mature Cheddar and Parmesan are particularly flavourful.

Chocolate

The different types of chocolate and their uses are discussed in detail in the introduction to Chapter 1, Glorious Chocolate Cakes (see *page 30*).

Spices

Ready-blended spices such as mixed spice are useful to have for general flavouring, but some recipes call for individual spices such as ground cinnamon, ginger and cloves. All spices should be as fresh as possible, and have an even better flavour when freshly ground. Buy in small quantities and replace often. Store them in the dark. Keep whole nutmeg in particular to grate freshly when needed.

Stem ginger is particularly useful in a few recipes. If you like the flavour use the ginger itself and the syrup lavishly!

Dried Fruit

Today, much of the dried fruit that we buy has been dried by artificial heat rather than the sun. Mineral oils are sometimes sprayed on to the fruits after drying to give them a glossy appearance and to prevent them sticking together. Try to buy dried fruit which has been treated with vegetable oils instead. Most dried fruit now comes ready washed, but it is wise to quickly pick over the fruit to remove any small pieces of stalk.

Dried fruit can dry out once the packet is opened, so store in an airtight container, or freeze in polythene bags to keep the maximum flavour. Mixed peel keeps better this way, and dried apricots don't darken in colour.

Whole candied peel has much more flavour than the ready mixed chopped peel and can be bought in good delicatessens and health-food stores. If the peel is hard and sugary, run it under the hot tap for a few seconds to soften it, then dry and chop. I use scissors to chop the peel roughly, and then a sharp knife if finer chopped peel is needed.

If you do a lot of baking, buy dried fruits separately – currants, raisins, peel etc. – and mix up your own mixed dried fruit. This can be cheaper, and means you have the individual proportions you particularly like.

Glacé cherries should be halved or quartered then washed and thoroughly dried before putting in a cake mixture, as this prevents them sinking to the bottom.

Nuts

A wide variety of nuts are used in cake baking and decorating, either whole, chopped, shredded, flaked or ground, to add flavour and texture. However, nuts are expensive and have a short shelf life, quickly going rancid in a warm kitchen. Use the freezer as an extra storecupboard, or keep small quantities in airtight containers, preferably in the fridge. Whole shelled nuts keep for up to five years in the freezer, flaked and ground almonds for one year. Shake out only what is required and pop the remainder back.

Nuts bought in their shells should feel heavy; if they are light, then they are probably stale.

Walnut pieces can now be bought, and they are cheaper than whole shelled nuts if they are to be chopped.

Toasting Nuts

The best way to toast nuts, such as flaked almonds, is under the grill, but they do need to be watched very carefully. You need to turn them frequently with a long-handled palette knife to obtain a good even colour and also to prevent them from burning.

Coconut is also best toasted in this way but be warned, it browns and then burns very quickly.

Whole hazelnuts are best browned in the oven to remove their skins. Rub them briskly in a tea towel to remove the skins and return any stubborn nuts to the oven for a little longer if necessary.

Essences and Flavourings

I see no reason why one should use an expensive essence when the real thing is so often close to hand – for instance, fresh lemons, or the alcohol itself (rum, brandy, Kirsch, sherry etc.). Vanilla and almond essences can play a part in baking, but often you could use some vanilla-flavoured sugar instead (see *Sugars* on *page 14*). Coffee essence can be bought, but liquid coffee is also good; or you could use instant coffee, powder or granules, but it has to be dissolved in a little hot water first.

Other Ingredients

There are many different cake-making ingredients apart from the basics above. Always try to buy the best – this will pay you dividends in texture and flavour.

Cereals

Bought cereals lend texture to many cakes, cake bases and other cake elements. These include rolled oats, medium oatmeal, muesli and All-Bran. Cornflakes and rice krispies are particularly useful for little children's cakes.

Biscuits

Bought biscuits are invaluable, mostly for cheesecake crusts or bases: I use digestive, chocolate digestive, ginger and coconut biscuits, and Hob Nobs. Each adds their own distinctive flavour and texture to the finished cheesecake.

Jams and Other Preserves

Jams and lemon curd are usually employed as fillings for cakes, and you should obviously use what you have: bought or home-made. Bought lemon curd is often like a thick synthetic lemon custard; instead buy lemon cheese which is more like home-made lemon curd. Vary the jams according to taste and to the season: a cake filled with blackcurrant jam would be lovely decorated with some fresh blackcurrants.

Marmalade is often used as an integral part of the cake itself, but you must choose the variety carefully. The better makes of marmalade are those with a high proportion of fruit. Check the labels for information.

Apricot jam is invaluable in cake making (see *page 29*).

Fresh Fruit

I use a surprisingly large amount of fresh fruit in my cake making, as toppings and fillings, and often as an integral part of the cake itself (banana, for instance). Choose fruits in season and use them lavishly.

Vegetables

In a few recipes, I use vegetables as a flavouring or major ingredient. Carrots are well known for their inclusion in sweet cakes, but I also use potatoes and marrow or courgettes in lovely savoury recipes.

Gelatine

I use the powdered variety when making uncooked cheesecakes. I describe how to use this in the introduction to Chapter 5, Cheesecakes (see *page 110*).

Cake-making Equipment

Specialist equipment is not necessary for cake making, but there are a few basic essentials which help to make life so much easier.

Baking Equipment

A lot of equipment you will already have, and some you can improvise. Always buy the best you can possibly afford; this will be worthwhile in the long run.

Cake Tins

Choose good quality, strong, solid cake tins, as these will last you a lifetime. Cheap cake tins are likely to be very thin, may warp with use and do not conduct heat evenly.

Non-stick cake tins are easy to clean, but it is wise still to follow the recipe instructions for greasing and lining, and not to rely solely on the tin's non-stick properties. Choose black-lined tins, as these conduct the heat better.

Loose-bottomed cake tins are excellent for cake making, but avoid the ones with thick insulated bases as they stop the cake cooking evenly in a modern cooker. They're meant to prevent cakes burning on the bottom, but they also slow the cooking down.

Choosing the correct size of cake tin for the recipe is of paramount importance. So often a cake fails simply because the cake tin was the wrong size. The depth of a cake tin is particularly important for sponge cakes; if the cake tin is too shallow for the cake mixture, then the cake will spill over and lose its shape. Too deep a cake tin will give a pale, flat-looking cake. If you do not have the size of tin specified, then choose a cake tin which is slightly larger and test the cake 5–10 minutes earlier, as the shallower cake will take less time to cook.

If you want to adapt a recipe to a different sized tin or container, the easiest way to do this is to fill the specified cake tin with water up to the top of where the cake mixture would be and then pour it into the tin that you want to use. If the water overfills the tin then it is obviously too small. Remember also that cakes cooked in different shaped tins may take a longer or shorter time to cook; the cooking time for a cake in a ring mould will be less than in a deep cake tin as the many sides of the tin conduct the heat more efficiently through the cake.

All the recipes in this book use one or other of the following cake tins.

2 × 7 in (18 cm) deep round sandwich tins
3 × 8 in (20 cm) deep round sandwich tins
2 × 9 in (23 cm) deep round sandwich tins
These should preferably be non-stick, and are best with loose bases.

8–9 in (20–23 cm) flan tins
11 in (28 cm) flan tin
If you do a lot of baking get both deep and shallow, and they're best with loose bases.

1 × 6 in (15 cm) deep round cake tin
1 × 7 in (18 cm) deep round cake tin
1 × 8 in (20 cm) deep round cake tin
1 × 9 in (23 cm) deep round cake tin
1 × 12 in (30 cm) deep round cake tin
All these should preferably be non-stick, and are best with loose bases.

1 × 8 in (20 cm) round loose-bottomed or spring-release tin
1 × 9 in (23 cm) round loose-bottomed or spring-release tin
1 × 10 in (25 cm) round loose-bottomed or spring-release tin

1 × 7 in (18 cm) shallow square cake tin

1 × 7 in (18 cm) deep square cake tin

12 × 9 in (30 × 23 cm) roasting tin (for traybakes)

$14\frac{1}{2} \times 11\frac{1}{2}$ in (36×29 cm) roasting tin (for traybakes)

11 × 7 in (28 × 18 cm) Swiss roll tin
13 × 9 in (33 × 23 cm) Swiss roll tin

2 × 1 lb (450 g) loaf tins
2 × 2 lb (900 g) loaf tins

3 pt (1.75 litre) capacity ring mould

At least 2 bun or patty tins (these can have from 12–20 containers, and can be fluted or plain). If you make mince pies you may like to choose fairly deep ones.

12 deep muffin tins

1 French madeleine tray

at least 6 dariole moulds – if you are likely to use them!

If you haven't any cake tins – but I hope that after reading some of the recipes in the book you'll want to invest in some – you can improvise. Look for something like an oven glass soufflé dish with straight sides and cover it on the outside with a double layer of foil, folding and pressing it in to fit snugly. Take the foil 'baking dish' off the glass dish and stand it on a baking tray. Grease it well and fill it as you would a conventional cake tin. Similarly, if you have only one cake tin or roasting tin, and the recipe requires two, you can make its twin as above.

Baking Trays

At least three baking trays are essential. I like these to be flat, or perhaps with a slight turn-up at one end. They should be rigid and heavy – and the right size for your oven!

Wire Racks

At least two are vital for cooling cakes once they have been baked: round ones are available which look quite attractive when hung on the wall, but large rectangular ones are better. Or you can, of course, use the rack from your grill pan.

Griddle

If you make a lot of drop scones or griddle cakes, a griddle is invaluable, and a variety of types are available. But a heavy-based, non-stick frying-pan will do just as well.

Ovens

Finally, although perhaps it should be first, an absolutely essential piece of baking equipment is your oven.

Regrettably, no two ovens are the same whether they are gas, electric or fan assisted. All the recipes in this book were tested in a conventional oven. Particular care is needed with the timing of fan ovens as they can all too quickly dry out a cake by overcooking. Most fan oven manufacturers recommend lowering the specified temperature in the recipe by 10° C, but you may find lowering by 20° C is more successful. Make a note beside each recipe of the exact time the cake took to cook in *your* oven. If the time varies enormously, then check your oven with an oven thermometer.

Some cookers have timers which are very useful when baking cakes, but separate digital ones are useful.

For the techniques of baking in an Aga refer to *The Aga Book* which comes free with a new Aga or can be bought from your local Aga distributor. If you have any problems getting one you can write to Aga-Rayburn at their UK base, PO Box 30, Ketley, Telford, Shropshire TF1 4DD (0952 642000).

I'm not too enthusiastic about basic microwave ovens because I don't think they are as efficient for baking; they don't brown cakes neither do they save all that much time. However, they are good when used as an *appliance*: for juicing a lemon, and melting butter or chocolate etc. Of course, if you have a combination oven it can be used as a normal oven for baking.

Preparation Equipment

Like baking equipment, most of the utensils needed for preparing cakes will already be in your kitchen.

Scales

A good set of scales is vital for making cakes. Your granny may never have used scales, yet made perfect cakes each time, but she would have probably used the same cup or spoon, allied with instinct and experience. Unless you are similarly endowed, you'll need to be more accurate for, more than any other branch of cookery, baking involves chemistry – exact proportions of ingredients reacting with each other – and it would be a shame to spoil a mixture for want of a little initial patience.

Whichever you use – the old-fashioned balance scales with weights, which I favour, or electronic or battery scales – test for accuracy by putting something on them which has its weight printed on it, an unopened bag of flour or sugar, say.

Measures

A set of accurate measuring spoons, preferably plastic, is vital for tablespoons and teaspoons. All the amounts given in the recipes here are for *level* spoonfuls unless otherwise stated. For liquids, use a jug which is see-through, heat-proof, and which shows both metric and imperial measures.

Bowls

I like to have a selection of these, from large down to the very smallest, preferably made of oven glass, which will fit one inside the other. This makes for economical storage. They should have rounded bottoms so that you can get to every bit of a mixture with your whisk, spoon or spatula.

Food Mixers

A large table-mixer is good for large cake mixtures, and is very quick and easy to clean. They take up a lot of space, though.

Electric hand-held mixers usually just have attachments to whip cream or egg whites, but some of the more expensive types have beaters for mixing and creaming thick cake mixtures. The great advantage of these is that they are portable, and you can move the beaters to different parts of the bowl. I'll never forget one demonstration when a student was helping me whip up some egg whites for meringues. She did everything my recipe said, but the whites still weren't whipped until exceedingly stiff and shiny. When I went over the procedure with her, I discovered that she had held the beaters in the one place all the time, rather than moving them about the large bowl which I had suggested to get at and aerate every part of the egg white!

Food Processors

These have become extremely popular, and they are very time-saving. But as they are so fast, you must be very careful not to *over*mix a mixture; things like nuts or dried fruit can be processed to nothing in no time at all! These are better folded in by hand after the mixing.

Great care must be taken when using processors in cake making as they don't get air into a mixture in the same way: it's a *combining* process, rather than a *beating* one. However, if you are very careful and take great care not to overmix, very good results can be achieved and it certainly is quicker.

Whisks

I like to use balloon whisks in two sizes, a bigger one for blending egg together, and a small spiral one for small amounts of mixture – rather easier in many cases than using an electrical gadget, and they can get into a corner or the bend of a bowl.

Spoons

One wooden spoon at least is vital, but it should have a rounded bottom (no need for a hole) to get into the bends of bowls. A wooden spoon or spatula with a flat, cut-off end can be used in a pan. A large metal spoon is useful for mixing egg whites into a mixture, as its slimmer edges flatten the egg foam much less than a wooden spoon.

Spatulas

I now always use a rubber, bendy spatula. It's most useful for getting all of a mixture off the sides of a bowl into the tin. It must never be put in the dishwasher or in boiling liquid, or stored by a warm oven as the rubber quickly perishes with heat.

Knives

Palette knives are indispensable both to spread and smooth mixtures into tins or icings on to cakes, but also to lift biscuits off baking trays or loosen a cake from the sides of the tin before turning out. Keen cooks need three sizes.

You'll also need a long sharp serrated knife to cut a cake cleanly into horizontal layers.

Fish Slice

This is useful for lifting out traybakes and also for lifting biscuits off baking trays.

Sieves

I like the strong plastic sieves best, as they come in a variety of sizes and can be put in the dishwasher. (The wire can come out of wire sieves, and they can easily become misshapen.) It's vital to have a nylon sieve for fruit anyway, as fruit such as raspberries react with metal.

Sugar Thermometer

For a couple of recipes this is a useful piece of equipment.

Skewers

Long, thin metal skewers are vital for testing when a cake is done. They should be flattened, not spiral.

Pastry Utensils

A long wooden rolling pin with no handles is best, and I like to use a brush which is more like a paintbrush; this can brush a glaze on to pastry, or brush fat over a tin.

Baking beans can be bought (metal or ceramic), but you could just keep a jar of old pulses or rice with which to blind bake pastry cases.

Baking 'Papers'

I normally use non-stick paper for lining cake tins which don't have loose bottoms. It should be of good quality, and it is available in sheets or rolls.

Non-stick parchment is a must for things containing a high proportion of sugar, such as meringues. It can be used again, too. One company, Lakeland Ltd, is actually making circles for the bottom of conventional 6–9 in (15–23 cm) diameter cake tins, as well as mini rolls which can be used to line the sides of cake tins (good as soufflé collars too) – saves time if you make a lot of cakes!

I've lately been using what I call 'lift off' paper, a re-usable type of graphite paper. It can be used to line a baking tray, roasting tin or cake tin, then simply wiped over and stored, ready for use again. It withstands domestic oven temperatures, and the manufacturers claim it can last, with regular domestic use, for over two years. A thinner version is Bacoglide which is less expensive.

Aluminium foil can be used to line baking trays and roasting tins. Line a tin for a traybake with foil, leaving 'tails' at either end, then you can easily lift the whole thing out. Or you can make a doubled layer into a cake tin substitute (see *page 19*). I use foil in two widths – 12 in (30 cm) and 24 in (60 cm).

Cling film can't be used in actual baking, of course, but it is handy for lining tins and trays for some types of no-bake cakes. Leave flaps or 'tails' at the side, so that the cake can be eased out in one piece. It is also useful for covering yeast dough while it is rising.

Paper cases of all kinds are necessary if you

want to make well shaped little cakes. Various sizes are available, from *petits fours* through to the largest muffin cases. When I use these, I don't place them at random on a baking tray and then pour the mixture in; they can become misshapen. I put the cases inside bun or patty tins, and *then* fill and bake them.

Greaseproof cake and loaf tin liners are available in various sizes; ideal for cakes that you want to sell.

Cutters

I have one set of plain and one set of fluted round cutters, which range in size. The most useful are the 2 and 3 in (5 and 7.5 cm) ones. If you make a lot of biscuits, then a selection of shapes is available, among them gingerbread men. Metal cuts best, but do make sure metal cutters are absolutely dry before you put them back in their box. If you are without cutters use an appropriate-sized glass upside down.

Decorating Equipment

This is a very specialized area. I have a little box of metal icing nozzles, of all sizes, but for the recipes in this book you only need $\frac{1}{4}$ in (5 mm) and $\frac{1}{2}$ in (1 cm) plain nozzles, plus a large and a medium star nozzle.

You'll need a piping bag, obviously, and this should be in an easily washable material such as nylon. Plastic and polythene bags are available too.

You could make your own icing bag out of greaseproof paper. Cut a 10 in (25 cm) square of greaseproof, and then fold into two equal triangles (see *figure 1*). Roll one triangle into a cornet shape with a good point at the end (see *figure 2*). Fold over the top to hold together, then snip off the tip of the point to make a narrow or a larger hole (see *figure 3*).

Alternatively you could slot one small plastic bag inside another, then snip off the corners at one side.

If you like cake decorating, then you'll need further equipment such as a turntable, a leveller and a side scraper.

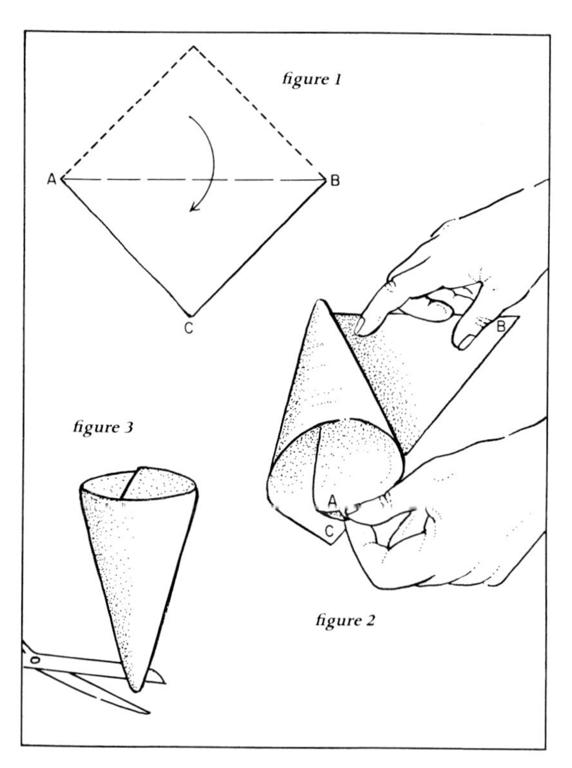

Storage Equipment

If cakes are not to be eaten straightaway, then a freezer is the best place to store fresh cakes. Some icings may weep a little on thawing. Kept in the freezer, they keep in perfect condition, away from temptation, and you will always have on hand something for an emergency. See *page 28* for further information on freezing.

Airtight Tins

These are vital for biscuits, so that they don't go soft. You can obviously buy special airtight tins for cake storage, but I most often use both square and round tins in which I've bought mixed commercial biscuits. If the tin lid isn't quite airtight, use a piece of foil to make the fit perfect.

Place a whole cake on the inside of the *lid* of the cake tin, and then place the bulk of the tin over the top. Otherwise the cake could be difficult to extract! (Cakes can be open-frozen on the lid, too, before being wrapped and stored in the freezer.)

Cake Wrappings

Cling film is useful here, too; it keeps the moisture in, and you can tell at a glance which cake it is!

Aluminium foil is a good wrapping as well, especially if you don't have airtight tins. Foil can also be used between layers of cakes in storage tins.

Polythene bags, especially the strong freezer ones, are as good as cling film and foil.

Cake-making Methods

Here are the principal methods of bringing together a cake mixture.

Creaming

This is the method that we all tend to learn first, for sponge cakes such as a Victoria sandwich. The fat and sugar are beaten together until pale and fluffy, eggs are gradually beaten in and then lastly flour is carefully folded into the creamed mixture.

The eggs must be at room temperature, added gradually, and beaten in thoroughly between each addition to prevent the mixture from curdling. A cake mixture which curdles holds less air, and therefore produces a heavy, dense cake. As a precaution against curdling, a spoonful of sifted flour can be added with each egg addition but the remaining flour needs to be very lightly folded in.

Using a Mixer

The creaming part is fine in a mixer but fold the flour in lightly by hand.

All-in-one

The all-in-one method means just that. All of the main ingredients go into the bowl at the same time to be mixed. There is no need for any creaming or rubbing in of the fat and no danger of the mixture curdling because of the egg being added too quickly. The fat must be a soft baking margarine which is of the correct consistency even when taken straight from the fridge. You can use block margarine or butter for this method of cake-making but it must be really soft, not oily.

Self-raising flour is used in all-in-one method cakes, often with the addition of baking powder to compensate for the air not being incorporated during the initial creaming stages.

This method is particularly suitable for making cakes in an electric mixer, but take care not to overbeat the mixture. Just beat enough to combine all ingredients to a smooth mixture.

Whisking

This method produces the lightest of all cakes. The classic whisked sponge contains no fat and is made by whisking together eggs and caster sugar and then carefully folding in the flour. The cake rises due to the air which is incorporated during the whisking of the eggs and sugar, and so it is very important not to lose the trapped air by stirring the flour in heavily.

To make a really light whisked sponge, the first whisking stage is the most crucial. The eggs and sugar must be whisked together until *really* thick. To test, lift the whisk out of the mixture: when ready, it should leave a trail. This is where the electric food mixer proves most useful as even on full speed the mixture does take a while to thicken. If you don't have an electric food mixer then stand a large bowl containing the eggs and sugar over a pan of hot water as this speeds up the thickening process, but don't let the bowl touch the water or it will get too hot. Whisk, preferably with a hand-held electric whisk, until the mixture is thick as before. Take the bowl off the hot water when ready and continue to whisk the mixture until the bowl is cold.

The Genoese sponge is a moister version of the classic whisked sponge, and it also keeps better. Melted butter is added with the flour, so extra care is needed with the folding to prevent air being lost. Make sure the butter is not too hot and add it in two batches, alternating with the flour. Pour the butter in around the edges of the mixtures, not straight into the middle where it is more likely to sink straight to the bottom. Don't substitute margarine for the butter or the flavour and texture will not be so good.

Traditionally, plain flour is used for whisked sponges, but it's more foolproof to use self-raising.

Rubbing-in

Many small cakes are made by the rubbing-in method. The fat is literally rubbed into the flour with the fingertips until the mixture resembles breadcrumbs. It helps to have cool hands and to lift the hands from the bowl whilst rubbing in, to incorporate some air. However, this method does not create enough air to make a cake rise, so the main raising agents are chemical. The rubbing in can be done in an electric mixer or processor.

Melting

Cakes such as gingerbreads are traditionally made by this method, which is very quick and simple. The moist and sticky texture of these cakes is due to the high proportion of sugary ingredients, including golden syrup and black treacle. Warm the tin of golden syrup or black treacle before using by standing it in a pan of hot water; it will then be easier to measure.

The fat and sugar and/or syrups are melted together before being added to the other ingredients. Do allow the mixture to cool a little or it will begin to cook the flour, resulting in a hard, tough cake.

Bicarbonate of soda is often used alone as the raising agent for these cakes, as the aromatic spices can counteract the slightly bitter flavour of the bicarbonate. The cake mixture should be the consistency of a thick batter; this can be poured into the tin where it will find its own level.

Cake Making

Most of the cake-making instructions are attached to individual recipes, but a few extra tips are gathered together here.

Preparing a Cake Mixture

First of all, check that you have time to make and bake the cake, particularly if it is a large rich fruit cake, as these can take quite a lot longer to cook than you realize. It is easy to begin with good intentions, only to be interrupted, and then it's time to collect the children from school! All-in-one mixtures and rich fruit cakes can be prepared and left in their tins to be baked later.

For the quickest and most successful results, read the recipe through carefully, checking that you have all the ingredients in the storecupboard. Weigh out the ingredients carefully, using measuring spoons for teaspoon and tablespoon measures for perfect accuracy. Follow the order given in the recipe listing, ticking them off so that nothing is accidentally forgotten.

Mix the ingredients by hand or in the processor or mixer, whichever you prefer, or following the recipe instructions. Continue mixing until the mixture is the specified colour or texture – the success of the finished cake depends on this.

Preparing and Lining Tins

I find melted white vegetable fat by far the best way to grease tins. Use a pastry brush to brush the melted fat evenly all over the tin.

It is useful to remember that you do not need to grease tins if you are baking with a pastry base. There is enough fat in the pastry to prevent it sticking.

Bases

Most cake mixtures require only the base of the tin to be greased and lined with greased greaseproof paper. Whatever the shape of the tin, place the base of the tin on the greaseproof paper, draw around it in pencil, then cut out just inside the pencil line. Loose-bottomed tins do not need to be lined unless particularly specified: simply grease the base and sides, and the cake is still easy to turn out.

If you do a lot of baking it is worth cutting out several bases at once and storing them flat in a polythene bag for future use (or buy them ready-cut, see *page 21*).

Sides

When making a rich cake mixture, such as a rich fruit cake, it is necessary to line the sides of the tin as well as the base. Cut a strip (or two strips if necessary) of greaseproof paper long enough to reach around the tin and overlap slightly and high enough to extend about 1 in (2.5 cm) above the top of the tin. Fold the bottom edge of the strip up by about 1 in (2.5 cm), creasing it firmly. Open out the fold and cut slanting lines into this narrow strip at intervals (see *figure 4*). Fit this strip into the greased tin, where the snipped edge will enable the paper to fit snugly into the base of any shaped tin. Fit the base disc over the cut part of the paper and the tin is then fully lined (see *figure 5*). Remember to grease well with a pastry brush (see *figure 6*).

Quick Tin-lining Method

If time is short, turn the tin to be lined upside down and mould a piece of foil over the top. Use this to line the tin and grease it well. This is useful too in loose-bottomed tins if a mixture is runny and might seep out.

Baking Cakes

Always pre-heat the oven before starting to make the cake so that it will be at the correct temperature by the time the cake is ready to go in. Check also that the shelves are in the right position. Unless specified otherwise, cook cakes in the centre of the oven.

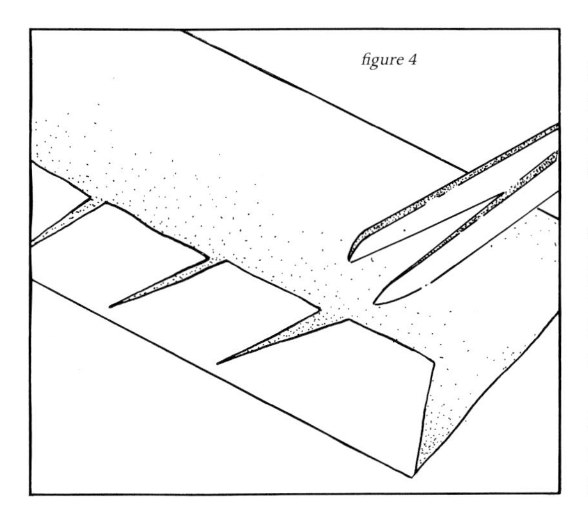

figure 4

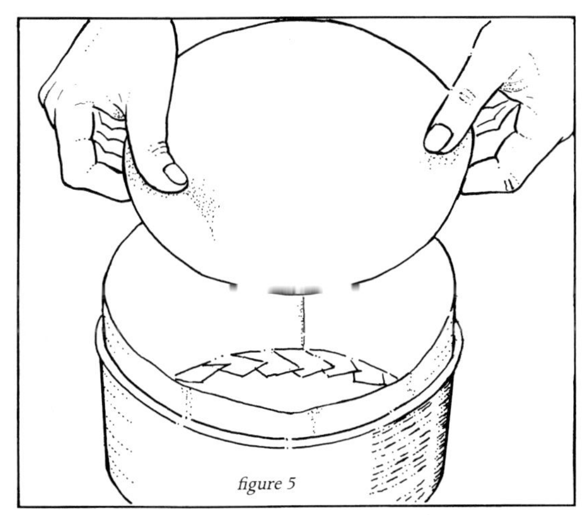

figure 5

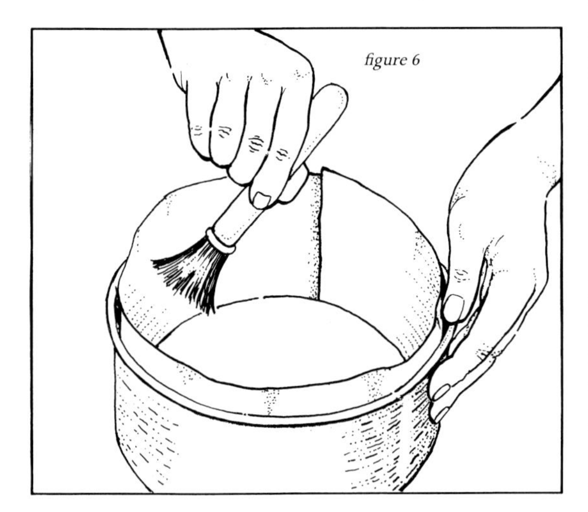

figure 6

Never open the oven door or move the cake tin during the first stages of baking, as both these actions will make the cake sink in the middle. (You don't have to worry so much about biscuits.)

Don't cram the oven with cakes or biscuits even if it is a fan oven, as there needs to be a good circulation of air around the tins. Remember that two or more cakes cooked in the same oven at once will take longer to cook than one cake.

It is probably a good idea to check your oven instruction handbook for baking cakes. In theory, a good oven should cook equally throughout; in practice ovens do differ. Always mark on the recipe, using pencil or a little yellow sticker, how the cake turned out – whether it took longer, whether it burned a little on the top etc.

If anything ever looks as though it might be browning too much too early, place a sheet of kitchen foil loosely over the top.

Baking Blind

Some of the recipes call for the pastry to be baked blind before the filling is added. The result is that the pastry is then really crisp underneath.

To bake blind, first preheat the oven to 200°C/400°F/Gas 6. Line a loose bottomed flan tin with pastry. Then line this with a large piece of greaseproof paper and fill with baking beans (or old raw pasta, pulses). Bake in the oven for 10–15 minutes. Remove the paper and beans and bake the pastry for a further 5 minutes to allow the pastry to dry out completely. The flan may then be filled with the chosen filling.

Testing to See if a Cake is Cooked

Most cakes are cooked when they begin to shrink away from the sides of the tin and when they spring back after being pressed lightly with the finger. The *look* of the cake gives an idea too; see each individual recipe for advice.

For fruit cakes, push a skewer into the centre of the cake; if it is done the skewer should come out clean. If there is still some cake mixture adhering to the skewer, the cake needs a little longer. Cover with kitchen foil if it's browning too much on the top, and perhaps turn the oven temperature down slightly.

Meringues should be crisp, or the colour specified in the recipe.

Biscuits and shortbreads should be checked by eye – are they the right colour? – and don't forget to check underneath as well.

COOLING CAKES

Particular cooling instructions are attached to individual recipes. In general, leave to cool for a few minutes in the tin, and then run a palette knife quickly around the edges of the cake tin and turn it out on to a wire rack.

Allow a sponge cake to cool in the tin for a few minutes before turning out so that it shrinks slightly from the sides of the tin, making it easier to turn out. I turn Victoria sponges out on to a rack, turn them the right way up, and then place the tins over them. This prevents the moisture evaporating while the cakes are cooling, but doesn't make them soggy.

Leave fruit cakes to cool completely in their tins.

To turn cakes out of loose-bottomed tins, stand the base on something like a large can so that the side can slip down, leaving the cake free, still standing on the tin base.

If the tin has been paper-lined, peel the paper off very carefully, as this can tear thinner cakes such as Swiss roll.

Leave meringues in the turned-off, slightly open oven to cool. This dries them out further. Then simply slip off the paper.

Don't leave biscuits on the tray to become stone cold or they'll stick. Remove with a palette knife or fish slice while still warm.

STORING AND FREEZING CAKES

In general, few cakes improve with keeping, except perhaps sticky gingerbread, Yorkshire parkin and, of course, rich fruit cakes. Lighter fruit cakes and creamed sponge cakes are definitely best eaten soon after making, but they can be kept fresh for a short time in an airtight tin, or wrapped in foil or cling film.

Whisked sponges do not keep well as they contain no fat; eat on the day of making if possible, or wrap well then fill and use the next day. However, they do freeze well and so can be made in advance. Genoese sponges keep better as they contain butter, but are still best eaten freshly made.

Cakes made by the rubbing-in method tend to have a low proportion of fat, and for this reason do not keep well. They are best eaten on the day that they are made, or frozen as soon as they are cool.

Sticky gingerbreads and other cakes made by the melting method do keep well; some actually improve with keeping. Make sure they are kept in an airtight container, though.

To keep a rich fruit cake moist, store it in its lining paper and then in greaseproof paper and kitchen foil. The cake must not come into direct contact with the foil or the acid in the fruit will corrode the foil.

Make sure that cakes and biscuits are not stored in the same tin, as the moisture from the cake will make the biscuits soggy.

Most cakes can be frozen either whole or in pieces, well wrapped in foil, cling film or polythene bags. Freeze cakes as soon as they are cold to keep the maximum freshness. Don't freeze for more than three months or they lose their flavour.

Open-freeze iced or delicate cakes until hard and then wrap well. Small cakes such as scones are best warmed through in a moderate oven after thawing.

ICING AND DECORATING CAKES

Icings, decorations and fillings can transform any cake, but the first necessity is that the cake must be stone cold.

Cut the cake cleanly, using a sharp knife, as the recipe specifies. Fill only when you are ready to serve, especially the softer cakes such as sponge.

Sometimes the simplest decorations are the most attractive – icing sugar sifted in a pattern, say, or a simple glacé icing made with icing sugar and liquid. I've given ideas in each of the recipes, where appropriate.

If you have time, brush a cake to be iced with some apricot glaze first. Apricot jam is gently heated to make it runny, then strained of lumps if it is for a special occasion. The glaze is then brushed over the cake, where it 'sets' preventing any stray crumbs working their way into the icing. Neither will the icing become dull; with the apricot layer in between, the moisture in the icing won't be absorbed by the cake. Apricot glaze is also useful as a 'glue' – helping the almond paste stick to a celebration cake, for instance.

You may want to decorate a special cake, the Sponge Christening Cake (see *page 106*) for example, and crystallized flowers make lovely decorations. These are very easy to prepare as they are simply real edible flowers covered in egg white. Quite a number of flowers are edible, including violets, pansies, japonica, primroses, little roses and polyanthus. You can also crystallize mint leaves and the herb borage in the same way.

Just beat a little egg white and brush this over the flowers (or leaves). Dust with caster sugar on both sides, then stand them on a wire cake rack in a warm place – over a radiator, at the back of an Aga, in the airing cupboard – until crisp and dry. This will take a few hours.

Should you want to decorate your Devil's Food Cake (see *page 36*) with an 'instant' American Frosting, try the following: measure 6 oz (175 g) caster sugar, an egg white, 2 tablespoons of hot water and a pinch of cream of tartar into a bowl over a pan of hot water and whisk for 10–12 minutes until thick. Use the frosting immediately to fill and ice the cake.

To fill a piping bag with icing – or cream with which to decorate a cake – stand the bag in a jug, point down, and bend the top edges of the bag over the top of the jug. You now have a large opening into which the mixture can easily be spooned.

Chapter 1

Glorious Chocolate Cakes

Everybody's favourite, rich and irresistible, chocolate is a luxurious and versatile ingredient for producing sensational cakes. The expression 'chocoholic' may be fairly new, but the passion for chocolate is much older, and widespread throughout the world. The Swiss are said to eat the most annually – some 10 kg (22 lb) per person – but the rest of us are not far behind!

About Chocolate

Chocolate is made from the bean of the cacao tree which grows in Central and South America. Through a process of drying, roasting and grinding, the cocoa beans are converted into a thick paste called chocolate liquor or mass, which is made up of cocoa solids and cocoa butter. This paste hardens on cooling and then goes through the processes of conching and tempering to produce the required texture and flavour of the chocolate. The blend of cocoa beans, the method of roasting and conching, and the proportion of cocoa butter are all important factors affecting the final flavour of the chocolate.

The quality of chocolate varies considerably; to be called chocolate, it must have a minimum of 34 per cent cocoa butter. The finest quality block chocolate always contains a high proportion of cocoa butter, on average 35 per cent but sometimes as much as 50 per cent. The more cocoa butter the chocolate contains, the softer and creamier it will be; the less it contains, the harder and more brittle it is; the more bitter the chocolate, the more chocolate flavour it has. In inferior types of chocolate, palm or vegetable oils or shortenings are substituted for the cocoa butter.

The exact composition of the different types of chocolate varies with each brand. Continental chocolates tend to contain higher levels of cocoa solids and therefore have a stronger flavour. Different types of chocolate have different melting and cooking properties, as well as different flavours. Therefore, don't substitute one for another, unless stated in the recipe.

Plain Chocolate

Plain chocolate, also called semi-sweet or bittersweet chocolate, has a rich, strong flavour, but contains enough sugar to make it palatable to eat alone. It is the chocolate most usually used in baking. There is no need to buy the expensive dessert chocolates unless particularly specified in the recipe. Add a little cream or vegetable oil to plain chocolate when using as a cake covering as this prevents it from setting too hard.

Plain chocolate is also available as chocolate 'chips' or 'polka dots' which are excellent for melting purposes or to use whole in cookies or cakes.

Milk Chocolate

Milk chocolate has the addition of full cream milk as well as sugar to the cocoa butter, and is sweeter. The flavour is therefore lost in baking. It is good for decoration and always popular with children. Milk chocolate is also available as 'chips' (see above).

White Chocolate

Good brands of white chocolate contain cocoa butter but the amount varies considerably – some inferior brands contain vegetable oil in place of the cocoa butter and therefore lack the taste of true chocolate. White chocolate does not contain any cocoa solids. White chocolate has inferior setting qualities; you need to add a little butter or use *more* chocolate to remedy this.

Cooking or Unsweetened Chocolate

Unsweetened, pure or cooking chocolate is often used by professionals in baking; it is not sweet enough to be eaten alone. It is available from specialist cake shops, many of which are also mail order suppliers, and is sold in block form or as chocolate chips.

Couverture

Couverture or coating chocolate is a high quality chocolate used primarily for dipping and moulding expensive hand-made chocolates and other high quality confectionery. It has a high proportion of cocoa butter which allows it to melt easily and smoothly, sets with a fine, smooth gloss and has an excellent flavour. Couverture chocolate is more expensive, the best coming from Belgium, Switzerland and France. It is available in semi-sweet, milk and white varieties. It is also available from specialist cake shops.

Chocolate-Flavoured Cake Covering

This is not a patch on the real thing. It contains cocoa solids but not cocoa butter, which is replaced by vegetable oils. This makes it easier to melt and handle, and it does make excellent curls and caraque, but the flavour is far inferior to real chocolate.

Cocoa Powder

Cocoa powder is pure chocolate liquor from which much of the cocoa butter has been extracted. It is then ground into a fine powder. This undoubtedly gives the most inexpensive, strongest and best chocolate flavour in baking. Sift with the other dry ingredients or blend with very hot water before using. Don't be tempted to substitute with drinking chocolate powder, as the added sugar in drinking chocolate will give a very mild, sweet flavour to the cake.

Carob

Carob is popular as a healthy substitute for chocolate as it contains less fat and no caffeine. Obtained from the carob or locust bean, it is available as powder, in bars or as carob 'drops' from health-food shops. Carob powder can be used to replace cocoa powder in recipes but neither the flavour nor the texture will be the same. Carob powder is much sweeter than cocoa powder so use only half as much in recipes. Make sure to dissolve the powder well or it will be very grainy. Take care when selecting carob bars or 'drops' as they are available sugar-free, milk and sugar-free, or simply described as dark. Cakes and biscuits made with carob are also much darker in colour.

WORKING WITH CHOCOLATE

Chocolate is not difficult to work with but there are certain guidelines to observe in order to avoid disasters.

MELTING CHOCOLATE

To melt chocolate successfully it is essential not to allow it to overheat. Break the chocolate into small pieces into a bowl which fits snugly over a pan of hot water, *not* boiling – if it is the chocolate will become solid and lose its shine. The bottom of the bowl should not actually touch the water. Allow the chocolate to melt slowly, not stirring but occasionally prodding the chocolate, until the chocolate becomes smooth and creamy.

Take care not to allow steam or water into the chocolate or it will 'seize', or become stiff and granular, and lose its gloss. For the same reason, ingredients with a high water or liquid content such as brandy, must be heated with the chocolate right at the beginning. 'Seized' chocolate can sometimes be rectified by adding a little blended white vegetable fat or vegetable oil. Cream and butter can be successfully melted with chocolate.

White chocolate has a tendency to separate on heating. Follow the method given above, being extra careful to keep the heat low.

Chocolate can also be melted in the microwave but care must be taken not to burn the chocolate. Use Defrost or Low power and always set the time for less than you think you will need. Burnt chocolate is irreversible and is only good for throwing away. (4 oz (100 g) plain or milk chocolate takes about 4 minutes on Defrost – check your own microwave instructions.)

TEMPERING CHOCOLATE

All chocolate that we buy has been 'tempered' during production to perfect its texture and appearance. Once melted, the chocolate can lose its 'temper', although it can be 're-tempered' for moulding and other specialist work. This process of heating, working, setting and re-heating the chocolate makes it more malleable and glossy, but it is not usually necessary to do this for home baking.

GRATING AND CHOPPING CHOCOLATE

On a warm day, chill the chocolate before grating or chopping. If chopping, make sure that the board and knife are completely dry. Chocolate can also be chopped in a food processor; use the pulse button, or the chocolate may become overworked and melt or stick together.

STORING CHOCOLATE

Chocolate is quick to absorb other flavours so keep it well wrapped in an airtight container. Milk and white chocolate contain more fat than plain chocolate, and therefore do not keep as long. Keep chocolate in a cool, dry place. If it is exposed to moisture it develops a white 'bloom' on the surface; this can also happen if melted chocolate is cooled rapidly in a damp place such as the fridge. Bars of chocolate which develop a 'bloom' can still be used for melting purposes.

CHOCOLATE DECORATIONS

There are many decorations or finishing touches that you can make and create with chocolate. They're fun to do and look most impressive.

CHOCOLATE CARAQUE

Chocolate caraque always looks so impressive and is not difficult to make. Pour a thin layer of melted chocolate on to a scratch-proof surface. Using a palette knife, spread the chocolate thinly until it begins to set and go cloudy. Leave until it no longer sticks to your hand when you touch it then, holding a long sharp flexible knife at an angle, shave the chocolate off the surface using a slight sawing action to form scrolls or flakes (see *figures* 7 and 8).

White chocolate needs to be more set than plain before it will form caraque.

CHOCOLATE SHAPES

These can easily be made by melting the chocolate as above and then cutting it into squares or triangles with a sharp knife; it helps to heat the knife or cutter first. Use a round plain or fluted cutter to stamp out circles.

CHOCOLATE LEAVES

Use a small paintbrush to spread melted chocolate evenly on to the undersides of clean, dry leaves. Leave to set and then gently peel the leaf away from the chocolate, not the other way round.

CHOCOLATE CURLS

These are very simply made by using a swivel peeler. Make sure the chocolate is at room temperature or it will simply flake rather than curl. Scrape the peeler along the flat side of the chocolate bar. Chocolate-flavoured cake covering is particularly good for this. Hold the chocolate bar in greaseproof paper if you find it becomes sticky.

LACY CHOCOLATE SHAPES

Simple shapes can be made by drizzling melted chocolate into irregular shapes on to a sheet of kitchen foil or preferably non-stick baking paper. For more definite shapes you will need an outline to follow. Trace your chosen shape on to paper and place a sheet of waxed or non-stick baking paper over the top. Melt the chocolate and pour into a paper piping bag. Cut off the tip of the bag and pipe over the outline of each shape. Leave to set.

Store all chocolate shapes in a cool, dry place and handle as little as possible.

INSTANT CHOCOLATE DECORATIONS

Cheats' chocolate decorations also have their place. Buy chocolate vermicelli or use the last few chocolate sticks in the box, a few Maltesers, chocolate buttons, or crumbled chocolate flakes to finish off a family birthday cake.

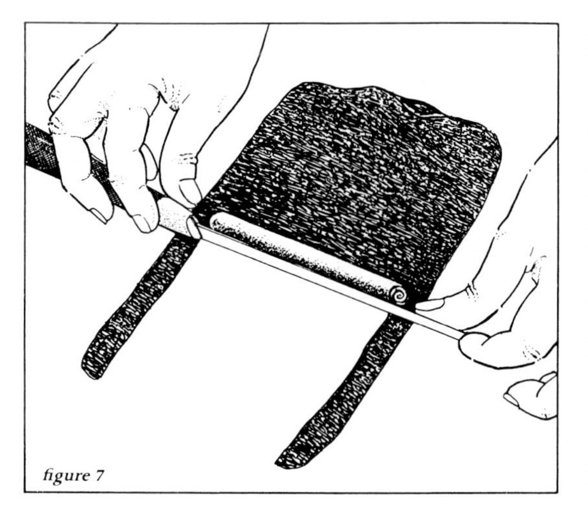

figure 7

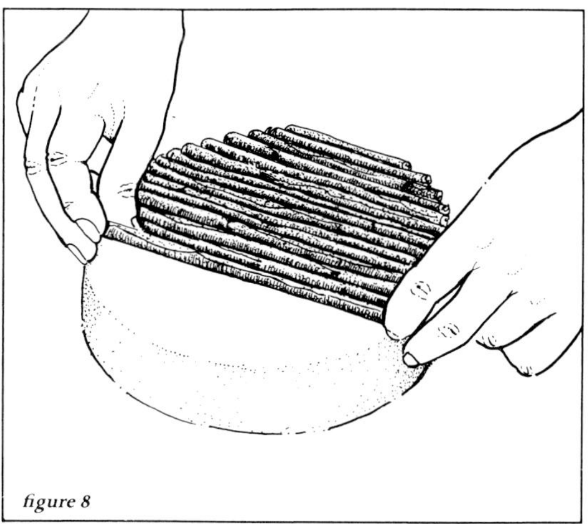

figure 8

Very Best Chocolate Roulade

Serves 8

This is a very special dessert cake for a party. Make it the day before, or in the morning ready for the evening. It must be kept damp, though. You could balance a long cake rack above the tin (without touching the cake), place a damp tea towel on top, and then pop the whole lot in a large plastic bag. To make the filling even more special, stir 2 tablespoons of brandy into the whipped cream.

8 oz (225 g) plain chocolate, broken into pieces

8 oz (225 g) caster sugar

8 eggs, separated

For the Filling

10 fl oz (300 ml) double cream

icing sugar

Pre-heat the oven to 180°C/350°F/Gas 4. Grease and line a 13 × 9 in (33 × 23 cm) Swiss roll tin with greased non-stick baking paper.

Melt the chocolate slowly in a bowl over a pan of hot water, then cool slightly.

Place the sugar and egg yolks into a bowl and whisk with an electric whisk on a high speed until light and creamy. Add the cooled chocolate and stir until evenly blended.

In a separate bowl, whisk the egg whites until stiff but not dry. Carefully fold into the chocolate mixture. Turn into the prepared tin and gently level the surface. Bake in the pre-heated oven for about 25 minutes until firm to the touch.

Remove the cake from the oven, leave in the tin and place a cooling rack over the top of the cake. Place a damp tea towel on top of the rack, place the whole lot into a plastic bag and leave for several hours or overnight in a cool place.

Whip the cream until it just holds its shape, and dust a large piece of greaseproof paper with icing sugar. Turn the roulade out on to the sugared paper and peel off the baking paper. Spread with the whipped cream and roll up like a Swiss roll, starting at the long edge and using the paper to help, rolling carefully but firmly. It may crack a little, but that's all part of its charm! Dust with more icing sugar.

Secrets of Success

If you have half a cream cake left over, cut into wedges, wrap individually and freeze. Take out a couple of wedges when someone drops in unexpectedly; they will thaw in 30 minutes.

Very Best Chocolate Roulade

Devil's Food Cake

Cuts into 8 Wedges

This classic American cake is moist and dark, and slightly bitter in flavour. The frosting is very sweet, though, crisp on the top and like marshmallow underneath. Proper American frosting requires the use of a sugar thermometer. Use the 'instant' American Frosting recipe given on page 29 if you don't have a sugar thermometer, or simply for speed.

2 oz (50 g) cocoa

$7\frac{1}{2}$ fl oz (225 ml) water

4 oz (100 g) soft margarine

10 oz (275 g) caster sugar

2 eggs

6 oz (175 g) plain flour

$\frac{1}{4}$ teaspoon baking powder

1 teaspoon bicarbonate of soda

For the American Frosting

1 lb (450 g) caster sugar

$4\frac{1}{2}$ fl oz (135 ml) water

2 egg whites

Pre-heat the oven to 180°C/350°F/Gas 4. Grease and base line 2 × 8 in (20 cm) sandwich tins with greased greaseproof paper.

Whisk the cocoa into the water until smooth. Set aside. Place the margarine in a bowl and gradually whisk in the sugar until the mixture is pale and fluffy. Lightly whisk the eggs, then gradually whisk into the creamed mixture until evenly blended.

Sift the flour with the baking powder and bicarbonate of soda and fold into the creamed mixture alternately with the cocoa and water.

Divide the mixture between the tins and level the surface. Bake in the pre-heated oven for about 30–35 minutes or until well risen and firm to the touch. Allow to cool in the tins for a few minutes then turn out and leave to cool completely on a wire rack.

For the American frosting, place the sugar in a large, heavy-based pan with the water and heat gently until the sugar has dissolved. Bring to the boil and boil to 115°C (240°F) as registered on a sugar thermometer.

Meanwhile, whisk the egg whites in a large deep bowl until stiff. Allow the bubbles to settle, then slowly pour the hot syrup on to the egg whites, whisking constantly. When all the sugar syrup has been added, continue whisking until the mixture stands in peaks and just starts to become matt around the edges.

Sandwich the cakes together with a little of the frosting. Spread the remainder over the top and sides, using a palette knife. Pull the frosting up into peaks all over. Work quickly as the icing sets rapidly. Leave to set in a cool place, but not in the fridge.

Marbled Chocolate Ring Cake

CUTS INTO ABOUT 10 SLICES

THIS FAMILY WEEKEND CAKE has a nice texture and looks spectacular, marbled with white and brown. It must be eaten fresh. (See photograph on pages 6–7)

8 oz (225 g) soft margarine
8 oz (225 g) caster sugar
4 eggs
8 oz (225 g) self-raising flour
2 teaspoons baking powder
$1\frac{1}{2}$ tablespoons cocoa
$1\frac{1}{2}$ tablespoons hot water

FOR THE ICING

5 oz (150 g) plain chocolate, broken into pieces
2 tablespoons water
4 oz (100 g) butter
2 oz (50 g) milk chocolate, broken into pieces

Pre-heat the oven to 180°C/350°F/Gas 4. Lightly grease a 3 pint (1.75 litre) capacity ring mould.

Place all the cake ingredients, except the cocoa and water, into a large bowl. Beat well until thoroughly blended. Dot about half of this mixture, in teaspoons, into the base of the prepared tin.

Mix the cocoa and water together in a small bowl and then mix into the remaining cake mixture. Dot this mixture over and between the plain mixture until all is used up. Swirl a little with a knife, then carefully level the surface.

Bake in the pre-heated oven for about 40 minutes or until well risen and springy to the touch. Allow to cool in the tin for a few minutes before turning out. Leave to cool completely on a wire rack.

For the icing, melt the plain chocolate slowly in a bowl with the water and the butter over a pan of hot water. Pour over the cake and then leave to set for about 1 hour.

Melt the milk chocolate slowly in a small bowl over a pan of hot water. Spoon into a paper piping bag, cut off the tip of the bag and drizzle the chocolate over the top of the plain chocolate icing. Leave to set.

SECRETS OF SUCCESS

A quick and easy way to pipe chocolate is to place the melted chocolate into two polythene bags which have been put together for strength. Snip off one corner and then simply drizzle the chocolate over the cake. Alternatively, make a greaseproof paper piping bag (see page 22).

Black Forest Cake

Cuts into 8–10 Wedges

This gâteau, originating in Germany, was popular in the 1960s, particularly in restaurants, but home-made cakes are far superior. Serve it as a dessert. Don't use fresh cherries in the cake as they would discolour – but a few on top as decoration would look good.

- 4 eggs
- 4 oz (100 g) caster sugar
- 3 oz (75 g) self-raising flour, sifted
- 1 oz (25 g) cocoa, sifted

For the Filling and Topping

- 2 × 15 oz (420 g) cans black cherries
- 2 tablespoons cornflour
- 3–4 tablespoons kirsch
- 1 pint (600 ml) double cream, whipped
- about 2 oz (50 g) flaked almonds, toasted
- plain chocolate caraque to decorate (pages 32–3)

Pre-heat the oven to 180°C/350°F/Gas 4. Grease and base line a 9 in (23 cm) deep round cake tin with greased greaseproof paper.

Break the eggs into a mixing bowl, add the sugar and whisk with an electric whisk until the mixture is pale and thick enough to leave a trail when lifted out of the bowl. Carefully fold in the sifted flour and cocoa. Turn the mixture into the prepared tin.

Bake in the pre-heated oven for about 40–45 minutes until the sponge is well risen and beginning to shrink away from the sides of the tin. Turn out on to a wire rack to cool.

Drain the cans of cherries, reserving the juice. Reserve a few whole cherries for the top and stone the remainder. Place the cornflour in a small saucepan and slowly stir in the cherry juice. Bring slowly to the boil, stirring until thickened, then simmer for 2 minutes. Remove from the heat and cool. Add the kirsch and the stoned cherries to the sauce.

Cut the sponge into three layers with a long sharp knife. Sandwich the layers together with three-quarters of the whipped cream and all of the cherry mixture. Spread a little of the remaining whipped cream around the sides of the cake and cover with the toasted flaked almonds. Pipe rosettes of cream around the top of the cake and decorate with chocolate caraque and fresh cherries if available.

Secrets of Success

The chocolate caraque can be made in advance, but keep it somewhere cool, and in a solid box with a lid to prevent accidental breakage.

Black Forest Cake

Mississippi Mud Pie

CUTS INTO 12 WEDGES

THE ORIGIN OF THIS pie is rather vague but it has become a very popular dessert in cafés and bistros. Like many American recipes it is rich, so serve in small slices.

FOR THE CRUMB CRUST BASE

4 oz (100 g) digestive biscuits, crushed

2 oz (50 g) butter, melted

1 oz (25 g) demerara sugar

FOR THE FILLING

14 oz (400 g) plain chocolate, broken into pieces

8 oz (225 g) butter

2 tablespoons instant coffee

2 tablespoons boiling water

10 fl oz (300 ml) single cream

12 oz (350 g) dark muscovado sugar

6 eggs

TO FINISH

5 fl oz (150 ml) whipping cream, whipped

Pre-heat the oven to 190°C/375°F/Gas 5. Lightly grease an 8 in (20 cm) loose-bottomed cake tin or spring-release tin.

First make the base. Mix together the crushed digestive biscuits, the melted butter and the sugar and spoon into the prepared tin. Level the biscuit mixture out evenly, using the back of a metal spoon.

For the filling, measure the chocolate, butter, instant coffee and water into a large pan and heat gently until the butter and chocolate have melted. Remove from the heat, and beat in the cream, sugar and eggs and then pour the mixture on to the biscuit crust.

Reduce the oven temperature to 180°C/350°F/Gas 4 and bake for $1\frac{1}{4}$–$1\frac{1}{2}$ hours or until set. Allow to cool before removing the tin, then decorate the top with the whipped cream.

Mini Chocolate Eclairs

Makes about 18

Eclairs are always delicious for afternoon tea or as a dessert, but especially when topped with good chocolate. The éclairs must be well cooked, though, until really firm and a good straw colour. They can be returned to the oven after splitting, at the lower temperature of 180°C/350°F/Gas 4, for a further 10 minutes.

Use a plain nozzle in the piping bag when piping in the cream filling. Make your éclairs larger if you like – the traditional length is 5–6 in (13–15 cm). Or make choux puffs, balls or profiteroles: these look wonderful piled up in a pyramid – a croquembouche *– at a buffet party.*

For the Choux Pastry

2 oz (50 g) margarine
5 fl oz (150 ml) water
2½ oz (65 g) plain flour, sifted
2 eggs, beaten

For the Filling

10 fl oz (300 ml) whipping cream, whipped

For the Icing

2 oz (50 g) plain chocolate, broken into pieces
2 tablespoons water
½ oz (15 g) butter
3 oz (75 g) icing sugar, sifted

Pre-heat the oven to 220°C/425°F/Gas 7. Lightly grease 2 baking trays.

To make the pastry, measure the margarine and water into a small pan. Allow the fat to melt and then bring slowly to the boil. Remove the pan from the heat, add the flour all at once, and beat until the mixture forms a soft ball. Allow to cool slightly, then gradually beat in the eggs, beating well between each addition to give a smooth shiny paste.

Spoon the mixture into a piping bag fitted with a ½ in (1 cm) plain nozzle and pipe into about 18 éclair shapes, about 3 in (7.5 cm) long, leaving room for them to spread. Bake in the pre-heated oven for about 10 minutes, then reduce the heat to 190°C/375°F/Gas 5 and cook for a further 20 minutes until well risen and a deep golden brown. Remove from the oven and split one side of the éclair to allow the steam to escape. Cool on a wire rack.

Fill each éclair with a little of the whipped cream, using a piping bag with a plain nozzle.

For the icing, melt the chocolate slowly in a bowl with the water and butter over a pan of hot water. Remove from the heat and beat in the sugar until smooth. Dip each éclair into the icing to coat the top, then leave to set.

Chocolate Rum Cake

Cuts into 8–10 Wedges

This is a moist chocolate cake laced with rum, filled and covered with a glossy chocolate icing which melts in the mouth. It is irresistible to chocoholics, and can be served as an afternoon cake, or as a pudding with single cream.

7 oz (200 g) plain chocolate, broken into pieces

4 oz (100 g) unsalted butter, cubed

3 eggs, separated

4 oz (100 g) dark muscovado sugar

2 fl oz (50 ml) dark rum

3 oz (75 g) self-raising flour, sifted

2 oz (50 g) ground almonds

For the Filling and Icing

8 oz (225 g) plain chocolate, broken into pieces

4 oz (100 g) unsalted butter, cubed

about 4 tablespoons apricot jam, warmed

For the Chocolate Ganache for Piping (Optional)

6 oz (175 g) plain chocolate, broken into pieces

4 tablespoons single cream

2 oz (50 g) butter, cubed

2 egg yolks

1 tablespoon rum

Pre-heat the oven to 180°C/350°F/Gas 4. Grease and base line an 8 in (20 cm) deep round cake tin with greased greaseproof paper.

Melt the chocolate and butter slowly in a bowl over a pan of hot water, then allow to cool slightly.

Place the egg yolks and the sugar into a large bowl and whisk with an electric whisk on full speed until pale and creamy. Add the cooled chocolate mixture and the rum and mix well. Gently fold in the flour and the ground almonds.

In a separate bowl, whisk the egg whites until stiff but not dry, then lightly fold into the mixture. Turn into the prepared tin and gently level the surface.

Bake in the pre-heated oven for about 45 minutes or until firm to the touch. Allow to cool in the tin for a few minutes then turn out and leave to cool completely on a wire rack.

For the filling and icing, melt the chocolate slowly in a bowl over a pan of hot water. Add the cubed butter and stir until the mixture has the consistency of thick pouring cream.

Split the cake in half horizontally and use a little of the icing to fill it. Warm the apricot jam then push through a sieve. Brush this over the top and sides of the cake and allow to set before pouring the icing over. Smooth the icing evenly with a palette knife and leave to set.

Chocolate Rum Cake

For the chocolate ganache (if using), melt the chocolate in a bowl with the cream over a pan of hot water. Cool slightly then beat in the butter a little at a time. Beat in the egg yolks and rum and then leave until cool and firm, stirring occasionally. When firm enough to hold its shape, spoon into a piping bag fitted with a star nozzle and pipe rosettes of the ganache to decorate the cake.

Secrets of Success

Piping can make all the difference to the finish of a cake, particularly if it is for a special occasion, and you don't need to have a vast array of piping bags and nozzles to achieve a good result. Strong plastic piping bags can be used and washed over and over again and a plain, small star and large star nozzle are all you need.

Bûche de Noël

Serves 8

This is a version of the Christmas log, which is suitable for serving as a dessert or with coffee.

1 unfilled Chocolate Swiss Roll (see page 205)

For the Filling

1 tablespoon coffee essence

4 tablespoons hot milk

8 oz (225 g) can unsweetened chestnut purée

2 oz (50 g) caster sugar

5 fl oz (150 ml) double cream, whipped

2 tablespoons brandy

For the Topping

10 fl oz (300 ml) double cream, whipped

cocoa to dust

holly leaves to decorate

First make the chocolate Swiss roll. Roll with paper inside and leave to cool.

For the filling, mix the coffee essence with the milk. Sieve the chestnut purée into a bowl and beat in the coffee mixture and the sugar until the mixture is smooth. Fold the whipped cream into the chestnut purée with the brandy.

Carefully unroll the Swiss roll, remove the paper, and spread the chestnut filling all over the cake, then re-roll. Cut a small slice off at an angle from one of the ends of the Swiss roll, place the Swiss roll on to a serving plate or board, and attach the slice to look like a branch.

Spread the whipped cream over the cake to cover completely, using a small palette knife in long strokes to give the bark effect. Dust lightly with cocoa and decorate with holly leaves.

Light Walnut and Chocolate Brownies

Makes about 24 Squares

These are lighter than the Dark Indulgent Chocolate and Walnut Brownies on page 50 in taste as well as colour. The flavour is very nutty and, curiously, rather sweeter than the dark brownies. Both types of brownie are very portable, so are perfect for a picnic or lunchbox.

3 oz (75 g) plain chocolate, broken into pieces

4 oz (100 g) margarine

3 eggs

12 oz (350 g) caster sugar

4½ oz (120 g) plain flour

1 teaspoon baking powder

6 oz (175 g) walnut pieces, chopped

Pre-heat the oven to 180°C/350°F/Gas 4. Grease and base line a 12 × 9 in (30 x 23 cm) roasting tin with greased greaseproof paper.

Melt the chocolate slowly in a bowl with the margarine over a pan of hot water, then cool a little.

In another bowl, whisk together the eggs and sugar until light. Add the cooled chocolate mixture and stir well to mix. Sift the flour and baking powder into the mixture and carefully fold in. Stir in the chopped nuts. Pour into the prepared tin and level the surface.

Bake in the pre-heated oven for about 40 minutes or until the cake is well risen and a dull crust has formed. The brownies should still be a little gooey in the centre. Allow to cool in the tin for a few minutes before turning out and leaving to cool completely on a wire rack. Cut into squares to serve.

Secrets of Success

Keep nuts, shelled and unshelled, in the freezer. Shelled whole nuts will keep for up to five years; ground or flaked for up to a year.

Chocolate Mousse Cake

Cuts into about 18 Wedges

You could use a chocolate whisked sponge for this cake, but a Genoese cake is moister and keeps better. Be very light handed when folding in the flour and butter, or the butter will sink and result in a heavy cake. There are quite a few stages to this cake, so it's not one to tackle if you're in a hurry! You can make the cake in advance and freeze it; the chocolate caraque can also be made in advance and stored in a cool, dry place. Eat as a dessert with a fork.

1 oz (25 g) butter

6 extra large eggs

6 oz (175 g) caster sugar

4 oz (100 g) self-raising flour

1 oz (25 g) cocoa

2 tablespoons cornflour

For the Mousse Filling

6 oz (175 g) plain chocolate, broken into pieces

2 tablespoons brandy

1 teaspoon powdered gelatine

2 eggs, separated

10 fl oz (300 ml) double cream

For the Decoration

7 oz (200 g) plain chocolate, broken into pieces

5 oz (150 g) white chocolate, broken into pieces

5 fl oz (150 ml) double cream

icing sugar for dusting

Pre-heat the oven to 180°C/350°F/Gas 4. Grease and base line a 9 in (23 cm) deep round loose-bottomed cake tin with greased greaseproof paper.

Place the butter in a small pan and heat gently until melted. Leave to cool slightly.

Whisk the eggs and sugar together using an electric whisk on full speed until the mixture is pale and creamy and thick enough to leave a trail when the whisk is lifted from the mixture.

Sift the flour, cocoa and cornflour together. Carefully fold half the flours into the egg mixture. Pour half the cooled butter around the edge of the mixture and carefully fold in. Gradually fold in the remaining flours and then the remaining butter. Pour the mixture into the prepared tin.

Bake in the pre-heated oven for about 35–40 minutes until well risen, firm to the touch and beginning to shrink away from the sides of the tin. Turn out on to a wire rack and leave to cool.

Cut the cake in half horizontally and place the bottom half back in the clean tin.

(Right) Chocolate Mousse Cake

To make the mousse filling, melt the chocolate with the brandy slowly in a bowl over a pan of hot water.

Meanwhile sprinkle the gelatine over 1 tablespoon of cold water in a small bowl and leave to sponge for about 10 minutes (see *page 110*). Stand the bowl in a pan of hot water and allow to dissolve gently.

Leave the melted chocolate to cool slightly and then stir in the egg yolks. Whip the cream until it just stands in soft peaks, then fold into the chocolate. Stir the dissolved gelatine into the chocolate mixture. Whisk the egg whites until stiff but not dry, and gently fold in.

Pour the mousse on top of the cake in the tin, gently level the surface and top with the remaining cake. Cover and leave to set in the fridge.

While the mousse is setting, melt the decoration chocolates separately, and use to make caraque (see *pages 32–3*).

When the mousse is set, ease around the sides of the mousse with a small palette knife and then stand the base of the cake tin on a large can. Ease the sides of the tin down, then slip the cake off the cake tin base and on to a serving plate. Whip the cream and cover the top and sides of the cake with it. Arrange the white and plain chocolate caraque to cover the cake completely: do so in any pattern you like! Dust with a little icing sugar.

Sunday Best Chocolate Fudge Cake

CUTS INTO 8 WEDGES

THIS CAKE IS IDEAL for a Sunday afternoon tea. To make it even more special, do take time to heat a little apricot jam to brush over it before icing. This keeps the cake moist. The icing is simple to make, but avoid getting it too hot as it loses its shine. If you make it ahead and it goes hard, just gently re-heat until runny.

$1\frac{1}{2}$ rounded tablespoons cocoa

3 tablespoons hot water

6 oz (175 g) soft margarine

6 oz (175 g) caster sugar

3 extra large eggs

6 oz (175 g) self-raising flour

$1\frac{1}{2}$ teaspoons baking powder

FOR THE FUDGE ICING

2 oz (50 g) margarine

1 oz (25 g) cocoa, sifted

about 2 tablespoons milk

8 oz (225 g) icing sugar, sifted

TO FINISH

a little warmed apricot jam (optional)

chocolate flake or grated chocolate

Pre-heat the oven to 180°C/350°F/Gas 4. Grease and base line 2 × 7 in (18 cm) sandwich cake tins with greased greaseproof paper.

Blend the cocoa with the hot water in a large bowl and leave to cool. Add the remaining cake ingredients to the bowl and beat thoroughly for 1–2 minutes. Divide between the tins and bake in the pre-heated oven for about 25–30 minutes or until the cakes have shrunk slightly from the sides of the tin and they spring back when pressed lightly with a finger. Turn out, remove the paper and leave to cool on a wire rack.

To make the icing, melt the margarine in a small pan, add the cocoa and cook for 1 minute. Remove from the heat and stir in the milk and icing sugar. Beat well until smooth. Cool a little until of a spreading consistency.

Spread a little warmed apricot jam on to the surface of one of the cakes (which will be the middle of the cake), and top with half the fudge icing. Place the remaining cake on top, brush with apricot jam as before and top with the remaining fudge icing, warmed if necessary. Decorate with chocolate flake or grated chocolate.

Dark Indulgent Chocolate and Walnut Brownies

Makes about 24 Squares

Brownies, like gingerbread, are likely to dip in the middle, but this all adds to their charm. Do not overcook as it's much preferable to have a slightly gooey texture. The outside crust should be on the crisp side though, because of the high proportion of sugar.

12 oz (350g) plain chocolate, broken into pieces

8 oz (225 g) margarine

2 teaspoons instant coffee

2 tablespoons hot water

3 extra large eggs

8 oz (225 g) caster sugar

1 teaspoon vanilla essence

3 oz (75 g) self-raising flour

6 oz (175 g) walnut pieces, chopped

8 oz (225 g) plain chocolate chips

Pre-heat the oven to 190°C/375°F/Gas 5. Grease and base line a 12 × 9 in (30 × 23 cm) roasting tin with greased greaseproof paper.

Melt the chocolate slowly in a bowl with the margarine over a pan of hot water, stirring occasionally. Allow to cool. Dissolve the coffee in the hot water.

In another bowl, mix together the coffee, eggs, sugar and vanilla essence. Gradually beat in the chocolate mixture. Fold in the flour, walnuts and chocolate chips, and then pour the mixture into the prepared tin.

Bake in the pre-heated oven for about 40–45 minutes or until firm to the touch and a dull crust has formed. Leave to cool in the tin. When the cake is completely cold cut into squares.

Dark Indulgent Chocolate and Walnut Brownies

Chapter 2

Meringues

Meringue is a mixture of whisked egg white and sugar. It is thought to have been invented by Gasparani, a Swiss pastry cook, in the early eighteenth century, in the town of Mehrinyghen, hence 'meringue'.

Meringue can be very slowly baked so that it dries out and becomes crisp and firm as in traditional meringues, usually sandwiched together with whipped cream, or baked quickly so that the outside of it is crisp and the inside soft and marshmallowy, like the topping of lemon meringue pie.

Types of Meringue

There is a variety of types of meringue, but the basics are always egg white and sugar.

Meringue Suisse (Swiss Meringue)

This is made by incorporating caster sugar into stiffly whisked egg white. The proportion of sugar to egg white is always 2 oz (50 g) sugar to 1 egg white. The sugar can be added in two halves, whisking in half of the sugar gradually and then folding in the remainder, or it can be added a little at a time. I definitely favour the latter method as it is foolproof. If not very careful, precious volume can be lost using the first method. The meringue mixture should be firm and have a glossy appearance.

This is the type of meringue most used in home baking – for meringue shells, cakes or the topping for meringue pies.

Meringue Cuite (Cooked Meringue)

This is made by whisking egg whites and icing sugar over a pan of hot water. The resulting mixture is white and glossy with a very smooth texture. This meringue holds its shape extremely well and is therefore used where a definite piped shape is required, for instance a meringue basket or nest. Baked *meringue cuite* is harder and more powdery than *meringue suisse.*

The proportion of sugar to egg whites is 2 oz (50 g) icing sugar to each egg white, although the weight of sugar can be slightly generous.

Meringue Italienne (Italian Meringue)

Made by whisking a hot sugar syrup into the egg whites, this method requires the use of a sugar thermometer and is very rarely used in home cooking. The resulting meringue is similar to *meringue cuite* but has a lighter and finer texture.

MAKING MERINGUES

The secret of making successful meringues is simple, providing a few straightforward rules are followed. All equipment must be scrupulously clean and dry, as egg white will not whisk properly if there are any traces of grease or moisture. The egg whites must, therefore, not contain even a speck of yolk.

As long as the sugar is beaten vigorously into the egg whites, in a large bowl, you can't fail. It really doesn't matter whether you use an electric whisk, rotary beater or the old-fashioned copper bowl and balloon whisk. Except when using an electric mixer with a fixed whisk, always move the beaters around the bowl to incoporate as much air into the mixture as possible.

For *meringue suisse*, the egg whites should first be whisked until they form stiff peaks, but no further otherwise the whites will become dry and lose bulk as water seeps out of them. To test the consistency, lift the whisk out of the bowl; the egg white sticking to it should stand in stiff peaks and not fall over at the top. Then add the sugar a teaspoonful at a time, whisking vigorously between each addition, until all the sugar has been incorporated. Add the sugar slowly at first, adding it more quickly towards the end when the egg whites will be more stable. Sugar added too quickly at the beginning without adequate whisking will result in a sticky meringue.

For *meringue cuite*, use a very low heat so that the meringue does not harden on the sides of the bowl or stiffen before enough air has been incorporated.

TIPS AND WATCHPOINTS

- Meringues are an ideal way to use up left-over egg whites. Egg whites can be stored in the fridge or frozen. Use 1 fl oz (25 ml) as a measure for 1 egg white.
- For maximum volume, use egg whites which are at room temperature.
- Cook *meringue suisse* straightaway, otherwise it will start to lose its bulk. *Meringue cuite* can stand for a little while before cooking.
- If the meringue is too runny to shape, the egg whites were probably not stiff enough before the sugar was added, or the sugar was not whisked in vigorously enough to begin with.
- Cracks and large air holes in the baked meringue are due to overwhisked egg whites.
- Sugar weeping out of the meringue once it is in the oven is usually caused by the sugar being added too quickly to the egg whites, or too much at once.

BAKING MERINGUES

Always use non-stick baking paper for meringues. It can be used again, simply wipe it over lightly. 'Lift off' paper is a black, stiff, polythene-type material which comes in sheets, is non-stick and can be used again and again. It is available from specialist suppliers (see *page 304*).

SERVING MERINGUES

Fill and assemble meringues with fruit and cream about two hours before serving to allow the meringue to soften slightly. This will prevent a meringue cake from splintering when cut into.

STORING AND FREEZING MERINGUES

Meringues can be made up to two weeks in advance. Store them carefully in polythene bags in an airtight tin. Or they can be frozen.

Many filled and layered meringues will also freeze: dust with icing sugar and pipe rosettes of cream on top when thawed. Do not freeze soft meringue toppings such as lemon meringue pie. Pavlova is best made on the day, or you can freeze it. Unfilled is best, but you could freeze it with a whipped cream filling. Never freeze a filling which contains fruit, as this makes the pavlova soggy.

Basic White Meringues

MAKES ABOUT 12 DOUBLE MERINGUES

AS MERINGUES ARE so brittle and easily broken, store them in a solid tin or polythene container with kitchen paper in between them. If you haven't got a large enough tin, store in a sealed polythene bag on a high shelf where they won't be bashed.

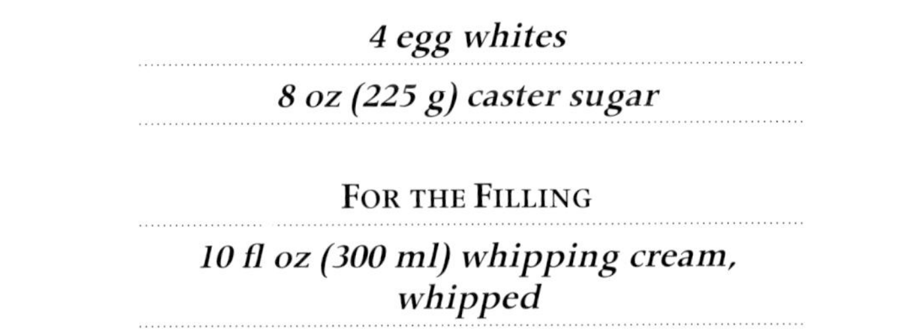

4 egg whites

8 oz (225 g) caster sugar

FOR THE FILLING

10 fl oz (300 ml) whipping cream, whipped

Pre-heat the oven to 130°C/250°F/Gas $\frac{1}{2}$. Line 2 baking trays with non-stick baking paper.

Place the egg whites in a large bowl and whisk on high speed with an electric or hand rotary whisk until stiff but not dry. Add the sugar, a teaspoonful at a time, whisking well after each addition, still on high speed, until all the sugar has been added.

Then, either pipe the meringue mixture into 'blob' shells (see *figure 9*) or 'coil' shells (see *figure 10*) using a $\frac{1}{2}$ in (1 cm) plain nozzle on to the lined baking trays, or shape the meringue into oval shells using 2 dessertspoons (see *figure 11*).

Bake in the pre-heated oven for about 1–1$\frac{1}{2}$ hours, or until they can be lifted easily from the paper without sticking. Turn off the oven, leave the door ajar and leave the meringues until cold.

To serve fill with whipped cream.

SECRETS OF SUCCESS

To dry meringue after baking, turn the oven off and leave the meringues in the oven with the door slightly open. *Leave pavlovas in the turned-off oven with the door* shut; *this will encourage the middle to develop the characteristic pavlova marshmallowiness.*

Brown Sugar Meringues

BROWN SUGAR GIVES meringues a lovely caramely flavour. Use half light muscovado sugar and half caster sugar for the most successful brown sugar meringues. Make and bake the meringues as in the Basic White Meringue recipe opposite.

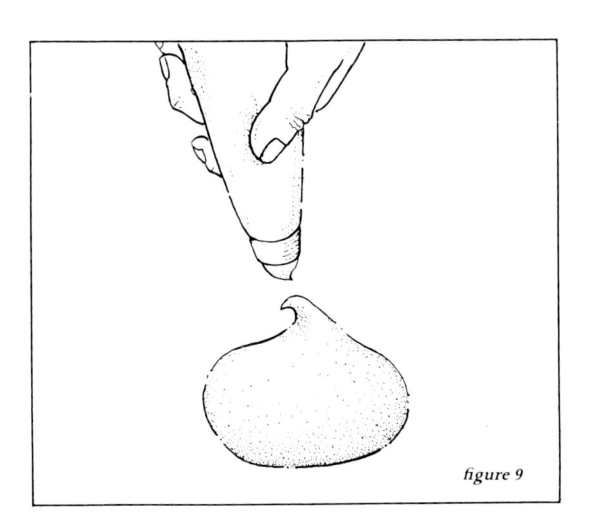

figure 9

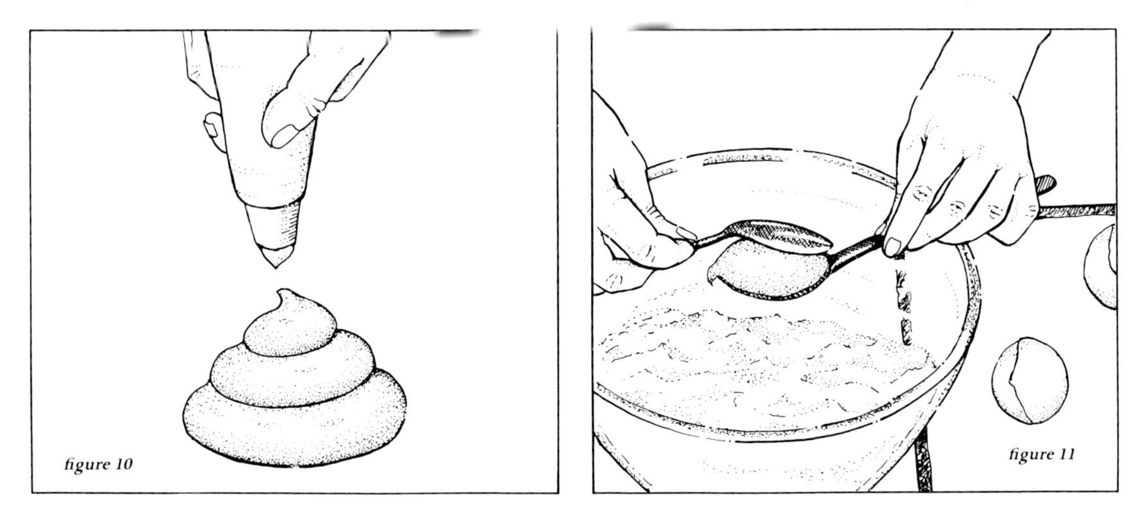

figure 10

figure 11

Hazelnut Meringue Cake

SERVES 6

THIS HAS BECOME A classic favourite, the raspberries and hazelnuts being a particularly good combination. Fill the meringue about 3 hours before serving; it will then cut into portions without splintering. Walnuts can be used in place of the hazelnuts in the meringue. Choose a fruit to complement the walnuts, such as strawberries or ripe peaches in season.

4½ oz (140 g) shelled hazelnuts

4 egg whites

9 oz (250 g) caster sugar

a few drops of vanilla essence

½ teaspoon white wine vinegar

FOR THE FILLING

10 fl oz (300 ml) whipping cream

8 oz (225 g) raspberries

icing sugar

Pre-heat the oven to 190°C/375°F/Gas 5. Lightly brush 2 ×8 in (20 cm) sandwich tins with oil and base line with non-stick baking paper.

Place the hazelnuts on a baking tray and put in the oven for about 10 minutes, then tip on to a clean tea towel and rub well together to remove the skins. (Some stubborn ones may need to go back into the oven but don't worry about getting every last bit of skin off, it's not necessary.) Place the nuts in a food processor or blender and grind.

Whisk the egg whites on maximum speed with an electric whisk until stiff. Add the sugar, a teaspoonful at a time, and continue whisking, still at top speed, until the mixture is very stiff, stands in peaks, and all the sugar has been added. Whisk in the vanilla essence and wine vinegar, then fold in the prepared nuts. Divide the mixture between the prepared tins and smooth the top with a palette knife.

Bake in the pre-heated oven for 30–40 minutes, but no longer. The top of the meringue will be crisp and the inside soft like a marshmallow. Turn out of the tins and allow to cool on a wire rack.

Whisk the cream until thick and use about two-thirds to fill the meringue along with the raspberries. Dust the top of the meringue with icing sugar and use the remaining cream to pipe rosettes on the top. Serve with Raspberry Coulis made with 8 oz (225 g) raspberries and 4 tablespoons (60 ml) sifted icing sugar (see *page 102*).

SECRETS OF SUCCESS

If you don't have sandwich tins, you can cook the mixture on 2 flat baking trays, spread out into 2 circles. It won't look quite so neat, but it tastes the same!

Apricot and Almond Meringue Gâteau

Serves 6

A lovely, delicately flavoured meringue, this is perfect for a very special dinner party. In season, you could use fresh apricots: stone about 12 oz (350 g), then cook and purée. Save a few quartered apricots as decoration.

4 egg whites

8 oz (225 g) caster sugar

3 oz (75 g) ground almonds

For the Filling and Sauce

4 oz (100 g) ready-to-eat dried apricots

a strip of lemon rind

10 fl oz (300 ml) water

4 oz (100 g) granulated sugar

juice of $\frac{1}{2}$ lemon

10 fl oz (300 ml) double cream

To Finish

icing sugar

about 5 fl oz (150 ml) double cream, whipped (optional)

Pre-heat the oven to 140°C/275°F/Gas 1. Line 2 baking trays with non-stick baking paper.

Whisk the egg whites on maximum speed with an electric whisk until stiff. Whisk in the caster sugar, a teaspoonful at a time, still on high speed. Fold in the ground almonds.

Divide the mixture between the baking trays and spread gently into 2 rounds 8 in (20 cm) in diameter. Bake in the pre-heated oven for about 1–1$\frac{1}{4}$ hours or until the paper peels away from the base of the meringue. (This meringue mixture is quite sticky so don't worry if it sticks a little in the middle.) Leave the meringues to cool on a wire rack.

For the filling, place the apricots in a small pan with the strip of lemon rind and half the water. Heat gently for about 20 minutes until the apricots are very tender. Place the apricots into a food processor or blender and process until smooth.

Gently dissolve the granulated sugar in the remaining water, add the lemon juice and boil for 3 minutes to make a sugar syrup.

Whip the cream until it holds its shape, and flavour with about one-third of the apricot purée. Use to fill the meringue. Dust the top of the meringue with icing sugar and decorate with rosettes of piped cream, if liked.

Dilute the remaining apricot purée with the sugar syrup and serve as a sauce.

Coffee and Banana Vacherin

SERVES 6

USE HALF CASTER SUGAR and half light muscovado sugar if you prefer a less caramely flavoured meringue.

4 egg whites

8 oz (225 g) light muscovado sugar

FOR THE FILLING

10 fl oz (300 ml) double cream

1 teaspoon instant coffee

2 ripe bananas

TO FINISH

icing sugar

5 fl oz (150 ml) double cream

Pre-heat the oven to 140°C/275°F/Gas 1. Line 2 baking trays with non-stick baking paper and mark each with an 8 in (20 cm) circle.

Place the egg whites in a large bowl and whisk on high speed with an electric whisk until stiff. Add the sugar, a teaspoonful at a time, whisking well at high speed after each addition, until all the sugar has been added.

Spoon the meringue mixture into a large nylon piping bag fitted with a $\frac{1}{2}$ in (1 cm) plain nozzle, and pipe the meringue into 2 circles in a spiral pattern, starting at the centre.

Bake in the pre-heated oven for 1–$1\frac{1}{4}$ hours or until the meringues are crisp and dry and lightly coloured. Allow to cool in the oven and then peel off the paper.

For the filling whip the cream until it holds its shape, and flavour with the coffee dissolved in a little water. Slice the bananas thinly and fold into the cream, making sure they are well coated to prevent discoloration. Spread over one meringue circle, and then place the other circle on top. Dust lightly with sieved icing sugar and decorate with rosettes of whipped cream.

SECRETS OF SUCCESS

You can make the meringue circles the day before, but don't keep the filled cake for too long as the bananas will eventually turn brown.

(Right) Coffee and Banana Vacherin

Strawberry Meringue Nests

Makes 6 Baskets

Ordinary meringue could be used for these nests, but they won't be quite so firm, nor will they store so well. Meringue cuite *is traditional because it holds its shape so well and is drier. Vary the fruit in these nests depending on the season.*

For the *Meringue Cuite*

4 egg whites

$8\frac{1}{2}$ oz (240 g) icing sugar

a few drops of vanilla essence (optional)

For the Filling

8 oz (225 g) fresh strawberries

about 2 tablespoons redcurrant jelly

Pre-heat the oven to 140°C/275°F/Gas 1. Line a baking tray with non-stick baking paper.

Place the egg whites into a large bowl and whisk until foaming. Sift the icing sugar through a fine sieve into the egg whites. Place the bowl over a pan of gently simmering water and whisk the whites and sugar together until very thick and holding their shape. Add the vanilla essence, if using, and whisk again to mix. Be careful not to let the pan get too hot or the meringue mixture will crust around the edges.

Spoon the mixture into a nylon piping bag fitted with a large star nozzle. Pipe into 6 baskets, starting in the centre and lastly building up the sides.

Bake in the pre-heated oven for about 45 minutes until crisp and dry. Carefully lift off the baking tray and allow to cool on a wire rack.

Halve the strawberries, if large, and use to fill the baskets. Warm the redcurrant jelly in a small pan and gently spoon over the strawberries to glaze.

Secrets of Success

To fill a piping bag stand the bag and nozzle point down in a jug and then fold the top edges of the bag over the top of the jug. That way it is much easier to spoon the cream or icing into the bag without getting it all over yourself!

Baby Meringues

MAKES ABOUT 30 FILLED MERINGUES

THESE ARE PERFECT for a party, the different shapes and fillings making a wonderful centrepiece for the dessert table. You could also make them with ordinary meringue (see page 54), but these will hold better once the fillings have been added.

FOR THE *MERINGUE CUITE*

4 egg whites

$8\frac{1}{2}$ oz (240 g) icing sugar

a few drops of vanilla essence (optional)

FOR THE FILLING

10 fl oz (300 ml) double cream

1 tablespoon brandy, or liqueur of your choice

about 1 oz (25 g) walnuts, finely chopped

small pieces of fresh fruit to decorate (small star fruit, strawberries, raspberries, kiwi fruit, grapes etc.)

Pre-heat the oven to 140°C/275°C/Gas 1. Line 3 baking trays with non-stick baking paper.

Place the egg whites into a large bowl and whisk until foaming. Sift the icing sugar through a fine sieve into the egg whites. Place the bowl over a pan of gently simmering water and whisk the whites and sugar together until very thick and holding their shape. Add the vanilla essence, if using, and whisk again to mix.

Be careful not to let the pan get too hot or the meringue mixture will crust around the edges.

Spoon the mixture into a nylon piping bag fitted with a large star nozzle. Pipe into tiny baskets, shells, spiral oblongs and fingers (see *figure 12*).

Bake in the pre-heated oven for about 45 minutes until crisp and dry. Carefully lift off the baking trays and allow to cool on a wire rack.

For the fillings, whip the cream with the brandy or liqueur until it holds its shape. Divide between 2 bowls. Stir the chopped nuts into one bowl, and leave the other cream plain. Sandwich the spiral oblongs and tiny shells with the cream with nuts; pipe a little plain cream into the baskets and use to sandwich the fingers together. Top the baskets and the sandwiched fingers with a small single piece of fruit, if liked.

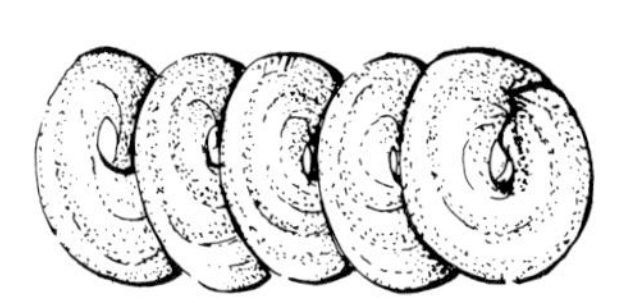
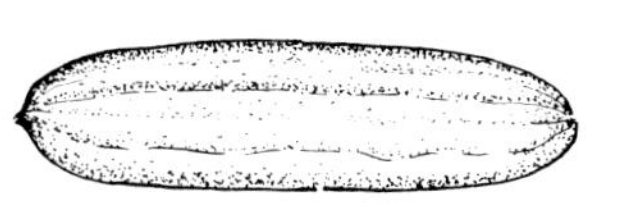

figure 12

Raspberry Meringue Roulade

Makes 8–10 Slices

This is rather an unusual idea, and it makes a generous roulade, an excellent size for a party. It also freezes extremely well: simply wrap in foil to freeze, then allow about 8 hours to thaw before serving.

5 egg whites

10 oz (275 g) caster sugar

2 oz (50 g) flaked almonds

For the Filling

10 fl oz (300 ml) whipping cream

12 oz (350 g) fresh raspberries

Pre-heat the oven to 200°C/400°F/Gas 6. Line a 13 × 9 in (33 × 23 cm) Swiss roll tin with greased non-stick baking paper.

Whisk the egg whites in an electric mixer on full speed until very stiff. Gradually add the sugar, a teaspoonful at a time, and still at high speed, whisking well between each addition. Whisk until very, very stiff and all the sugar has been included.

Spread the meringue mixture into the prepared tin and sprinkle with the almonds. Place the tin fairly near the top of the pre-heated oven and bake for about 8 minutes until pale golden. Then lower the oven temperature to 160°C/325°F/Gas 3 and bake the roulade for a further 15 minutes until firm to the touch.

Remove the meringue from the oven and turn almond side down on to a sheet of non-stick baking paper. Remove the paper from the base of the cooked meringue and allow to cool for about 10 minutes.

Meanwhile, whisk the cream until it stands in stiff peaks, and gently mix in the raspberries. Spread the cream and raspberries evenly over the meringue. Start to roll from the long end fairly tightly until rolled up like a roulade. Wrap in non-stick baking paper and chill before serving.

Secrets of Success

Left-over egg yolks should be stored in the fridge in a small container. Pour a tablespoon of cold water over the top, and then cover with cling film. Use within a week.

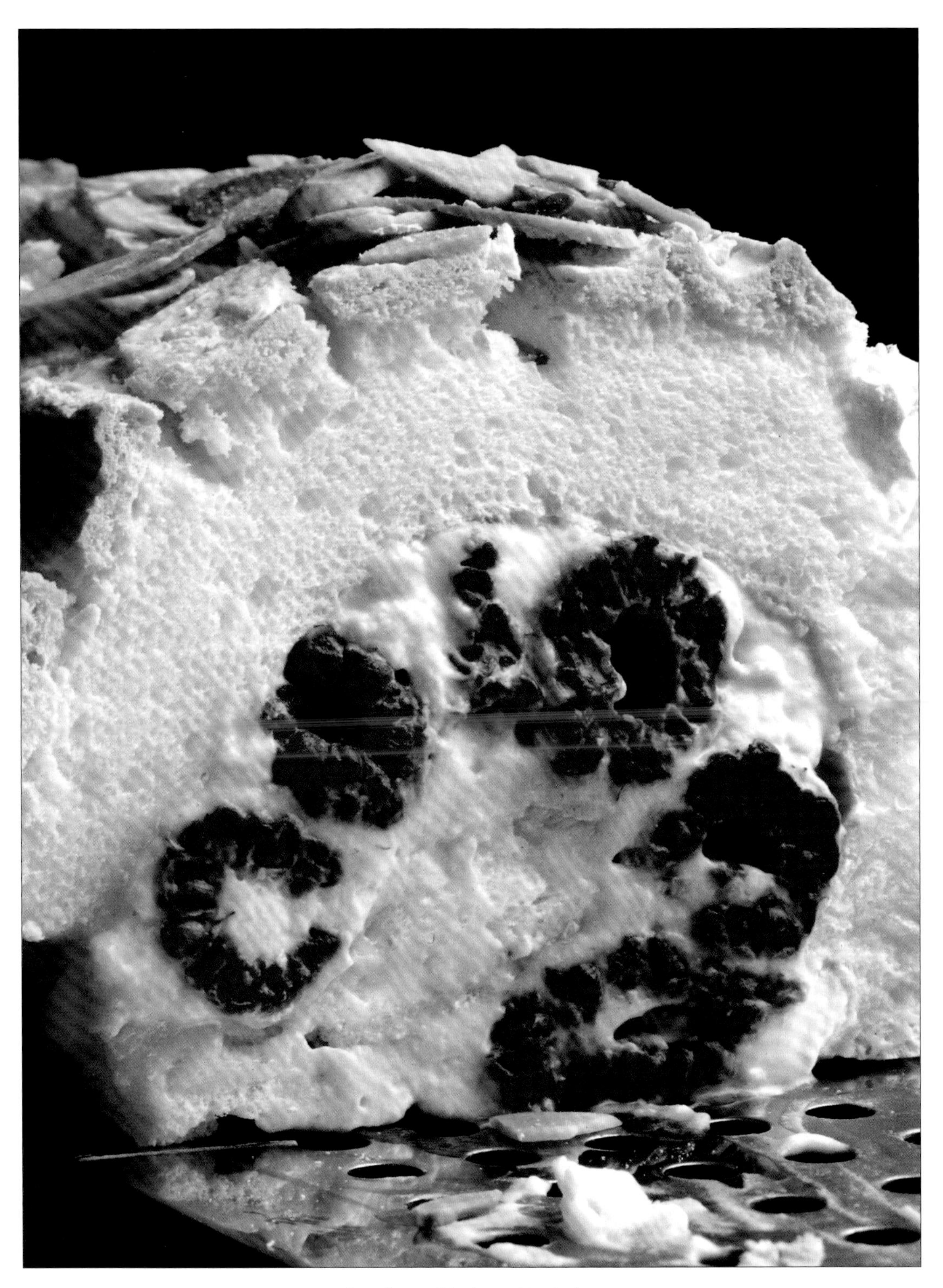

Raspberry Meringue Roulade

Fruit-filled Meringue Basket

SERVES 8–10

THIS RECIPE USES meringue cuite *which holds its shape better than ordinary meringue. The finished basket makes a wonderful centrepiece for a cold buffet or dessert table. Fill it with ice-cream for a change. The unfilled basket will freeze, or it will keep for about a week in an airtight container.*

FOR THE FIRST BATCH *MERINGUE CUITE*

4 egg whites

$8\frac{1}{2}$ oz (240 g) icing sugar

FOR THE SECOND BATCH *MERINGUE CUITE*

2 egg whites

$4\frac{1}{4}$ oz (110 g) icing sugar

FOR THE FILLING

10 fl oz (300 ml) whipping cream, whipped

about 1 lb (450 g) fresh fruits in season, such as strawberries, raspberries and redcurrants

Pre-heat the oven to 140°C/275°F/Gas 1. Line 2 baking trays with non-stick baking paper. Draw a 7 in (18 cm) circle on each piece of paper.

Make the first batch of *meringue cuite.* Place the egg whites into a large bowl and whisk until foaming. Sift the icing sugar through a fine sieve into the egg whites. Place the bowl over a pan of simmering water and whisk the whites and sugar together until the mixture is very thick and holding its shape. Be careful not to allow the bowl to get too hot or the meringue will crust around the edges.

Put about half the mixture into a nylon piping bag fitted with a $\frac{1}{2}$ in (1 cm) plain nozzle. Pipe a *solid round* on to the first baking tray, starting at the centre and piping around in a spiral motion. Pipe a *hoop* of meringue on to the second baking tray. Use the pencilled circles as guides for each (see *figure 13*). You'll have some meringue left over; cover it in the bowl with a damp cloth to prevent it from becoming hard.

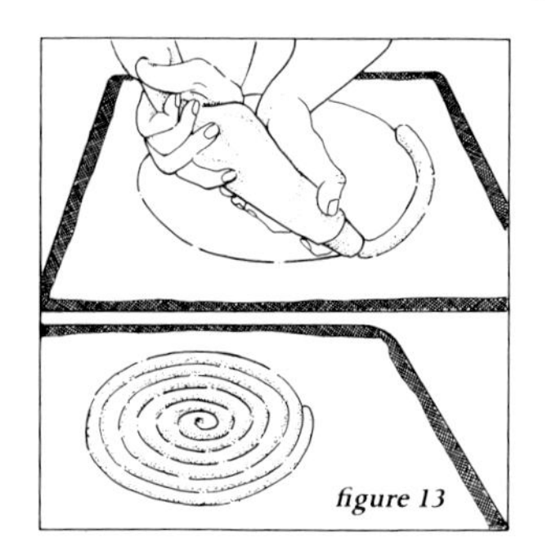

figure 13

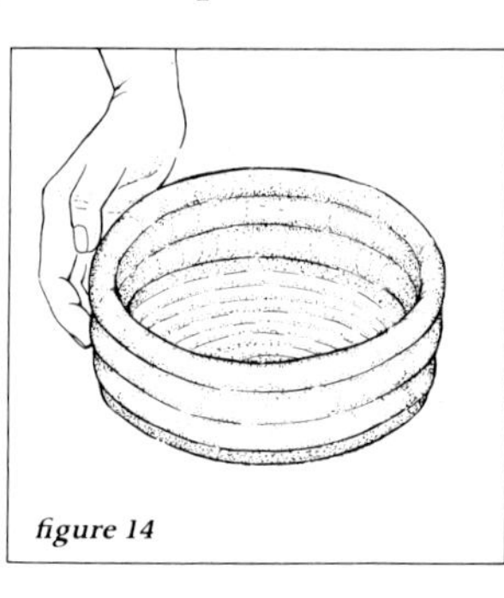

figure 14

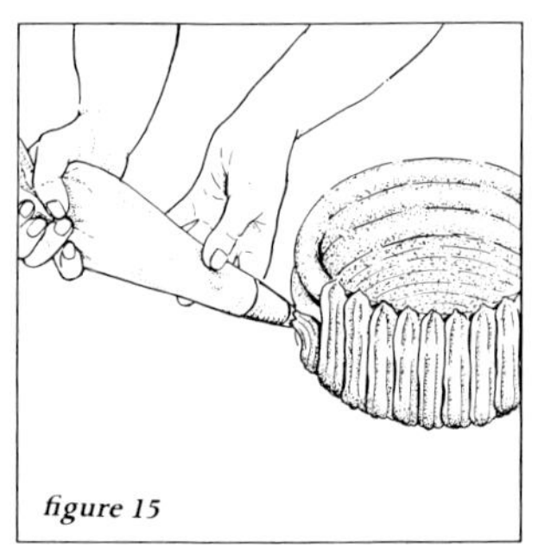

figure 15

(Right) Fruit-filled Meringue Basket

Bake in the pre-heated oven for about 45 minutes or until dry and crisp. Gently lift the baked meringue round and hoop off the baking trays and leave to cool on a wire rack. Turn the papers over and pipe two more *hoops* of meringue to the same size as before. Bake and cool as before.

Make up the second batch of meringue in the same way as above, and use a little of this to 'stick' the 3 hoops on to the round, one on top of the other (see *figure 14*). Fit the piping bag with a large star nozzle and then fill with the remaining meringue. Pipe vertically around the outside of the hoops to neaten and to give a decorative appearance (see *figure 15*). Pipe small stars on the top of the basket if you like. Bake the whole thing again at the same temperature for about 45 minutes until set and crisp.

Leave to cool completely then fill with the whipped cream and fruits to serve.

Pavlova

SERVES 8

THIS MARSHMALLOWY MERINGUE is believed to have been created in Australia in the 1930s to celebrate the visit of the ballerina, Anna Pavlova. Don't worry about cracks on the top – this is all part of the charm. (See photograph on pages 2–3.)

4 egg whites

8 oz (225 g) caster sugar

1½ teaspoons cornflour

1½ teaspoons white wine vinegar

FOR THE FILLING

12 oz (350 g) fresh fruits, such as blueberries, kiwi fruit and raspberries

15 fl oz (450 ml) whipping cream, whipped

Pre-heat the oven to 160°C/325°F/Gas 3. Lay a sheet of non-stick baking paper on a baking tray and mark a 9–10 in (23–25 cm) circle on it.

Whisk the egg whites with an electric whisk until stiff, then add the sugar, a teaspoonful at a time, still whisking at full speed. Blend the cornflour and wine vinegar together and whisk into the meringue mixture. Spread the meringue out to cover the circle on the baking tray, building up the sides so they are higher than the middle.

Place in the pre-heated oven but immediately reduce the temperature to 150°C/300°F/Gas 2. Bake the pavlova for about 1–1¼ hours until firm to the touch and a pale beige colour. Turn the oven off and allow the pavlova to become quite cold in the oven.

Remove the pavlova from the baking tray and slide on to a serving plate. Fill with the whipped cream and fruits. Leave in the fridge for about 1 hour before serving.

Key Lime Pie

Serves 8

This pie originates from Key West in Florida and it caters for those with a sweet tooth. For a sharper filling use 3 limes. It may look like a cheat's recipe, but it's authentic, and surprisingly simple to make.

For the Base

5 oz (150 g) digestive biscuits

2½ oz (65 g) butter

1 oz (25 g) demerara sugar

For the Filling

2 egg yolks

1 × 14 oz (397 g) can condensed milk

grated rind and juice of 2 limes

For the Meringue

2 egg whites

4 oz (100 g) caster sugar

Pre-heat the oven to 150°C/300°F/Gas 2.

Place the biscuits in a food processor and process until crushed, or put the biscuits into a plastic bag and crush with a rolling pin. Melt the butter in a small pan, add the crushed biscuits and the sugar and mix thoroughly. Place in an 8–9 in (20–23 cm) glass pie dish, pressing down well over the base and up the sides to form a case.

For the filling, place the egg yolks and condensed milk in a bowl and mix together, then stir in the lime rind and juice until the mixture thickens. Turn into the biscuit case and smooth the top.

For the meringue, whisk the egg whites in a large bowl with an electric whisk until they form stiff peaks. Add the sugar, a teaspoonful at a time, whisking well and at top speed between each addition, until all the sugar is used. Spoon or pipe on top of the filling.

Bake in the pre-heated oven for about 45 minutes or until the meringue is pale golden and crisp on the outside and soft and marshmallowy on the inside. Serve warm or cold.

Lemon Meringue Pie

Serves 6 and 12

As this is such a family favourite – it's perfect for a Sunday lunch – I have tested it in two sizes, one to serve six, one to serve twelve. There's quite a lot of washing up when making a lemon meringue pie, but the recipe itself isn't too complicated.

FOR A 9 IN (23 CM) PIE	FOR AN 11 IN (28 CM) PIE
For the Pastry	**For the Pastry**
6 oz (175 g) plain flour	*8 oz (225 g) plain flour*
½ oz (15 g) icing sugar	*1 oz (25 g) icing sugar*
3 oz (75 g) butter	*4 oz (100 g) butter*
1 egg yolk	*1 egg yolk*
about 1 tablespoon water	*about 2 tablespoons water*
For the Filling	**For the Filling**
2 large lemons	*4 large lemons*
1½ oz (40 g) cornflour	*3 oz (75 g) cornflour*
10 fl oz (300 ml) water	*1 pint (600 ml) water*
2 egg yolks	*4 egg yolks*
3 oz (75 g) caster sugar	*6 oz (175 g) caster sugar*
For the Meringue	**For the Meringue**
3 egg whites	*5 egg whites*
4½ oz (120 g) caster sugar	*8 oz (225 g) caster sugar*

Pre-heat the oven to 200°C/400°F/Gas 6.

To make the pastry, measure the flour and sugar into a bowl and rub in the butter until the mixture resembles fine breadcrumbs. Add the egg yolk and water and work to a firm dough – this may, of course, be done in a processor. Wrap in cling film and leave to rest in the fridge for about 30 minutes.

On a lightly floured work surface, roll out the pastry and use to line a 9 in (23 cm) or 11 in (28 cm) loose-bottomed, fluted flan tin. Prick the pastry lightly all over with a fork, line with greaseproof paper, fill with baking beans and bake blind (see *page 27*) in the pre-heated oven for about 20 minutes or until the pastry is pale golden and dried out, removing the paper and beans for the last 5 minutes.

Lemon Meringue Pie

Lower the oven heat to 150°C/300°F/Gas 2.

For the filling, finely grate the rinds from the lemons and squeeze out the juice. Put the rind, juice and cornflour into a small bowl and blend together. Bring the water to the boil, then stir into the cornflour mixture. Simmer gently, stirring, until it forms a thick custard. Mix the egg yolks and sugar together and stir into the custard. Bring back to the boil, whisking until just bubbling. Remove from the heat. Allow to cool a little then pour into the pastry case. Spread the mixture out evenly.

For the meringue, whisk the egg whites in a large bowl with an electric whisk until they form stiff peaks. Whisk in the caster sugar, a teaspoonful at a time, whisking well and at high speed between each addition. Spoon the meringue over the top of the lemon filling, spreading it out evenly and swirling it into peaks. Make sure there are no gaps.

Bake at the lower oven temperature for about 45 minutes for the 9 in (23 cm) pie and about 1 hour for the 11 in (28 cm) pie or until the meringue is crisp and pale beige on the outside and soft and marshmallowy underneath. Serve warm or cold.

Meringue Tranche

SERVES 6

ATTRACTIVE SHAPE AND easy to slice, you can fill the meringue with any fresh fruit in season.

3 egg whites

6 oz (175 g) caster sugar

FOR THE FILLING

10 fl oz (300 ml) whipping cream, whipped

8 oz (225 g) fresh raspberries or strawberries

Pre-heat the oven to 130°C/250°F/Gas ½. Line 2 baking trays with non-stick baking paper and mark each piece with an oblong 4½ in (11.5 cm) wide and 11 in (28 cm) long.

Place the egg whites in a large bowl and whisk on high speed with an electric or hand rotary whisk until stiff but not dry. Add all the sugar, a teaspoonful at a time, whisking well after each addition, still on high speed.

Spoon the mixture into a large piping bag fitted with a ½ in (1 cm) star nozzle. Pipe 2 oblongs of meringue on to the prepared baking trays, using the pencil marks as a guide, taking the piping bag in a zig-zag fashion across the width of the oblong (see *figure 16*).

Bake in the pre-heated oven for about 1–1½ hours or until dried out. Turn off the oven, leave the door ajar and leave the meringues until cold.

Place one oblong upside down on to a serving plate and top with the whipped cream and fruit. Place the other meringue on top and dust with icing sugar to serve.

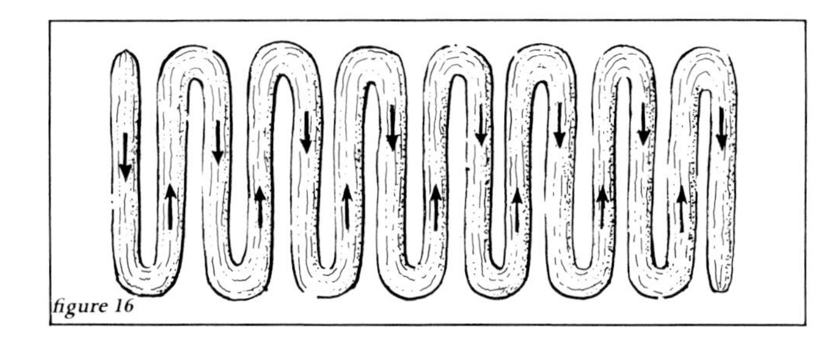

figure 16

Chocolate Ganache Meringue

SERVES 8

GANACHE IS A RICH chocolate and cream mixture, a classic filling for chocolate cakes and chocolate tartlet cases. Add fruit such as black cherries to the cream filling if you like.

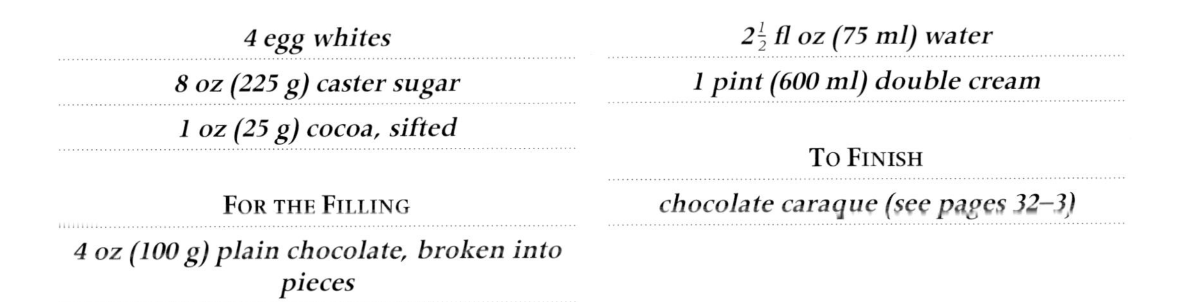

4 egg whites

8 oz (225 g) caster sugar

1 oz (25 g) cocoa, sifted

FOR THE FILLING

4 oz (100 g) plain chocolate, broken into pieces

$2\frac{1}{2}$ fl oz (75 ml) water

1 pint (600 ml) double cream

TO FINISH

chocolate caraque (see pages 32–3)

Pre-heat the oven to 140°C/275°F/Gas 1. Line 3 baking trays with non-stick baking paper and mark 2 of them with a 7 in (18 cm) circle.

Place the egg whites in a large bowl and whisk on high speed with an electric or hand rotary whisk until they are stiff but not dry. Add the sugar, a teaspoonful at a time, whisking well after each addition, still at high speed, until all the sugar has been added. Carefully fold the cocoa into the meringue mixture.

Pipe about one-third of the meringue mixture using a $\frac{1}{2}$ inch (1 cm) plain nozzle, into 8 small shells, about 2 in (5 cm) in diameter, on the prepared baking trays. Pipe the remaining mixture into 2 solid circles following the pencilled outlines, or spread out carefully using a palette knife. Bake in the pre-heated oven for about 1–$1\frac{1}{4}$ hours, or until the meringues are dry and crisp.

For the filling, melt the chocolate slowly with the water in a small pan, then allow to cool. Whisk the cream until it holds its shape, then fold in the cooled chocolate.

Place one meringue round on a serving plate and spread over half the chocolate cream. Top with the second round and spread the remaining chocolate cream evenly over the top. Arrange the meringue shells on top and decorate with chocolate caraque.

Baked Alaska

Serves About 10

Impressive to serve but surprisingly easy to make, this makes an instant birthday cake, and you can decorate it with lit sparklers. For adults, spoon a little booze over the cake.

For the Sponge Base

2 extra large eggs

3 oz (75 g) caster sugar

2 oz (50 g) self-raising flour

For the Filling

1 tablespoon sherry (optional)

8 oz (225 g) strawberries

$1\frac{3}{4}$ pints (1 litre) strawberry ice-cream

For the Meringue Topping

4 egg whites

8 oz (225 g) caster sugar

2 oz (50 g) flaked almonds

icing sugar

Pre-heat the oven to 190°C/375°F/Gas 5. Lightly grease and base line a 9 in (23 cm) sandwich cake tin with greased greaseproof paper.

For the sponge, measure the eggs and sugar into a large bowl and whisk at full speed with an electric whisk until the mixture is pale in colour and thick enough to just leave a trail when the whisk is lifted. Sift the flour over the surface of the mixture and gently fold in with a metal spoon or spatula. Turn into the prepared tin and tilt the tin to allow the mixture to spread evenly to the sides.

Bake in the pre-heated oven for about 20–25 minutes until springy to the touch and beginning to shrink from the sides of the tin. Turn out and leave to cool on a wire rack.

Place the sponge on an ovenproof serving dish, sprinkle it with the sherry, if using, then scatter with the strawberries, leaving a small gap around the edge. Slice the ice-cream and arrange it in a dome shape over the strawberries. Put into the freezer while you are making the meringue.

Pre-heat the oven to 230°C/450°F/Gas 8.

To make the meringue, whisk the egg whites at full speed until they are stiff but not dry. Add the sugar, a teaspoonful at a time, still whisking at high speed, until all the sugar has been added and the meringue is thick and glossy.

Take the cake and ice-cream from the freezer and pile the meringue on top and over the sides, making sure that all the ice-cream and sponge have been covered. Sprinkle over the flaked almonds. Bake immediately in the pre-heated oven for about 3–4 minutes or until well browned. Dust with icing sugar and serve immediately. If you like, you can push lit sparklers into the top to serve. Keep a strict eye on the sparklers when lit and stand the baked Alaska on a large board or tray.

Baked Alaska

Chapter 3

Traybakes

What I have always called traybakes must be the easiest of all cakes to make, and they are so economical in time, energy and space. The basic mixture is brought together in minutes in a food mixer, then it is baked, cooled *and* iced in one large tin (a roasting tin is perfect). You do not have to bother with turning the cake out on to a cooling rack, which saves on space in a busy kitchen and you avoid having to clear up the spills and mess afterwards; the icing is simply poured over the cooled cake *in the tin*, then smoothed over with a palette knife and left to set. Ultimately all you have to wash up is the tin! If you've lined the tin with foil you don't even have to do that!

The cake can then be cut into whatever size pieces you prefer – large for hungry teenagers, or small, two-bite-sized pieces for younger children. In general I specify 21 pieces for a medium traybake, but this is just a rough guide. Two traybakes can easily be baked at the same time, which means you can be making about 40 portions in one go – much more than you would get from two conventional Victoria sponges, say. After you've cut into portions, lift them out with a palette knife.

Traybakes are ideal for large numbers – for parties, bazaars, coffee mornings and school fêtes, for instance. I used to make many a traybake for children's parties because they required so little effort or trouble that it left me free to concentrate on other, more complicated, party specialities. Cut children's traybakes very small as there is less possibility of any wasted cake. I still make them for bazaars and the like because of the ease of transportation and because they can serve so many portions. (If you line the tin or tins with foil, that can be the container in which to transport the cake if you don't want to lose your roasting tin!)

You can also make a *layered* cake with traybakes. Make two, then sandwich them together with a filling of your choice. This is perfect for something like a cricket tea.

The possible variety of traybakes is enormous. Here I have given a basic sponge traybake recipe, and then lots of variations on the same theme. There are also several other ideas which are as easy and just as delicious.

In this chapter I have lined the tins with greased greaseproof paper. You could use non-stick baking paper or greased foil.

Basic All-in-one Sponge Traybake

Cuts into 21 Small Pieces

This is the simplest of cakes to make. Measure the ingredients straight into the bowl and beat just until smooth. When cooked and cold, sieve over icing sugar, if liked.

8 oz (225 g) soft margarine	***2 teaspoons baking powder***
8 oz (225 g) caster sugar	***4 eggs***
10 oz (275 g) self-raising flour	***4 tablespoons milk***

Pre-heat the oven to 180°C/350°F/Gas 4. Grease and base line a 12 × 9 in (30 × 23 cm) roasting tin with greased greaseproof paper.

Measure all the ingredients into a large bowl and beat well for about 2 minutes until well blended. Turn the mixture into the prepared tin and level the top.

Bake in the pre-heated oven for about 35–40 minutes or until the cake has shrunk from the sides of the tin and springs back when pressed in the centre with your fingertips. Leave to cool in the tin.

Large Basic All-in-one Sponge Traybake

Cuts into 32 Small Pieces

This is the same as the recipe above, but for a large cake, so it is perfect for a fête or a party.

12 oz (350 g) soft margarine	***3 teaspoons baking powder***
12 oz (350 g) caster sugar	***6 eggs***
1 lb (450 g) self-raising flour	***6 tablespoons milk***

Pre-heat the oven to 180°C/350°F/Gas 4. Grease and base line a $11\frac{1}{2} \times 14\frac{1}{2}$ in (29 × 36 cm) roasting tin with greased greaseproof paper.

Measure all the ingredients into a large bowl and beat well for about 2 minutes until well blended. Turn the mixture into the prepared tin and level the top.

Bake in the pre-heated oven for about 40–45 minutes or until the cake has shrunk from the sides of the tin and springs back when pressed in the centre with your fingertips. Leave to cool in the tin.

Iced Lemon Traybake

CUTS INTO 21 SMALL PIECES

YOU CAN VARY A basic traybake quite simply – in this case by adding a subtle lemon flavour and a lemon glacé icing. (See photograph on pages 80–81.)

8 oz (225 g) soft margarine
8 oz (225 g) caster sugar
10 oz (275 g) self-raising flour
2 teaspoons baking powder
4 eggs
4 tablespoons milk
grated rind of 2 lemons

FOR THE ICING

about 3 tablespoons lemon juice
8 oz (225 g) icing sugar, sifted

Pre-heat the oven to 180°C/350°F/Gas 4. Grease and base line a 12 × 9 in (30 × 23 cm) roasting tin with greased greaseproof paper.

Measure all the ingredients into a large bowl and beat well for about 2 minutes until well blended. Turn the mixture into the prepared tin and level the top.

Bake in the pre-heated oven for about 35–40 minutes or until the cake has shrunk from the sides of the tin and springs back when pressed in the centre with your fingertips. Leave to cool in the tin.

Mix together the lemon juice and icing sugar to give a runny consistency. Spread out evenly over the cake and leave to set.

Iced Chocolate Traybake

Cuts into 21 Small Pieces

Chocolate cakes are always popular, and this is a particularly simple version which is great for family teas or lunchboxes. *(See photograph on pages 80–81.)*

4 tablespoons cocoa
4 tablespoons hot water
8 oz (225 g) soft margarine
8 oz (225 g) caster sugar
10 oz (275 g) self-raising flour
2 teaspoons baking powder
4 eggs
1 tablespoon milk

For the Icing and Decoration

4 tablespoons apricot jam
5 oz (150 g) plain chocolate, broken into pieces
6 tablespoons water
12 oz (350 g) icing sugar, sifted
1 teaspoon sunflower oil
chocolate curls (see page 33)

Pre-heat the oven to 180°C/350°F/Gas 4. Grease and base line a 12 × 9 in (30 × 23 cm) roasting tin with greased greaseproof paper.

Blend together the cocoa and water then allow to cool slightly.

Measure all the ingredients into a large bowl and beat well for about 2 minutes until well blended. Turn the mixture into the prepared tin and level the top.

Bake in the pre-heated oven for about 35–40 minutes or until the cake has shrunk from the sides of the tin and springs back when pressed in the centre with your fingertips. Leave to cool in the tin.

For the icing, warm the apricot jam in a pan and brush all over the cake. Place the chocolate and water in a pan and heat gently until melted and smooth. Allow to cool slightly, then beat in the icing sugar and oil. Pour over the cake and smooth over gently with a palette knife. Allow to set for about 30 minutes. Cut into squares and decorate with chocolate curls.

Secrets of Success

If time allows, do brush the cake with apricot jam. It gives the cake a lovely flavour and prevents crumbs from the cake getting into the icing.

Chocolate Chip and Vanilla Marble Cake

CUTS INTO 21 SMALL PIECES

A POPULAR TRAYBAKE for parties, children particularly enjoy the fun of making marble cakes. (See photograph on pages 80–81.)

8 oz (225 g) soft margarine
8 oz (225 g) caster sugar
10 oz (275 g) self-raising flour
2 teaspoons baking powder
4 eggs
2 tablespoons milk
½ teaspoon vanilla essence
1½ tablespoons cocoa
2 tablespoons hot water
2 oz (50 g) plain chocolate chips

FOR THE ICING

2 oz (50 g) plain chocolate, broken into pieces
2 oz (50 g) white chocolate, broken into pieces

Pre-heat the oven to 180°C/350°F/Gas 4. Grease and base line a 12 × 9 in (30 × 23 cm) roasting tin with greased greaseproof paper.

Measure the margarine, sugar, flour, baking powder, eggs, milk and vanilla essence into a large bowl and beat well for about 2 minutes until well blended. Spoon half the mixture into the prepared tin, dotting the spoonfuls apart.

In a small bowl, blend the cocoa and hot water. Cool slightly, then add it to the remaining cake mixture with the chocolate chips. Spoon this chocolate mixture in between the plain cake mixture to fill the gaps.

Bake in the pre-heated oven for about 35–40 minutes or until the cake has shrunk from the sides of the tin and springs back when pressed in the centre with your fingertips. Leave to cool in the tin.

Melt the plain and white chocolate separately. Spoon into two separate small plastic bags, snip off the corner of the bags and drizzle the chocolates all over the top of the cake to decorate. Leave to set for about 30 minutes before cutting into squares.

Sultana and Orange Traybake

CUTS INTO 21 SMALL PIECES

THE ORANGES AND THE sultanas go well together. You can sprinkle the cake with demerara sugar to give a crusty, sugary top, or as an alternative, you can omit the demerara sugar and instead ice the cake with orange glacé icing made with 8 oz (225 g) of sifted icing sugar and about 3 tablespoons of orange juice. *(See photograph on pages 80–81.)*

8 oz (225 g) soft margarine

8 oz (225 g) caster sugar

10 oz (275 g) self-raising flour

2 teaspoons baking powder

4 eggs

2 tablespoons milk

10 oz (275 g) sultanas

grated rinds of 2 oranges

demerara sugar

Pre-heat the oven to 180°C/350°F/Gas 4. Grease and base line a 12 × 9 in (30 × 23 cm) roasting tin with greased greaseproof paper.

Measure all the ingredients except the demerara sugar into a large bowl and beat well for about 2 minutes until well blended. Turn the mixture into the prepared tin and level the top.

Bake in the pre-heated oven for about 25 minutes then sprinkle the top with demerara sugar and return to the oven for a further 10–15 minutes or until the cake has shrunk from the sides of the tin and springs back when pressed in the centre with your fingertips. Leave to cool in the tin.

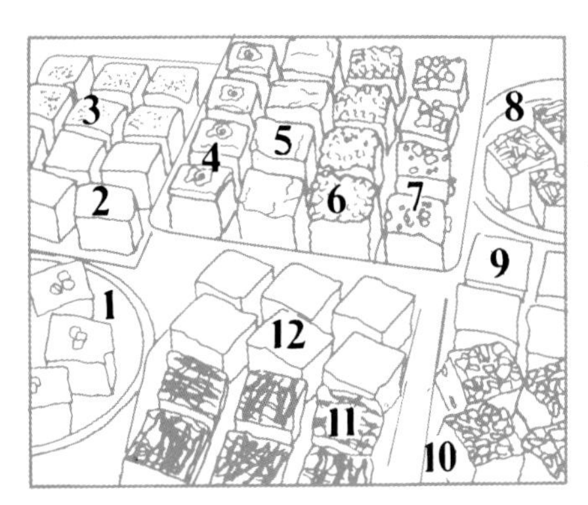

Traybakes

1 *Gingerbread Traybake (page 89)*

2 *Iced Lemon Traybake (page 76)*

3 *Sultana and Orange Traybake (page 79)*

4 *Coffee and Walnut Traybake (page 83)*

5 *Devonshire Apple Cake (page 85)*

6 *American Spiced Carrot Traybake (page 88)*

7 *Marmalade Traybake (page 86)*

8 *Iced Chocolate Traybake (page 77)*

9 *Date and Walnut Traybake (page 87)*

10 *Cherry and Almond Traybake (page 84)*

11 *Chocolate Chip and Vanilla Marble Cake (page 78)*

12 *Treacle Spice Traybake (page 82)*

Treacle Spice Traybake

CUTS INTO 21 SMALL PIECES

THIS IS ONE FOR those who like the rich flavour of treacle in baking. Don't be too worried if the traybake dips in the centre – it just means you were a little generous with the treacle. *(See photograph on pages 80–81.)*

8 oz (225 g) soft margarine
6 oz (175 g) caster sugar
8 oz (225 g) black treacle
10 oz (275 g) self-raising flour
2 teaspoons baking powder
2 teaspoons mixed spice
4 eggs
4 tablespoons milk

TO FINISH
icing sugar

Pre-heat the oven to 180°C/350°F/Gas 4. Grease and base line a 12 × 9 in (30 × 23 cm) roasting tin with greased greaseproof paper.

Measure all the ingredients into a large bowl and beat well for about 2 minutes until well blended. Turn the mixture into the prepared tin and level the top.

Bake in the pre-heated oven for about 40 minutes or until the cake has shrunk from the sides of the tin and springs back when pressed in the centre with your fingertips. Leave to cool in the tin. Dust with sifted icing sugar to serve.

Coffee and Walnut Traybake

CUTS INTO 21 SMALL PIECES

COFFEE AND WALNUTS go particularly well together, but you can use other nuts for this recipe if you prefer. (See photograph on pages 80–81.)

8 oz (225 g) soft margarine
8 oz (225 g) light muscovado sugar
10 oz (275 g) self-raising flour
2 teaspoons baking powder
4 eggs
2 tablespoons milk
2 tablespoons coffee essence
3 oz (75 g) walnuts, chopped

FOR THE ICING

3 oz (75 g) soft margarine
8 oz (225 g) icing sugar, sifted
2 teaspoons milk
2 teaspoons coffee essence
walnut halves

Pre-heat the oven to 180°C/350°F/Gas 4. Grease and base line a 12 × 9 in (30 × 23 cm) roasting tin with greased greaseproof paper.

Measure all the ingredients into a large bowl and beat well for about 2 minutes until well blended. Turn the mixture into the prepared tin and level the top.

Bake in the pre-heated oven for about 35–40 minutes or until the cake has shrunk from the sides of the tin and springs back when pressed in the centre with your fingertips. Leave to cool in the tin.

For the icing, beat together the margarine with the icing sugar, milk and coffee essence. Spread evenly over the cake using a palette knife, then decorate with the walnut halves.

SECRETS OF SUCCESS

If you like, you can use instant coffee instead of coffee essence, 1 teaspoon to 1 tablespoon of water.

Cherry and Almond Traybake

CUTS INTO 21 SMALL PIECES

IN SEASON, YOU CAN use fresh stoned cherries instead of glacé, but you must eat the cake up quickly. It won't keep so well because it will be moister. You'll need about 1 lb (450 g) of sweet black cherries, stoned. *(See photograph on pages 80–81.)*

8 oz (225 g) glacé cherries
10 oz (275 g) self-raising flour
2 teaspoons baking powder
8 oz (225 g) soft margarine
8 oz (225 g) caster sugar
finely grated rind of 2 lemons
3 oz (75 g) ground almonds
5 eggs
1 oz (25 g) flaked almonds

Pre-heat the oven to 180°C/350°F/Gas 4. Grease and base line a 12 × 9 in (30 × 23 cm) roasting tin with greased greaseproof paper.

Cut each cherry into quarters, put in a sieve and rinse under running water. Drain well then dry thoroughly on kitchen paper.

Measure all the remaining ingredients, except the flaked almonds, into a large bowl and beat well for 1 minute to mix thoroughly. Lightly fold in the cherries. Turn into the prepared tin and sprinkle over the flaked almonds.

Bake in the pre-heated oven for about 40 minutes or until well risen, golden brown and a skewer inserted into the centre comes out clean. Leave to cool in the tin for 10 minutes then turn out, remove the paper and finish cooling on a wire rack.

SECRETS OF SUCCESS

If you transport cakes in your own tins to bazaars or fêtes, mark their bases indelibly with something – your initials in bright pink nail varnish, perhaps – so that you can reclaim them later.

Devonshire Apple Cake

SERVES 12

THIS APPLE CAKE LOOKS a little unappetizing when cold but is quite delicious served warm with cream or fromage frais. *(See photograph on pages 80–81.)*

1 lb (450 g) cooking apples

juice of ½ lemon

12 oz (350 g) self-raising flour

2 teaspoons baking powder

12 oz (350 g) caster sugar

4 eggs

1 teaspoon almond essence

8 oz (225 g) butter, melted

a generous scattering of shredded, flaked or chopped almonds

caster sugar to sprinkle

Pre-heat the oven to 180°C/350°F/Gas 4. Grease and base line a 12 × 9 in (30 × 23 cm) roasting tin with greased greaseproof paper.

Peel, core and thinly slice the apples and squeeze the lemon juice over them.

Measure the flour, baking powder and sugar into a large bowl. Beat the eggs together with the almond essence and stir into the flour with the melted butter. Mix well then spread half this mixture into the tin. Arrange the apples over the top of the cake mixture. Carefully top with the rest of the mixture; don't worry if the apples show through a little. Sprinkle over the almonds.

Bake in the pre-heated oven for about 1¼ hours or until the cake is golden, firm to the touch and slightly shrunk away from the sides of the tin. Leave to cool for 15 minutes and then turn out and remove the paper. Sprinkle over the caster sugar and serve warm with cream or *fromage frais.*

Marmalade Traybake

CUTS INTO 21 SMALL PIECES

BE CAREFUL WHEN measuring the marmalade. If you put too much in, the traybake will dip in the centre. *(See photograph on pages 80–81.)*

6 oz (175 g) soft margarine
6 oz (175 g) caster sugar
6 oz (175 g) sultanas
6 oz (175 g) currants
3 eggs, beaten
9 oz (250 g) self-raising flour
1½ teaspoons baking powder
2 oz (50 g) glacé cherries, quartered
2 tablespoons chunky marmalade, chopped
3 tablespoons milk
nibbed sugar to decorate

Pre-heat the oven to 180°C/350°F/Gas 4. Grease and base line a 12 × 9 in (30 × 23 cm) roasting tin with greased greaseproof paper.

Measure all the ingredients, except the nibbed sugar, into a large bowl and mix well until thoroughly blended. Turn into the prepared tin and smooth the top, sprinkle with nibbed sugar.

Bake in the pre-heated oven for 40–45 minutes or until well risen, golden brown and firm to the touch. Leave to cool in the tin for about 10 minutes before turning out and leaving to cool completely on a wire rack.

SECRETS OF SUCCESS

Instead of nibbed sugar, you could use crushed sugar cubes.

Date and Walnut Traybake

CUTS INTO 21 SMALL PIECES

THIS IS A DELICIOUSLY nutty and rich traybake. (See photograph on pages 80–81.)

9 oz (250 g) dates, stoned and chopped
1½ oz (40 g) soft margarine
12 fl oz (350 ml) boiling water
2 eggs
7 oz (200 g) dark muscovado sugar
5 oz (150 g) ground almonds
5 oz (150 g) walnuts, chopped
12 oz (350 g) self-raising flour
1½ teaspoons ground cinnamon

FOR THE ICING

8 oz (225 g) icing sugar, sifted
grated rind and juice of 1 lemon
walnut pieces to decorate

Pre-heat the oven to 180°C/350°F/Gas 4. Grease and base line a 12 × 9 in (30 × 23 cm) roasting tin with greased greaseproof paper.

Measure the dates and margarine into a small bowl and pour over the boiling water. Leave to cool.

Beat the eggs and sugar together in a large bowl, then add the cooled date mixture and the remaining cake ingredients. Stir well to mix then pour into the prepared tin.

Bake in the pre-heated oven for about 1 hour 10 minutes or until the cake is firm to the touch and golden brown in colour. Allow to cool in the tin for about 10 minutes then turn out on to a wire rack and allow to cool completely.

For the icing, mix the icing sugar and lemon together, adding a little hot water to make a spreading consistency. Pour over the cake and gently spread out evenly with a palette knife. Decorate with walnut pieces and leave to set.

American Spiced Carrot Traybake

CUTS INTO 21 SMALL PIECES

BOUGHT MIXTURES OF chopped nuts usually include a high proportion of peanuts. I always prefer to make up my own mix from shelled nuts. (See photograph on pages 80–81.)

10 oz (275 g) self-raising flour
12 oz (350 g) caster sugar
2 teaspoons baking powder
3 oz (75 g) mixed nuts, chopped
3 teaspoons ground cinnamon
2 teaspoons ground ginger
10 fl oz (300 ml) sunflower oil
10 oz (275 g) carrots, grated
4 eggs
1 teaspoon vanilla essence

FOR THE TOPPING

14 oz (400 g) low fat soft cheese
4 teaspoons clear honey
2 teaspoons lemon juice
mixed chopped nuts to decorate

Pre-heat the oven to 180°C/350°F/Gas 4. Grease and base line a 12 × 9 in (30 × 23 cm) roasting tin with greased greaseproof paper.

Measure all the dry ingredients into a large bowl. Add the oil, grated carrots, eggs, one at a time, and vanilla essence mixing well between each addition. Pour into the prepared tin.

Bake in the pre-heated oven for about 50–60 minutes or until the cake is well risen, golden brown in colour and firm to the touch. Allow to cool in the tin for about 10 minutes before turning out on to a wire rack and allowing to cool completely.

For the topping, mix together the cheese, honey and lemon juice. Spread evenly over the cake with a palette knife and sprinkle over the mixed chopped nuts to decorate. Store in the fridge for up to 2 weeks.

Gingerbread Traybake

Cuts into 21 Small Pieces

This gingerbread is equally delicious without the icing. It is perfect for a packed lunch. *(See photograph on pages 80–81.)*

10 oz (275 g) golden syrup
10 oz (275 g) black treacle
8 oz (225 g) light muscovado sugar
8 oz (225 g) soft margarine
1 lb (450 g) self-raising flour
2 teaspoons mixed spice
2 teaspoons ground ginger
4 eggs, beaten
4 tablespoons milk

For the Icing

8 oz (225 g) icing sugar
about 2 tablespoons water
2 oz (50 g) crystallized or stem ginger, finely chopped

Pre-heat the oven to 160°C/325°F/Gas 3. Grease and base line a 12 × 9 in (30 × 23 cm) roasting tin with greased greaseproof paper.

Measure the syrup, treacle, sugar and margarine into a large pan and heat gently until the fat has melted. Remove the pan from the heat and stir in the flour and spices. Add the lightly beaten eggs and milk, and beat well until smooth. Pour into the prepared tin.

Bake in the pre-heated oven for about 45–50 minutes or until well risen and beginning to shrink away from the sides of the tin. Allow to cool in the tin for a few minutes before turning out and cooling on a wire rack.

For the icing, sift the icing sugar into a bowl, add the water, a little at a time, and mix until smooth. Mix in the chopped ginger, spoon over the cake and leave to set.

Secrets of Success

Heat the syrup and other ingredients through very gently. If they are too hot when the flour is stirred in, it could go lumpy. If it does, you'll have to rub it through a sieve.

Chapter 4

Celebration Cakes

Special occasions demand celebration, and celebrations call for special cakes! Whether it's Christmas or Easter, a birthday, major anniversary, wedding or christening, a home-baked cake will catch and enhance the festive mood.

Christmas is a time when even the most timid cook might turn his or her hand to making a cake, and my Classic Rich Christmas Cake recipe is virtually foolproof. Even if you've never attempted to make a fruit cake before, you'll find it easy, as I've carefully worked out every possible permutation – the ingredient quantities, timings, all the extras such as almond paste and icings – for the usual shapes and sizes of cake tins. For those who may not have time to make this classic cake, I've included a cake which can be cooked quickly at the last minute, and a Victorian Christmas Cake. Both are lighter than the classic rich fruit one, and are delicious.

All families have their own ideas of what a celebration cake should consist of, and I've found that it is usually the older generations who like fruity cakes. Younger people now seem to prefer sponges, which is why I've included a chocolate birthday cake. This can be adapted to make a chocolate wedding cake for the less traditional bride; serve with a sauce such as raspberry coulis for dessert, as the Americans do.

Other calendar celebrations include Easter, for which I've created a traditional Simnel cake, and New Year, for which a 'tipsy' cake seems more than appropriate! Sporting occasions such as Wimbledon can be celebrated, too, as can christenings and birthdays, whether the star of the day is three months, three years or thirty!

SECRETS OF SUCCESS

The biggest mistake with rich fruit cakes is to overbake them. They shouldn't be too dark. They will become darker as they are fed with brandy and left to mature.

Classic Rich Christmas Cake

Makes 1 × 8 in (20 cm) Cake

This is a wonderful, rich traditional cake. Make it well in advance to give it time to mature. There is no need to skin the almonds. (See photograph on pages 96–7.)

10 oz (275 g) currants
6 oz (175 g) sultanas
6 oz (175 g) raisins
4 oz (100 g) glacé cherries, rinsed, dried and quartered
4 oz (100 g) ready-to-eat dried apricots, snipped into pieces
2 oz (50 g) mixed candied peel, finely chopped
3 tablespoons brandy
8 oz (225 g) plain flour
¼ teaspoon freshly grated nutmeg
½ teaspoon mixed spice
8 oz (225 g) soft margarine or softened butter
8 oz (225 g) dark muscovado sugar
4 extra large eggs
2 oz (50 g) whole almonds, chopped
1 scant tablespoon black treacle
grated rind of 1 lemon
grated rind of 1 orange

To Finish

brandy to feed
10 in (25 cm) round silver cake board
1½ lb (675 g) almond paste (see page 93)
1½ lb (675 g) fondant or ready-to-roll icing
almond paste (left-over from putting over the cake)
green food colouring
ribbon, Christmas roses, holly and candle to decorate

Begin this cake the night before you want to bake it. Measure the prepared fruits into a large bowl, mix in the brandy, cover and leave in a cool place overnight.

Pre-heat the oven to 140°C/275°F/Gas 1. Grease and line an 8 in (20 cm) deep round cake tin with a double layer of greased greaseproof paper.

Measure the flour, spices, margarine or butter, sugar, eggs, almonds, treacle and lemon and orange rinds into a large bowl. Beat well to mix thoroughly, then fold in the soaked fruits. Spoon the mixture into the prepared tin and spread out evenly with the back of a spoon. Cover the top of the cake loosely with a double layer of greaseproof paper.

Bake in the pre-heated oven for about 4½–4¾ hours or until the cake feels firm to the touch and a skewer inserted into the centre comes out clean. Allow the cake to cool in the tin.

When cool, pierce the cake at intervals with a fine skewer and feed with a little brandy. Wrap the completely cold cake in a double layer of greaseproof paper and again in foil and store in a cool place for up to 3 months, feeding at intervals with more brandy.

Don't remove the lining paper when storing as this helps to keep the cake moist.

Almond paste the cake about a week before icing as directed on pages 93–4.

Cover the cake with fondant (or ready-to-roll) icing as directed on page 95.

Colour the almond paste (left over from putting the almond paste on to the cake) dark green. Roll out on a board which has been lightly sprinkled with icing sugar and cut into 1 in (2.5 cm) wide strips. Cut these into diamonds and then, with the base of an icing nozzle, remove half circles from the sides of the diamonds to give holly-shaped leaves. Make vein marks on the leaves with a sharp knife, bend the leaves over the handles of wooden spoons and leave to dry.

Decorate the top of the cake with the Christmas roses, holly and candle, and finish by tying a ribbon around the sides of the cake.

Classic Fruit Celebration Cake

Below is a table of ingredients for the usual size and shape of classic fruit cake. Simply choose the size and follow the recipe for Classic Rich Christmas Cake on page 91.

	6" Round 5" Square	*7" Round 6" Square*	*8" Round 7" Square*	*9" Round 8" Square*	*10" Round 9" Square*	*11" Round 10" Square*	*12" Round 11" Square*	*13" Round 12" Square*
Currants	5 oz (150 g)	7 oz (200 g)	10 oz (275 g)	14 oz (400 g)	1 lb (450 g)	1¼ lb (550 g)	1½ lb (750 g)	1¾ lb (800 g)
Sultanas	3 oz (75 g)	4 oz (100 g)	6 oz (175 g)	8 oz (225 g)	10 oz (275 g)	12 oz (350 g)	1 lb (450 g)	1¼ lb (550 g)
Raisins	3 oz (75 g)	4 oz (100 g)	6 oz (175 g)	8 oz (225 g)	10 oz (275 g)	12 oz (350 g)	1 lb (450 g)	1¼ lb (550 g)
Glacé cherries	2 oz (50 g)	3 oz (75 g)	4 oz (100 g)	5 oz (150 g)	6 oz (175 g)	8 oz (225 g)	10 oz (275 g)	12 oz (350 g)
Ready-to-eat dried apricots	2 oz (50 g)	3 oz (75 g)	4 oz (100 g)	5 oz (150 g)	6 oz (175 g)	8 oz (225 g)	10 oz (275 g)	12 oz (350 g)
Candied peel	1 oz (25 g)	1½ oz (40 g)	2 oz (50 g)	2½ oz (65 g)	3 oz (75 g)	4 oz (100 g)	5 oz (150 g)	6 oz (175 g)
Brandy	1½ tbsp	2 tbsp	3 tbsp	4 tbsp	5 tbsp	6 tbsp	7 tbsp	8 tbsp
Plain flour	4 oz (100 g)	6 oz (175 g)	8 oz (225 g)	10 oz (275 g)	14 oz (400 g)	1 lb (450 g)	1 lb 2 oz (500 g)	1¼ lb (550 g)
Grated nutmeg	⅛ tsp	scant ¼ tsp	¼ tsp	scant ½ tsp	½ tsp	½ tsp	¾ tsp	1 tsp
Ground mixed spice	¼ tsp	scant ½ tsp	½ tsp	¾ tsp	¾ tsp	1 tsp	1¼ tsp	1½ tsp
Soft margarine	4 oz (100 g)	6 oz (175 g)	8 oz (225 g)	10 oz (275 g)	14 oz (400 g)	1 lb (450 g)	1lb 2 oz (500 g)	1¼ lb (550 g)
Dark musc. sugar	4 oz (100 g)	6 oz (175 g)	8 oz (225 g)	10 oz (275 g)	14 oz (400 g)	1 lb (450 g)	1lb 2 oz (500 g)	1¼ lb (550 g)

Eggs	2	3	4	5	7	8	9	10
Whole almonds	1 oz (25 g)	1½ oz (40 g)	2 oz (50 g)	2½ oz (65 g)	3 oz (75 g)	4 oz (100 g)	5 oz (150 g)	6 oz (175 g)
Black treacle	½ tbsp	rounded ½ tbsp	1 scant tbsp	1 tbsp	1½ tbsp	2 tbsp	3 tbsp	4 tbsp
Rind lemon	½	½	1	1½	2	2	3	3
Rind orange	½	½	1	1½	2	2	3	3
Baking times (approx.)	3½ hrs	4 hrs	4½ hrs	4¾ hrs	5 hrs	5½ hrs	6 hrs	6½ hrs

Almond Paste

MAKES ABOUT 1½ LB (675 G)

YOU CAN NOW BUY very good ready-prepared almond paste, but if you do like to make your own, here is the basic recipe.

8 oz (225 g) ground almonds

8 oz (225 g) caster sugar

8 oz (225 g) icing sugar, sifted

4 egg yolks, or 2 whole eggs

about 6 drops almond essence

Mix the ground almonds and sugars together in a bowl, then add the yolks or whole eggs and almond essence. Knead together to form a stiff paste. Do not over-knead as this will make the paste oily. Wrap in cling film and store in the fridge until required.

TO COVER A CAKE WITH ALMOND PASTE

The best method to cover a cake with almond paste really depends on the type of icing you are going to use. Fondant or ready-to-roll icing is best put over almond paste with rounded edges, using the first method given. For royal icing, it is usually better to use the second method as it gives sharper corners to the cake, essential if you want to smooth the top and sides of the icing with an icing ruler.

Stand the cake on a cake board which is 2 in (5 cm) larger than the size of the cake. Brush the cake all over with a little apricot glaze made by warming a little sieved apricot jam.

FIRST METHOD

Lightly dust a work surface with sifted icing sugar then roll out the almond paste to about 2 in (5 cm) larger than the surface of the cake. Brush the cake all over with apricot jam. Carefully lift the almond paste over the cake with the help of a rolling pin (see *figure 17*). Gently level and smooth the top of the paste with a rolling pin, then ease the almond paste down the sides of the cake, smoothing it at the same time (see *figure 18*). Neatly trim excess almond paste off at the base (see *figure 19*). (Keep this, wrapped in cling film, for making holly leaves and berries.)

SECOND METHOD

Lightly dust a work surface with sifted icing sugar, then roll out one-third of the almond paste to a circle slightly larger than the top of the cake (see *figure 20*). Using your cake tin base as a guide, cut the almond paste to the exact size (see *figure 21*). Brush the top and sides of the cake with apricot jam (see *figure 22*). Lift the almond paste on to the cake and smooth over gently with a rolling pin. Neaten the edges (see *figure 23*).

Cut a piece of string the height of the cake plus the almond paste, and another to fit around the cake. Roll out the remaining almond paste and, using the string as a guide, cut the almond paste to size (see *figure 24*). Brush a little more jam on the top edge of the strip as a seal, then roll up the strip loosely, place one end against the side of the cake and unroll to cover the sides of the cake completely (see *figure 25*). Use a small palette knife to smooth over the sides and the joins of the paste.

See table at bottom of page opposite for quantities of almond paste to cover both the sides and top of the cake.

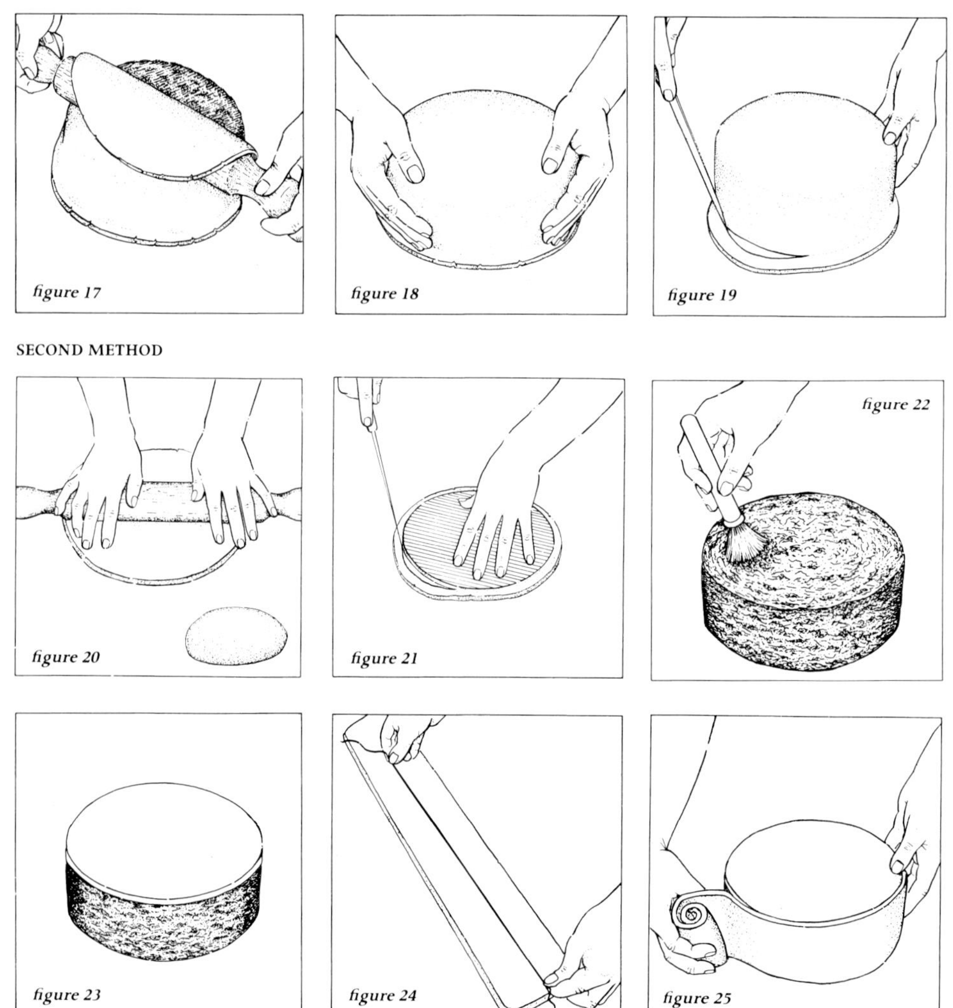

Home-Made Fondant Icing

MAKES ABOUT $1\frac{1}{4}$ LB (550 G)

THERE ARE SOME EXCELLENT makes of fondant or ready-to-roll icing available today. However, if you prefer to make your own, here is the recipe. Liquid glucose is available from good chemists.

about 1 lb 2 oz (500 g) icing sugar

1 generous tablespoon liquid glucose

1 egg white

Sift the icing sugar into a large mixing bowl, make a well in the centre and add the liquid glucose and egg white. Knead together until the mixture forms a soft ball. Turn on to a work surface lightly dusted with icing sugar, and knead for about 10 minutes until smooth and brilliant white. Keep adding sifted icing sugar if the mixture is a bit on the sticky side. Wrap in cling film and store in the fridge until required.

TO COVER A CAKE WITH FONDANT ICING
Brush the almond pasted cake with a little sherry, rum or kirsch (this has a sterilizing effect and also helps the fondant icing to stick).

Roll out the icing on a work surface lightly dusted with icing sugar, to about 2 in (5 cm) larger than the top of the cake. Lift the icing on to the cake, using the rolling pin for support. Smooth out evenly over the top of the cake with your hand, easing the icing down the sides of the cake. Trim any excess icing from the base of the cake, then finish smoothing with a plastic cake smoother, or carefully with your hand. Leave to dry out at room temperature for about 1 week before decorating.

See table below for quantities of fondant icing to cover both the sides and top of the cake.

Round tin	Square tin	Almond Paste	Fondant icing
6 in (15 cm)	5 in (13 cm)	12 oz (350 g)	12 oz (350 g)
7 in (18 cm)	6 in (15 cm)	1 lb (450 g)	1 lb (450 g)
8 in (20 cm)	7 in (18 cm)	$1\frac{1}{2}$ lb (675 g)	$1\frac{1}{2}$ lb (675) g)
9 in (23 cm)	8 in (20 cm)	$1\frac{3}{4}$ lb (800 g)	$1\frac{3}{4}$ lb (800 g)
10 in (25 cm)	9 in (23 cm)	2 lb (900 g)	$2\frac{1}{4}$ lb (1 kg)
11 in (28 cm)	10 in (25 cm)	$2\frac{1}{4}$ lb (1 kg)	$2\frac{3}{4}$ lb (1.2 kg)
12 in (30 cm)	11 in (28 cm)	$2\frac{1}{2}$ lb (1.1 kg)	3 lb (1.3 kg)
13 in (33 cm)	12 in (30 cm)	3 lb (1.3 kg)	$3\frac{1}{2}$ lb (1.6 kg)

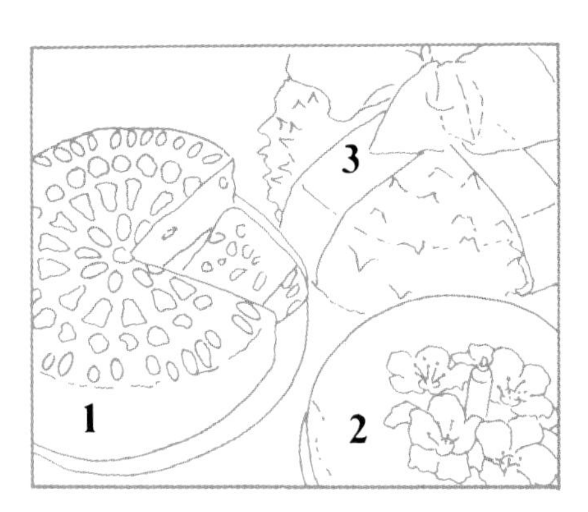

1 Victorian Christmas Cake (page 98)

2 Classic Rich Christmas Cake (page 91)

3 Fast Christmas Cake (page 99)

Royal Icing

You can easily buy 'instant' royal icing. However, if you do like to make your own, the recipe below makes sufficient to decorate an 8–9 in (20–23 cm) round cake.

- ***2 egg whites***
- ***1 lb 2 oz (500 g) icing sugar, sifted***
- ***about 4 teaspoons lemon juice***

Put the egg whites into a large mixing bowl and whisk lightly with a fork until bubbles begin to form on the surface. Add about half the icing sugar and the lemon juice, and beat well with a wooden spoon for about 10 minutes until brilliant white. Gradually stir in the remaining icing sugar until the correct consistency for piping.

Once made, keep the icing covered with a damp cloth to prevent it drying out.

Makes 1 × 9 in (23 cm) Cake

Unlike traditional Christmas cakes, this mixture produces a light, succulent and moist cake. *(See photograph on pages 96–7.)*

- ***12 oz (350 g) glacé cherries***
- ***1 × 8 oz (227 g) can pineapple in natural juice***
- ***12 oz (350 g) ready-to-eat dried apricots***
- ***4 oz (100 g) whole blanched almonds***
- ***finely grated rind of 2 lemons***
- ***12 oz (350 g) sultanas***
- ***9 oz (250 g) self-raising flour***
- ***9 oz (250 g) caster sugar***
- ***9 oz (250 g) soft margarine***
- ***3 oz (75 g) ground almonds***
- ***5 eggs***

To Decorate

- ***whole almonds***
- ***glacé cherries***
- ***glacé pineapple***

To Finish

- ***4 oz (100 g) icing sugar, sifted***

Pre-heat the oven to 160°C/325°F/Gas 3. Grease a 9 in (23 cm) deep round cake tin and line the base and sides with a double layer of greased greaseproof paper.

Cut each cherry into quarters, rinse and drain well. Drain and roughly chop the pineapple, then dry both the cherries and pineapple very thoroughly on kitchen paper. Snip the apricots into pieces. Roughly chop the almonds. Place the prepared fruit and nuts in a bowl with the grated lemon rind and sultanas and gently mix together.

Place the remaining ingredients in a large bowl and beat well for 1 minute until smooth. Lightly fold in the fruit and nuts then turn the mixture into the prepared cake tin. Level the surface and decorate the top with blanched whole almonds, halved glacé cherries and pieces of glacé pineapple.

Bake in the pre-heated oven for about $2\frac{1}{4}$ hours or until golden brown. A skewer inserted into the centre of the cake should come out clean. Cover the cake loosely with foil after 1 hour to prevent the top becoming too dark in colour. Leave to cool in the tin for about 30 minutes then turn out and cool completely on a wire rack.

Mix the icing sugar with water, and drizzle over the cake to glaze.

Fast Christmas Cake

Makes 1 × 8 in (20 cm) Cake

The simplest and quickest decoration for a Christmas cake is 'instant' royal icing, pulled to a rough peak texture, and a ribbon and bow. (See photograph on pages 96–7.)

5 oz (150 g) soft margarine
5 oz (150 g) light muscovado sugar
2 eggs
8 oz (225 g) self-raising flour
1 × 14 oz (400 g) jar luxury mincemeat
6 oz (175 g) currants
2 oz (50 g) whole almonds, chopped

To Decorate

10 in (25 cm) round silver cake board
$1\frac{1}{2}$ lb (675 g) almond paste (see page 93)
1 quantity of royal icing (see page 98)
ribbon to decorate

Pre-heat the oven to 160°C/325°F/Gas 3. Grease and line the base and sides of an 8 in (20 cm) deep round cake tin with greased greaseproof paper.

Measure all the ingredients into a large bowl and beat well for 1 minute until thoroughly mixed. Turn into the prepared tin and level the surface.

Bake in the pre-heated oven for about $1\frac{3}{4}$ hours or until a skewer inserted into the centre comes out clean and the cake is shrinking from the sides of the tin. Cover the cake with foil after 1 hour if beginning to brown too much. Allow to cool in the tin for about 10 minutes before turning out and cooling completely on a wire rack.

Almond paste the cake about a week before icing, as directed on page 93.

Make up the royal icing as directed on page 98, spread some of the icing thickly over the sides of the cake, smoothing with a palette knife or cake side smoother. Spoon more royal icing on to the top of the cake, smooth a strip in the centre (this is where the ribbon will go) then pull the remainder into peaks with the back of a spoon. Allow the icing to harden for a few hours. Then decorate with ribbon.

American Chocolate Wedding Cake

Serves about 100

Served with raspberry coulis (see page 102) this makes a super dessert for a wedding breakfast. Don't be surprised that the recipe has no flour – it still works. Be warned, you do need huge bowls to make this cake. If you wish to make one layer at a time, to test the recipe before the big day, see page 300 for individual quantities. The icing should be made the day before the wedding, otherwise it loses its sheen.

30 eggs, separated

8 whole eggs

2 lb 13 oz (1.27 kg) caster sugar

3 lbs 9 oz (1.6 kg) good quality plain chocolate, broken into pieces and melted

1 lb 14 oz (840 g) ground almonds

7½ teaspoons black coffee

8 oz (225 g) apricot jam, sieved

For the Icing

2½ lb (1.25 kg) plain chocolate, broken into pieces

1 lb (450 g) unsalted butter

To Decorate

foliage and flowers

Pre-heat the oven to 190°C/375°F/Gas 5. Lightly grease and line a 6 in (15 cm), a 9 in (23 cm) and a 12 in (30 cm) deep round cake tins with greased greaseproof paper.

Measure the yolks, whole eggs and sugar into a large bowl and whisk until thick and light. Add slightly cooled chocolate with the almonds and the coffee.

In a separate bowl, whisk the egg whites until stiff but not dry. Fold carefully into the chocolate mixture, then divide the mixture between the prepared tins.

Bake in the pre-heated oven. The small cake will take about 45 minutes, the medium cake about 1 hour and the large cake about 1½ hours (cover loosely after 1 hour). They can all go into the oven at once; put the large cake on the middle shelf and the two smaller cakes on the top shelf. Test the centre of each with a skewer which should come out just about clean. Turn on to a wire rack to cool completely. At this point, the cakes can be frozen. Turn the cakes upside down so that the flat side is uppermost. Brush over the tops and sides of the cakes with the warmed sieved jam.

For the icing, melt the chocolate slowly in a bowl over a pan of hot water, add the butter and stir until the butter has melted. Place each cake on a cooling rack, with a baking tray underneath to catch the drips, and pour over the chocolate icing. Smooth the top and sides with a palette knife and then leave to set in a cool place.

Place the largest cake on a cake board or serving plate and stack the other two cakes on top. Decorate, *in situ*, with fresh flowers and foliage. Serve with Raspberry Coulis.

(Right) American Chocolate Wedding Cake

Raspberry Coulis

Serve this with the American Chocolate Wedding Cake (see page 100), or with ice-cream or plain desserts.

5 lb (2.3 kg) raspberries	*1 lb (450 g) icing sugar, sifted*

Place the raspberries in a food processor and blend until they form a purée, then push the purée through a nylon sieve into a bowl to remove the seeds. Gradually whisk in the icing sugar.

Wimbledon Cake

Makes 1 × 8 in (20 cm) Cake

Perfect not just for Wimbledon, but for all special summer occasions, the semolina gives this cake a slightly crunchy, close texture. It must be eaten on the day of filling. (See photograph on pages 2–3.)

3 eggs, separated	For the Filling
4 oz (100 g) caster sugar	*4 oz (100 g) fresh strawberries*
grated rind and juice of 1 orange	*1 passion fruit*
3 oz (75 g) semolina	*5 fl oz (150 ml) whipping cream, whipped*
	icing sugar to finish

Pre-heat the oven to 180°C/350°F/Gas 4. Grease and base line an 8 in (20 cm) deep round cake tin with greased greaseproof paper.

Place the egg yolks, sugar, grated orange rind and juice and the semolina into a bowl and beat well until thoroughly blended.

In a separate bowl, whisk the egg whites until they are stiff but not dry, then gently fold into the orange and semolina mixture. Turn into the prepared tin.

Bake in the pre-heated oven for about 30–35 minutes until well risen and pale golden brown. The top of the cake should spring back when lightly pressed with a finger. Allow the cake to cool in the tin for a few minutes then turn out and leave to cool completely on a wire rack.

Reserve a few whole strawberries if wished and slice the remainder. Halve the passion fruit and scoop out the pulp. To fill, split the cake in half horizontally and fill with the sliced strawberries, passion fruit pulp and the whipped cream. Just before serving, sift some icing sugar over the top and decorate with the reserved sliced or whole strawberries.

Divine Chocolate Birthday Cake

Serves about 10

This is a very close-textured 'fudgy' cake which needs no filling. There is no flour in this recipe, ground almonds give the flavour and texture. Use a good quality chocolate (see page 30). Decorate with crystallized flowers (see page 29) and candles.

6 eggs, 5 of them separated

$7\frac{1}{2}$ oz (215 g) caster sugar

$9\frac{1}{2}$ oz (265 g) plain chocolate, broken into pieces

1 teaspoon instant coffee

1 teaspoon hot water

5 oz (150 g) ground almonds

For the Icing

about 4 tablespoons apricot jam

8 oz (225 g) plain chocolate, broken into pieces

4 oz (100 g) unsalted butter

Pre-heat the oven to 190°C/375°F/Gas 5. Grease and base line a 9 in (23 cm) deep round cake tin with greased greaseproof paper.

Place the egg yolks and whole egg in a large bowl with the sugar and whisk together until thick and light in colour.

Melt the chocolate slowly in a heatproof bowl over a pan of hot water. Dissolve the coffee in the water and add to the melted chocolate. Cool slightly, then stir into the egg mixture with the ground almonds.

In a separate bowl whisk the egg whites until stiff but not dry. Carefully fold into the egg and chocolate mixture. Turn into the prepared tin and gently level the surface.

Bake in the pre-heated oven for about 50 minutes or until well risen, and a skewer inserted into the centre comes out clean. Allow to cool for 10 minutes in the tin before turning out. Leave to cool completely on a wire rack.

Measure the apricot jam into a small saucepan and allow to melt over a low heat. Brush over the cake.

For the icing, melt the chocolate slowly in a bowl over a pan of hot water. Add the butter and stir until the icing has the consistency of thick pouring cream.

Place the cake on a cooling rack and pour over the icing, smoothing it over top and sides with a palette knife. Allow to set, then decorate if you like.

Easter Simnel Cake

Makes 1 × 8 in (20 cm) Cake

This has become the traditional Easter cake, but originally it was given by servant girls to their mothers when they went home on Mothering Sunday.

8 oz (225 g) soft margarine
8 oz (225 g) light muscovado sugar
4 eggs
8 oz (225 g) self-raising flour
8 oz (225 g) sultanas
4 oz (100 g) currants
4 oz (100 g) glacé cherries, washed, dried and quartered
2 oz (50 g) mixed candied peel, chopped
grated rind of 2 lemons
2 teaspoons mixed spice

For the Filling and Topping

1 lb (450 g) almond paste (see page 93)
about 2 tablespoons apricot jam
1 egg, beaten, to glaze

Pre-heat the oven to 150°C/300°F/Gas 2. Grease and line the base and sides of an 8 in (20 cm) deep round cake tin with greased greaseproof paper.

Measure all the cake ingredients into a large mixing bowl and beat well until thoroughly blended. Place half the mixture into the prepared tin and level the surface.

Take one-third of the almond paste and roll it out to a circle the size of the tin and then place on top of the cake mixture. Spoon the remaining cake mixture on top and level the surface.

Bake in the pre-heated oven for about $2\frac{1}{2}$ hours until well risen, evenly brown and firm to the touch. Cover with foil after 1 hour if the top is browning too quickly. Allow the cake to cool in the tin for about 10 minutes before turning out and cooling on a wire rack.

When the cake is cool, brush the top with a little warmed apricot jam and roll out half of the remaining almond paste to fit the top. Press firmly on the top and crimp the edges to decorate. Mark a criss-cross pattern on the almond paste with a sharp knife. Form the remaining almond paste into 11 balls to represent the Apostles (not counting Judas). Brush the almond paste with the beaten egg and arrange the almond paste balls around the outside. Brush the tops of the balls with beaten egg, too, and then place the cake under a hot grill to turn the almond paste golden. Decorate with crystallized primroses, or jonquils and violets, if liked.

(Right) Easter Simnel Cake

Sponge Christening Cake

Makes 1 × 9 in (23 cm) Cake

A lemon cake is perfect for a christening. Colour the icing pale pink for a girl or pale blue for a boy if you like or maybe a pale primrose colour: (See photograph on pages 108–9.)

3 oz (75 g) butter

6 extra large eggs

6 oz (175 g) caster sugar

5 oz (150 g) self-raising flour

2 tablespoons cornflour

For the filling

10 fl oz (300 ml) whipping cream, whipped

about 4 tablespoons lemon curd

To Finish

2 lb (900 g) ready-to-roll icing

crystallized flowers and ribbon to decorate

Pre-heat the oven to 180°C/350°F/Gas 4. Grease and base line a 9 in (23 cm) deep round cake tin with greased greaseproof paper.

Melt the butter in a small pan and then leave it to cool slightly.

Measure the eggs and sugar into a large bowl and whisk over hot water with an electric whisk on high speed until the mixture becomes pale and creamy and thick enough to leave a trail on the surface when the whisk is lifted. Remove the bowl from the pan and continue to whisk until the mixture is cold. (Or whisk at high speed in a food mixer.)

Sift the flours together into a bowl. Fold half the flour into the egg mixture with a metal spoon, then carefully pour half the cooled butter around the edge of the mixture and lightly fold in. Fold in the remaining flour and butter alternately.

Pour into the prepared tin and bake in the pre-heated oven for about 40 minutes or until well risen, firm to the touch and beginning to shrink away from the sides of the tin. Allow to cool in the tin for a few minutes before turning out on to a wire rack and leaving to cool completely.

Split the cake into 3 horizontally. Reserve 3–4 tablespoons of the whipped cream then mix the remainder with the lemon curd and use to fill the cake. Place on a serving plate or board.

Spread the reserved cream around the sides and over the top of the cake, just enough to make them sticky. Dust the work surface with icing sugar and roll out the icing large enough to cover the cake completely. Fold the icing over the rolling pin and carefully lift on to the cake, gently smoothing the sides. Trim the extra icing from the base of the cake. Decorate with ribbon and crystallized flowers (see *page 29*).

SERVES 8–10

POTATO FLOUR IS AVAILABLE from health-food shops and good delicatessens. (See photograph on pages 108–9.)

5 extra large eggs, 2 of them separated

10 oz (275 g) caster sugar

$2\frac{1}{2}$ oz (65 g) self-raising flour, sifted

$2\frac{1}{2}$ oz (65 g) potato flour (fecule) or cornflour, sifted

grated rind of 1 lemon

FOR SOAKING THE CAKE

2 oz (50 g) granulated sugar

3 tablespoons water

5 fl oz (150 ml) sweet white wine

1 tablespoon brandy

FOR THE FILLING AND DECORATION

about 8 oz (225 g) red summer fruits

15 fl oz (450 ml) double cream, whipped

Pre-heat the oven to 180°C/350°F/Gas 4. Grease and base line a 9 in (23 cm) deep round cake tin with greased greaseproof paper.

Place the 3 whole eggs, the 2 egg yolks and the sugar into a large bowl and whisk over hot water until thick and mousse-like, and the mixture leaves a trail when the whisk is lifted. (Or whisk at high speed in a food mixer.)

In a separate bowl, whisk the egg whites until stiff but not dry and fold into the mixture with the flours and the grated lemon rind. Turn into the prepared tin.

Bake in the pre-heated oven for about 45–50 minutes or until the cake is well risen, golden and the surface springs back when lightly pressed with the fingertip. Allow to cool in the tin for about 10 minutes before turning out and leaving to cool completely on a wire rack.

Meanwhile, gently dissolve the granulated sugar in the water in a small pan. When completely dissolved, bring the syrup to the boil and allow to boil for 2 minutes. Allow to cool, then add the wine and the brandy.

When the cake is cold, use a serrated knife to make a cut in the top around the cake about 1 in (2.5 cm) in from the edge and about $1\frac{1}{2}$ in (4 cm) deep. Holding the knife almost horizontally, cut towards the centre of the cake to remove a wedge of sponge and leave a sponge flan case shape with a lid. Put the lid to one side.

Soak the cake with two-thirds of the sugar syrup and fill with the fruit and half the cream. Replace the 'lid' and moisten with the remaining syrup. Mask the whole cake with the remaining cream and decorate with more fresh fruits.

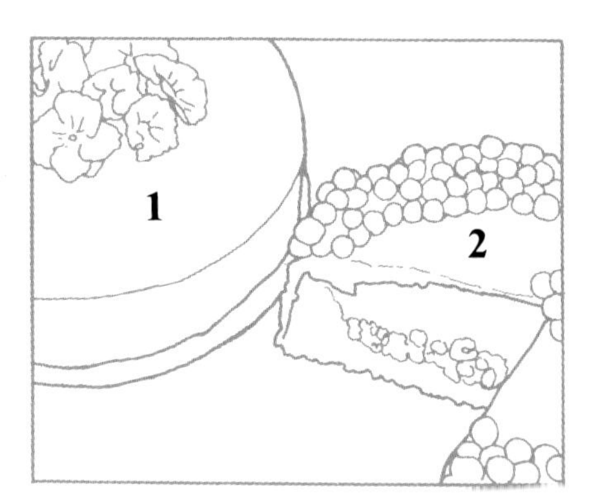

Celebration Cakes

1 Sponge Christening Cake (page 106)

2 New Year Tipsy Cake (page 107)

Chapter 5

Cheesecakes

The cheesecake originated long ago in Russia and Eastern Europe, and consisted of the local soft cheese, some sugar and eggs, baked in a pastry case. I suppose at one time it was a traditional and delicious means of using up eggs and a little bit of cheese. Cooked cheesecakes are still a speciality of countries like Austria, Germany and France, although there is a long tradition in Britain too, dating from at least the thirteenth century.

Cooked cheesecakes that are made at home are a far cry from any you will find in run-of-the-mill restaurants or sandwich bars. They can be cooked in pastry or sponge flan cases, or in a tin just like a cake. They can also have crushed biscuit bases – very quick and easy! They are rich, so only a small slice is needed per portion. They also freeze very well.

Gelatine-set, uncooked cheesecakes have become even more popular, and they are a modern American invention. They are usually lighter in texture than the European cooked varieties. Their bases can also be pastry, biscuit crust or sponge, but these must, of course be pre-baked.

The success of these cheesecakes depends on using gelatine properly. (Powdered gelatine is easier to find and use than leaf gelatine.) The gelatine must always be added to the liquid (water, juice, alcohol) and not the other way round. Sprinkle it over the liquid in a cup or small bowl, swirl to mix, and then leave it to 'sponge', or swell and begin to dissolve. To complete the dissolving process, stand the cup or bowl in a pan of hot water and heat very gently; the gelatine is ready for use when it becomes clear. Check by stirring with a metal spoon: there should be no undissolved granules visible on the spoon. Cool the dissolved gelatine before mixing in, because if it is too hot, it can form lumps and threads, and ruin the texture of the cheesecake.

Gelatine-set cheesecakes can be frozen but, like mousses, not for very long, only for up to a week. Many shrink back a bit on thawing. Freeze *without* any topping. And do remember that some cheesecakes may begin to 'melt' in a warm room. Bring only to room temperature, or keep chilled.

Serve cheesecakes, cooked or uncooked, as a dessert cake, or with coffee. The majority are eaten with a fork.

Easy Lemon Cheesecake

Serves 8

An excellent quick cheesecake, always popular with the family.

For the Base

10 digestive biscuits, crushed
2 oz (50 g) butter, melted
1 oz (25 g) demerara sugar

For the Cheesecake

5 fl oz (150 ml) single cream
1 × 14 oz (397 g) can condensed milk
6 oz (175 g) low-fat soft cheese, softened
grated rind and juice of 3 large lemons

For the Topping

5 fl oz (150 ml) whipping cream, whipped
fresh strawberries

Mix together the biscuits, butter and demerara sugar for the biscuit crust. Turn into a 9 in (23 cm) flan dish and press evenly over the base and sides. Leave to set.

For the cheesecake filling, mix together the cream, condensed milk, soft cheese and lemon rind, then add the lemon juice a little at a time, whisking until the mixture thickens. Pour the mixture into the flan case and leave to chill in the fridge for 3–4 hours or overnight.

Decorate with swirls of cream and fresh strawberries.

Sharp Lemon Cheesecake

SERVES 8

A VERY SMOOTH, fresh cheesecake, this is the second easiest to make in this chapter. It uses a lemon jelly as the setting agent for the cheesecake filling.

FOR THE BASE

4 oz (100 g) Hob Nob biscuits, coarsely crushed

2 oz (50 g) butter, melted

1 oz (25 g) demerara sugar

FOR THE CHEESECAKE

1 × 1 pint (600 ml) packet lemon jelly

juice of 1 lemon

12 oz (350 g) full-fat soft cheese

4 oz (100 g) caster sugar

5 fl oz (150 ml) whipping cream, whipped

TO DECORATE

5 fl oz (150 ml) whipping cream, whipped

pared rind of 1 lemon

Lightly oil an 8 in (20 cm) round, loose-bottomed cake tin or spring-release tin.

Separate the jelly into squares. Dissolve in 5 fl oz (150 ml) of boiling water then add the juice of the lemon to make up to 10 fl oz (300 ml). Put in a cold place until the jelly is thick and nearly set.

Meanwhile, mix together the ingredients for the base and spread over the bottom of the prepared tin, pressing down evenly.

Mix the soft cheese with the sugar and the almost-set jelly and then fold in the whipped cream. Turn into the tin on top of the crumbs and put in a cool place to set.

For the decoration, cut the pared lemon rind into very fine shreds with a sharp knife. Blanch in boiling water for 1 minute, then rinse under the cold tap and dry thoroughly on kitchen paper.

To serve, loosen the sides of the cheesecake from the tin and push up the base, or remove the sides of the spring-release tin and slide the cheesecake on to a plate. Spread the top with a thin layer of cream if liked and pipe rosettes of whipped cream around the top edge of the cheesecake. Decorate with the shreds of lemon rind.

Sharp Lemon Cheesecake

Grapefruit Cheesecake

SERVES 8

A GOOD, DEEP CHEESECAKE with a lovely, refreshingly sharp flavour, the biscuit crust for this cake is made after the cheesecake mixture and placed on top to set: this gives a very crisp crust.

FOR THE CHEESECAKE

½ oz (15 g) powdered gelatine
3 tablespoons cold water
1 lb (450 g) full-fat soft cheese
7 oz (200 g) carton frozen concentrated unsweetened grapefruit juice, thawed
3 oz (75 g) caster sugar
10 fl oz (300 ml) whipping cream

FOR THE BASE

4 oz (100 g) Hob Nob biscuits, coarsely crushed
2 oz (50 g) butter, melted
1 oz (25 g) demerara sugar

TO DECORATE

fresh grapefruit segments from 2 white grapefruit

Lightly oil an 8 in (20 cm) cake tin, preferably loose-based, and place a circle of greaseproof paper in the base.

Sprinkle the gelatine over the cold water in a small basin and leave to 'sponge' for about 10 minutes. Place the bowl in a pan of simmering water and leave to dissolve until the gelatine has become clear. Allow to cool slightly.

Cream the cheese until soft and gradually beat in the grapefruit juice and caster sugar. Stir in the cooled gelatine. Whisk the cream until it is thick but not too stiff and fold into the cheesecake mixture. Turn into the prepared tin and place in the fridge to set.

Mix together the ingredients for the base and press this mixture evenly over the cheesecake. Leave in the fridge for several hours.

Turn the cheesecake out on to a serving plate and remove the greaseproof paper. Decorate the top with segments of fresh grapefruit.

SECRETS OF SUCCESS

Make an orange cheesecake in the same way, substituting frozen orange juice and orange segments.

American Cheesecake

Serves 6–8

This is a very quick and easy cheesecake to make. It's delicious to eat as well, as the yoghurt gives the filling a wonderfully fresh flavour.

For the Base

6 oz (175 g) digestive biscuits, crushed

3 oz (75 g) butter, melted

$1\frac{1}{2}$ oz (40 g) demerara sugar

For the Cheesecake

8 oz (225 g) full-fat soft cheese

1 oz (25 g) caster sugar

5 fl oz (150 ml) double cream

5 fl oz (150 ml) Greek yoghurt

juice of $1\frac{1}{2}$ lemons

For the Topping

6 oz (175 g) raspberries or other soft fruits

about 4 tablespoons redcurrant jelly

Mix together the ingredients for the base and, using a metal spoon, press over the base and sides of an 8 in (20 cm) round loose-bottomed cake tin or a spring-release tin.

Measure the cheese and sugar into a large bowl (or food processor) and mix well to blend thoroughly. Add the cream and yoghurt and mix again. Gradually add the lemon juice, whisking all the time; a hand-held electric mixer is useful for this. (If using a food processor, pour the lemon juice into the mixture through the funnel.) Turn the mixture into the tin on top of the biscuit crust and leave in the fridge to set overnight.

Carefully loosen the sides of the biscuit crust with a small palette knife, then push up the base or remove the sides of the spring-release tin and slide the cheesecake on to a serving plate.

Arrange the fruit on top of the cheesecake. Heat the redcurrant jelly in a small saucepan until it has melted, and then carefully brush over the fruit. Leave to set. Serve chilled.

Gooseberry and Elderflower Cheesecake

Serves 10

This is an unusual, and unusually sharp cheesecake. If you like, you can add a dash of green vegetable colouring to the cheesecake mixture.

For the Base

2 oz (50 g) butter

1 oz (25 g) demerara sugar

4 oz (100 g) ginger biscuits, crushed

For the Cheesecake

½ oz (15 g) powdered gelatine

3 tablespoons water

about 1 lb (450 g) fresh gooseberries

2½ fl oz (75 ml) elderflower cordial

3 tablespoons clear honey

8 oz (225 g) full-fat soft cheese

5 fl oz (150 ml) soured cream

2 eggs, separated

4 oz (100 g) caster sugar

For the Topping

about 10 fl oz (300 ml) whipping cream, whipped

Lightly grease a loose-bottomed 9 in (23 cm) round cake tin or spring-release tin.

Melt the butter for the base, then add the demerara sugar and the crushed biscuits. Mix together and use to line the prepared tin.

Sprinkle the gelatine over the water in a bowl and leave for 10 minutes to 'sponge'.

Place the gooseberries in a pan with the elderflower cordial, bring to the boil then simmer gently for about 5 minutes or until the gooseberries are tender. Push through a nylon sieve to remove the seeds and make a purée. Turn into a food processor and add the honey, cheese, soured cream and egg yolks. Process together until smooth.

Stand the bowl of gelatine in a pan of gently simmering water and allow to dissolve. Mix into the gooseberry mixture in the processor.

Whisk the egg whites until frothy, then add the caster sugar, a little at a time, until the mixture is very stiff. Turn the gooseberry mixture into the meringue and blend well together. Pour on to the biscuit crust and chill in the fridge to set.

Loosen the side edges of the tin using a small palette knife if necessary. Push up the base of the tin and slip the cheesecake on to a serving plate. Pipe a lattice of whipped cream on top of the cheesecake to decorate. Serve chilled.

Gooseberry and Elderflower Cheesecake

American Chocolate Ripple Cheesecake

Serves 8–10

Serve this cheesecake in small portions as it is quite sweet and rich. Expect the cheesecake to crack on cooling.

For the Base

4 oz (100 g) plain chocolate digestive biscuits, crushed

2 oz (50 g) butter, melted

For the Cheesecake

5 oz (150 g) plain chocolate, broken into pieces

1½ lb (700 g) full-fat soft cheese

8 oz (225 g) caster sugar

½ teaspoon vanilla essence

2 extra large eggs

Pre-heat the oven to 160°C/325°F/Gas 3. Lightly grease an 8 in (20 cm) loose-bottomed cake tin or spring-release tin.

Mix together the ingredients for the base and press into the prepared tin.

For the cheesecake filling, melt the chocolate in a bowl over a pan of hot water. Cool slightly.

Measure the cheese into a large bowl and beat until soft. Add the sugar and beat again until well mixed. Beat in the vanilla essence and then the eggs, one at a time. Spoon half the cheese mixture on to the biscuit crust, separating the spoonfuls. Add the melted chocolate to the remaining cheesecake mixture and stir well to mix. Spoon this mixture in between the cheesecake mixture already in the tin. Swirl the top to give a marbled effect.

Bake the cheesecake in the pre-heated oven for about 30 minutes or until the cheesecake becomes puffy around the edges but is still very soft in the centre. Turn off the oven but leave the cheesecake in the oven to cool.

Chill well and then loosen the cheesecake from the sides of the tin using a small palette knife. Serve well chilled.

Austrian Curd Cake

Serves 10

This makes a good, deep cheesecake. It is very moist, so there is no need for cream.

5 oz (150 g) butter, softened
10 oz (275 g) caster sugar
$1\frac{1}{4}$ lb (550 g) curd cheese
4 eggs, separated
4 oz (100 g) ground almonds
4 oz (100 g) sultanas
2 oz (50 g) semolina
grated rind and juice of 2 lemons
icing sugar to dust

Pre-heat the oven to 190°C/375°F/Gas 5. Lightly grease and base line a 9 in (23 cm) spring-release tin or loose-bottomed cake tin with greased greaseproof paper.

Soften the butter in a large bowl and then add the sugar and the curd cheese. Beat well together until light and creamy. Beat the egg yolks into the mixture one at a time, then stir in the ground almonds, sultanas, semolina and the grated lemon rind and juice. Leave the mixture to stand for about 10 minutes; this allows the mixture to thicken so that the sultanas don't sink to the bottom of the cake when baking.

In a separate bowl, whisk the egg whites until stiff but not dry and fold lightly into the mixture. Turn the mixture into the prepared tin.

Bake in the pre-heated oven for about 1 hour or until firm to the touch. Cover the top of the cheesecake loosely with foil about half-way through the cooking time to prevent the top becoming too brown.

When cooked, turn off the oven but leave the cheesecake in to cool for about 1 hour. Allow to cool completely, then loosen the sides of the cake with a palette knife and remove the side of the tin. Invert the cheesecake, remove the base of the tin and the paper and turn back the right way to serve. Dust with sieved icing sugar before serving.

Secrets of Success

Instead of curd cheese, you can use cottage cheese. Process in the food processor or rub through a sieve to make it smooth.

Chocolate, Brandy and Ginger Cheesecake

SERVES 8

A SOPHISTICATED CHEESECAKE, if you like, you can add a little more brandy to the cheesecake filling. If ginger is a great favourite, that quantity can be increased as well.

FOR THE BASE

4 oz (100 g) ginger biscuits, crushed

2 oz (50 g) butter, melted

1 oz (25 g) demerara sugar

FOR THE CHEESECAKE

4 oz (100 g) plain chocolate, broken into pieces

½ oz (15 g) powdered gelatine

3 tablespoons cold water

2 eggs, separated

2 oz (50 g) caster sugar

8 oz (225 g) full-fat soft cheese

5 fl oz (150 ml) soured cream

4 tablespoons brandy

2 pieces stem ginger, chopped, about 1 oz (25 g)

TO DECORATE

5 fl oz (150 ml) whipping cream, whipped (optional)

chocolate caraque or curls (see pages 32 and 33)

stem ginger, sliced

Lightly grease a loose-bottomed 8 in (20 cm) round cake tin or spring-release tin.

Make the base by mixing the crushed biscuits, melted butter and sugar together. Press into the base of the prepared tin and leave to set.

Melt the chocolate slowly in a bowl over a pan of hot water. Allow to cool slightly.

Sprinkle the gelatine over the measured water in a small bowl and leave for 10 minutes to 'sponge'. Stand the bowl over a pan of gently simmering water until the gelatine has completely dissolved. Leave to cool slightly. Beat together the egg yolks, sugar and cheese in a large bowl. Add the soured cream and cooled chocolate. Stir in the dissolved gelatine. Whisk the egg whites until frothy and fold into the cheese mixture with the brandy and chopped stem ginger. Pour on to the biscuit base and chill to set.

Carefully remove the cheesecake from the tin before decorating with whipped cream if liked, chocolate caraque or curls, and slices or pieces of stem ginger.

Chocolate, Brandy and Ginger Cheesecake

Angel Sponge Cheesecake

Serves 8–10

A good cheesecake for a party, the sponge can be made in advance and frozen. Keep the cheesecake chilled once made, as it contains no gelatine and will soon soften in a warm room. *(See photograph on pages 124–5.)*

For the Sponge

2 eggs

3 oz (75 g) caster sugar

2 oz (50 g) self-raising flour

For the Cheesecake

4 oz (100 g) unsalted butter, softened

5 oz (150 g) caster sugar

3 size 2 eggs, separated

finely grated rind and juice of 2 oranges

7 oz (200 g) low- or medium-fat soft cheese

10 fl oz (300 ml) whipping cream

For Decoration

icing sugar for dusting

orange wedges

lemon balm leaves

Pre-heat the oven to 180°C/350°F/Gas 4. Lightly grease and base line a 9 in (23 cm) loose-bottomed round cake tin or spring-release tin with greased greaseproof paper.

First make the sponge. Measure the eggs and sugar into a large bowl and whisk at full speed with an electric whisk until the mixture is thick and light in colour and leaves a trail when the whisk is lifted out of the mixture. Sift the flour into the whisked mixture and fold in lightly using a large metal spoon or spatula.

Turn the mixture into the prepared tin and tilt the tin to allow the mixture to spread evenly to the sides. (Don't worry that there appears to be little mixture for the size of the tin.) Bake in the pre-heated oven for about 20–25 minutes or until the cake springs back when lightly pressed with the finger and has shrunk slightly from the sides of the tin. Turn out and leave to cool on a wire rack.

Wash and dry the cake tin and then line the base and sides with non-stick baking paper. When the cake is completely cold, split in half horizontally using a serrated knife. Place one layer into the prepared cake tin, cut side up.

For the cheesecake filling, measure the butter into a large bowl and beat it well until thoroughly softened. Add the sugar and beat until light and fluffy. Next add the egg yolks, finely grated orange rind, the strained orange juice and the cheese, and beat well until smooth and thoroughly mixed. Whip the cream until it just holds its shape and fold into the cheese mixture. In a separate bowl, whisk the egg whites until stiff but not dry and fold them into the mixture.

Spoon the cheesecake mixture into the tin on top of the sponge and level the surface.

Gently place the remaining sponge on top, cut side on to the cheesecake mixture, cover with cling film and chill for about 4 hours or until the cheesecake mixture is firm.

To serve, carefully remove the sides of the tin and then gently peel away the paper. Using a palette knife or fish slice, ease the cake on to a serving plate. Dust the top with sifted icing sugar and mark into sections with the back of a knife. Decorate with orange wedges and lemon balm leaves.

Buttermilk and Honey Cheesecake

Serves 8

This is a lovely, subtly flavoured cooked cheesecake. You'll find buttermilk with the yoghurts and creams in larger supermarkets.

For the Base

1 sponge flan case, about 8 in (20 cm) in diameter

For the Cheesecake

8 oz (225 g) full-fat soft cheese

3 eggs, separated

3 oz (75 g) caster sugar

2 rounded tablespoons clear honey

2 oz (50 g) ground almonds

1½ oz (40 g) plain flour

10 fl oz (300 ml) buttermilk

a handful of flaked almonds

For the Topping

about 1 tablespoon clear honey

Pre-heat the oven to 160°C/325°F/Gas 3. Lightly grease an 8 in (20 cm) loose-bottomed cake tin or spring-release tin.

Slip the sponge flan case into the prepared tin, trimming the cake to fit if necessary.

Measure the cheese into a large bowl and beat until soft. Beat in the egg yolks with 1 oz (25 g) of the sugar, the honey, ground almonds, flour and the buttermilk.

In a separate bowl, whisk the egg whites until stiff, then whisk in the remaining caster sugar. Fold into the cheese mixture. Spoon the mixture on top of the sponge flan case and sprinkle the flaked almonds over the surface.

Bake in the pre-heated oven for about 1¼ hours or until firm but still spongy to the touch. Turn off oven, open the door and leave cheesecake to cool inside.

Ease the cheesecake away from the sides of the tin with a small palette knife and slide on to a serving plate. Gently heat the honey in a small pan and brush over the top of the cheesecake to glaze.

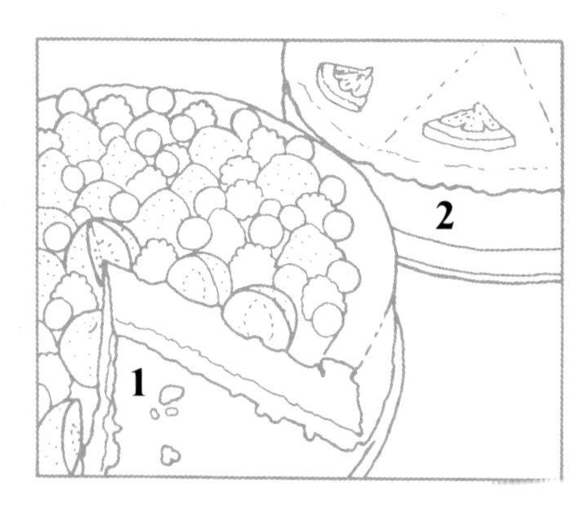

Cheesecakes

1 *Continental Cheesecake (page 127)*

2 *Angel Sponge Cheesecake (page 122)*

Yorkshire Cheesecake Tartlets

MAKES ABOUT 24

Try to use the deeper bun tins if you can for these, that way you get more filling! Serve whilst still warm.

For the Pastry

8 oz (225 g) plain flour

2 oz (50 g) butter or margarine

2 oz (50 g) white vegetable fat

about 2–3 tablespoons cold water

For the Filling

4 oz (100 g) curd cheese

2 oz (50 g) butter, softened

1 egg, beaten

1 egg yolk

2 oz (50 g) fresh white breadcrumbs

2 oz (50 g) caster sugar

6 oz (175 g) mixed dried fruit

1 tablespoon double cream

grated rind of 1 lemon

1 tablespoon brandy

Pre-heat the oven to 220°C/425°F/Gas 7.

First make the pastry. Measure the flour into a bowl and rub in the fats with the fingertips until the mixture resembles fine breadcrumbs. Bind to a soft but not sticky pastry with the water. Roll out the pastry thinly on a lightly floured work surface, and use a 3 in (7.5 cm) cutter to stamp out about 24 rounds. Use these to line the prepared bun trays and chill.

For the filling, mix the cheese with the butter and then stir in all the remaining ingredients (the mixture will be fairly wet). Spoon generously into the chilled pastry cases and bake in the pre-heated oven for about 15 minutes or until the cheesecakes are beginning to brown on top. Allow to cool slightly, before serving warm.

Secrets of Success

For perfect pastry, cold hands, chilled fat, cold water and a cold rolling-out surface are best. The air trapped in the making of the dough will expand more if it is cold, making the pastry rise well. For this reason, too, chill pastry dough for about 30 minutes before baking.

Continental Cheesecake

SERVES 12

A TRADITIONAL COOKED cheesecake, this recipe is a good large size, excellent for a party. Use frozen mixed summer fruits, available from good supermarkets, if fresh are unavailable. No need to use all the fruits suggested for the topping, maybe just raspberries, redcurrants and blackcurrants. The centre of the cooked cheesecake dips a little on cooling – perfect to hold the fruit! *(See photograph on pages 124–5.)*

FOR THE BASE

4 oz (100 g) digestive biscuits, crushed

2 oz (50 g) butter, melted

1½ oz (40 g) demerara sugar

FOR THE CHEESECAKE

2½ oz (65 g) soft margarine

8 oz (225 g) caster sugar

1¼ lb (550 g) curd cheese

1½ oz (40 g) plain flour

finely grated rind and juice of 2 lemons

4 eggs, separated

7 fl oz (200 ml) double cream, lightly whipped

FOR THE TOPPING

1 lb (450 g) mixed summer fruits (strawberries, raspberries, red and blackcurrants, blackberries)

caster sugar to taste

1 teaspoon arrowroot

5 fl oz (150 ml) double cream, whipped

Pre-heat the oven to 160°C/325°F/Gas 3. Lightly oil a 10 in (25 cm) loose-bottomed round cake or spring-release tin, and line with greased greaseproof paper.

Mix together the ingredients for the base, spread over the base of the tin and press down firmly with the back of a metal spoon. Leave to set.

For the cheesecake, measure the margarine, sugar, curd cheese, flour, lemon rind and juice, and egg yolks into a large bowl. Beat until smooth. Fold in the cream. Whisk the egg whites stiffly then fold into the mixture. Pour on to the biscuit crust.

Bake in the pre-heated oven for about 1½ hours or until set. Turn off the oven and leave the cheesecake in the oven for a further 1 hour to cool. Run a knife around the edge of the tin to loosen the cheesecake and push the base up through the cake tin. Remove the side paper.

For the topping, cook the redcurrants, blackcurrants and blackberries in 2 tablespoons of water and sweeten to taste. Blend the arrowroot with 2 more tablespoons of cold water, add the cooked fruit and liquid from the pan. Return to the pan, allow to thicken and then leave to cool. Stir the raspberries and strawberries in to the other fruits then pile on top of the cheesecake, levelling out evenly. Decorate the edge of the cheesecake with piped or spooned whipped double cream.

Chapter 6

Scones and Teabreads

Scones piled high with cream and jam and teabreads lavishly spread with butter are classic essentials for a proper afternoon tea.

The principal beauty of scones – whether baked in the oven or on top of the stove, or on a griddle – is that they are quick and easy to put together and make. If faced suddenly with a lot of hungry people, a batch of scones takes no time at all, and most of the ingredients will already be in the store-cupboard. Most of the ingredients are inexpensive, too.

To be at their best, scones should be freshly baked, and served warm. But they can be frozen, immediately after cooling, then refreshed in a moderate oven before serving.

Another advantage is that a big plain scone can serve as a bread. If there is no bread in the house, make up a suitable amount of scone mix and bake in a loaf tin as bread, or in a mound on a baking sheet like a soda bread. You can use white or brown flour.

Teabreads are usually enriched with fruit and nuts, and they keep well, the richer the longer. They are generally served buttered, and are not only good at teatime, but are excellent for lunchboxes or picnics as they remain moist. There are many traditional recipes from around Britain, some of which I have included here. I find them so useful for hungry children or husbands, or unexpected guests, that I usually make two at the same time, one to use, and one to freeze.

Makes about 12 Scones

Butter gives the best flavour to scones, but margarine can be used instead. Handle the mixture lightly to ensure light scones. *(See photograph on pages 134–5.)*

8 oz (225 g) self-raising flour

2 teaspoons baking powder

2 oz (50 g) butter

1 oz (25 g) caster sugar

1 egg

milk

Pre-heat the oven to 220°C/425°F/Gas 7. Lightly grease 2 baking trays.

Measure the flour and baking powder into a bowl, then add the butter and rub in with the fingertips until the mixture resembles fine breadcrumbs. Stir in the sugar.

Break the egg into a measuring jug, then make up to 5 fl oz (150 ml) with milk. Stir the egg and milk into the flour – you may not need it all – and mix to a soft but not sticky dough. Turn out on to a lightly floured work surface, knead lightly and then roll out to a thickness of $\frac{1}{2}$ in (1 cm).

Cut into rounds with a fluted 2 in (5 cm) cutter and place them on the prepared baking trays. Brush the tops with a little extra milk, or any egg and milk left in the jug, and bake in the oven for about 10 minutes or until they are a pale golden brown. Lift on to a wire rack to cool. Eat as fresh as possible.

Brown Scones

Use wholemeal self-raising flour instead of white. You may need to use a little more liquid.

Secrets of Success

If you have any left-over scones, slice in half and toast them for breakfast.

Cheese Scone Round

MAKES 1 SCONE ROUND

SERVE WARM WITH COLD meats, soup or a cheese board – with butter, of course! (See photograph on pages 134–5.)

8 oz (225 g) self-raising flour
½ teaspoon salt
½ teaspoon mustard powder
¼ teaspoon cayenne pepper
1 teaspoon baking powder
1 oz (25 g) butter or margarine
5 oz (150 g) mature Cheddar, grated
1 egg
milk

Pre-heat the oven to 220°C/425°F/Gas 7. Lightly grease a baking tray.

Measure the flour, salt, mustard powder, cayenne and baking powder into a bowl. Add the butter or margarine and rub in with the fingertips until the mixture resembles fine breadcrumbs. Stir in 4 oz (100 g) of the grated cheese.

Break the egg into a measuring jug and make up to 5 fl oz (150 ml) with milk. Stir the egg and milk into the dry ingredients and mix to a soft but not sticky dough. Turn out on to a lightly floured work surface and knead lightly. Roll out to a 6 in (15 cm) circle and mark into 6 wedges. Brush with a little milk and sprinkle with the remaining grated cheese.

Bake in the pre-heated oven for about 15 minutes or until golden brown and firm to the touch. Slide on to a wire rack to cool. Eat as fresh as possible.

Potato Scones

Makes about 12 Scones

These scones are particularly moist, excellent if you want to keep them a day or two. They can be made sweet or savoury: for savoury potato scones, omit the sugar and add ½ teaspoon of salt to the flour. (See photograph on pages 134–5.)

6 oz (175 g) plain flour

3 teaspoons baking powder

2 oz (50 g) butter or margarine

1½ oz (40 g) caster sugar

4 oz (100 g) freshly boiled mashed potato

about 3 tablespoons milk

Pre-heat the oven to 220°C/425°F/Gas 7. Lightly grease 2 baking trays.

Measure the flour and baking powder into a bowl, add the butter or margarine and rub in with the fingertips until the mixture resembles fine breadcrumbs. Stir in the sugar and the mashed potato, mixing with a fork to prevent the potato from forming lumps. Add enough milk to form a soft but not sticky dough.

Turn the mixture out on to a lightly floured work surface and knead very lightly. Roll out to a thickness of about ½ in (1 cm) and cut into rounds using a 2 in (5 cm) fluted cutter (use a plain cutter for savoury scones). Place on the prepared baking trays and bake in the oven for about 12–15 minutes or until well risen and golden brown. Serve warm and buttered.

Scotch Pancakes

MAKES ABOUT 21 PANCAKES

THESE ARE ALSO KNOWN as drop scones. Wrap in a clean tea towel as they come off the griddle to keep them soft and moist. (See photograph on pages 134–5.)

6 oz (175 g) self-raising flour

1 teaspoon baking powder

1½ oz (40 g) caster sugar

1 extra large egg

about 7 fl oz (200 ml) milk

Prepare a griddle or heavy-based frying-pan (preferably non-stick) by heating and greasing with oil or white vegetable fat.

Measure the flour, baking powder and sugar into a bowl, make a well in the centre and then add the egg and half the milk. Beat to a smooth thick batter, then beat in enough of the remaining milk to make the batter the consistency of thick cream.

Drop the mixture in spoonfuls on to the hot griddle, spacing the mixture well apart. When bubbles rise to the surface, turn the scones over with a palette knife and cook them on the other side for a further 30 seconds to 1 minute until they are golden brown. Lift off on to a wire rack and cover them with a clean tea towel to keep them soft.

Continue cooking until all the batter has been used up, then serve warm with butter and golden syrup.

Welshcakes

MAKES ABOUT 18 CAKES

FOR SWEET CAKES IT IS traditional to use a fluted cutter, but you may find a plain cutter easier for these as it will cut through the fruit in the dough more easily. *(See photograph on pages 134–5.)*

12 oz (350 g) self-raising flour
2 teaspoons baking powder
6 oz (175 g) margarine
4½ oz (115 g) caster sugar
4 oz (100 g) currants
¾ teaspoon mixed spice
1 extra large egg
about 2 tablespoons milk
caster sugar to finish

Prepare a griddle or heavy-based frying-pan (preferably non-stick) by heating and lightly greasing with oil or white vegetable fat.

Measure the flour and baking powder into a large bowl and rub in the margarine until the mixture resembles fine breadcrumbs. Add the sugar, currants and spice. Beat the egg with the milk, then add this to the mixture and mix to form a firm dough, adding a little more milk if necessary.

Roll out the dough on a lightly floured work surface to a thickness of ¼ in (5 mm) and cut into rounds with a 3 in (7.5 cm) plain round cutter.

Cook the Welshcakes on the griddle on a low heat for about 3 minutes on each side until golden brown. (Be careful not to cook them too fast, otherwise the centres will not be fully cooked through.)

Cool on a wire rack then dust with caster sugar. They are best eaten on the day of making. Serve buttered.

SECRETS OF SUCCESS

If you have an Aga, you can cook Welshcakes, drop scones, or any of the other griddle cakes directly on the simmering plate.

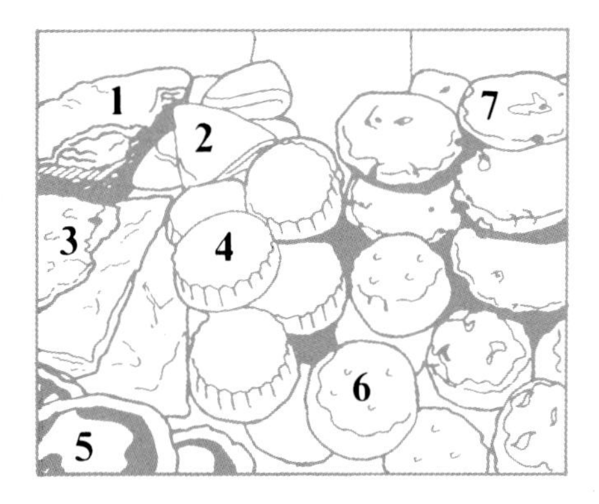

Scones and Teabreads

1 *Cheese Scone Round (page 130)*

2 *Griddle Scones (page 137)*

3 *Singin' Hinny (page 136)*

4 *Potato Scones (page 131)*

5 *Scotch Pancakes (page 132)*

6 *Scones (page 129)*

7 *Welshcakes (page 133)*

Singin' Hinny

Serves 4–6

This Northumberland griddle cake 'sings' or sizzles as it cooks on the griddle, hence its name. 'Hinny' is Northern slang for honey, an endearment especially for children and young women. Traditionally the Singin' Hinny is made in one large round, but you can make two or three smaller ones in the same way. (See photograph on pages 134–5.)

12 oz (350 g) plain flour

½ teaspoon bicarbonate of soda

1 teaspoon cream of tartar

3 oz (75 g) lard or white vegetable fat

4 oz (100 g) currants

about 7 fl oz (200 ml) milk

Prepare a griddle or large heavy-based frying-pan (preferably non-stick) by heating and lightly greasing it with oil or white vegetable fat.

Measure the flour, bicarbonate of soda and cream of tartar into a bowl, add the lard or white vegetable fat and rub in until the mixture resembles fine breadcrumbs. Stir in the currants. Mix to a soft but not sticky dough with the milk and turn out on to a lightly floured work surface. Knead lightly then roll out to a large round about ¼ in (5 mm) thick.

Lift the scone round on to the prepared griddle and cook on a gentle heat for about 5 minutes on one side, then carefully turn over and cook on the other side for a further 5 minutes or until both sides are a good brown.

Slide the Singin' Hinny on to a wire rack to cool slightly, then split and butter, sandwich back together and serve hot.

Griddle Scones

Makes 12 Scones

Make these with white or wholemeal flour and eat really fresh spread with butter. You will need to add a little more milk to the mixture when you use the wholemeal flour. *(See photograph on pages 134–5.)*

8 oz (225 g) plain flour

1 teaspoon bicarbonate of soda

2 teaspoons cream of tartar

1 oz (25 g) margarine

1 oz (25 g) caster sugar

about 5 fl oz (150 ml) milk

Prepare a griddle or heavy-based frying-pan (preferably non-stick) by heating and lightly greasing with oil or white vegetable fat.

Measure the flour, bicarbonate of soda and cream of tartar into a bowl, add the margarine and rub into the dry ingredients with the fingertips until the mixture resembles fine breadcrumbs. Stir in the sugar and gradually add the milk, mixing the dough with a round bladed knife to a soft but not sticky dough.

Divide the dough in half and knead each piece very lightly on a lightly floured work surface. Roll each piece into a round about ½ in (1 cm) thick, then cut each round into 6 equal wedges. Cook in batches on the prepared griddle for about 5 minutes each side until the scones are evenly brown on each side. Lift on to a wire rack to cool. Eat as fresh as possible.

Secrets of Success

It is traditional to use bicarbonate and cream of tartar, but you can use self-raising flour and 2 teaspoons of baking powder.

Bara Brith

Makes 1 × 2 lb (900 g) Loaf

There are many versions of this traditional teabread, which can be made with or without yeast. In Welsh, 'bara brith' means 'speckled bread'. Similar breads are made in different parts of Britain: barm brack in Ireland and Selkirk bannock in Scotland.

6 oz (175 g) currants

6 oz (175 g) sultanas

8 oz (225 g) light muscovado sugar

10 fl oz (300 ml) strong hot tea

10 oz (275 g) self-raising flour

1 egg, beaten

Measure the fruit and sugar into a bowl, pour over the hot tea, cover and leave overnight.

Pre-heat the oven to 150°C/300°F/Gas 2. Lightly grease and base line a 2 lb (900 g) loaf tin with greased greaseproof paper.

Stir the flour and egg into the fruit mixture, mix thoroughly then turn into the prepared tin and level the surface.

Bake in the pre-heated oven for about $1\frac{1}{2}$–$1\frac{3}{4}$ hours or until well risen and firm to the touch. A fine skewer inserted into the centre should come out clean. Allow to cool in the tin for about 10 minutes before turning out and leaving to cool completely on a wire rack. Serve sliced and buttered.

Bara Brith

All-Bran Teabread

MAKES 1 × 2 LB (900 G) LOAF

THIS IS VERY EASY to make, and is a good way of using up the last bit of All-Bran in the box.

4 oz (100 g) All-Bran breakfast cereal
2 oz (50 g) light muscovado sugar
10 oz (275 g) mixed dried fruit
10 fl oz (300 ml) milk
1 egg, beaten
4 oz (100 g) self-raising flour
1 teaspoon mixed spice

Measure the All-Bran, sugar and dried fruit into a bowl, pour over the milk, stir to mix, then cover and leave in a cool place overnight.

Pre-heat the oven to 180°C/350°F/Gas 4. Lightly grease and base line a 2 lb (900 g) loaf tin with greased greaseproof paper.

Stir the egg, flour and mixed spice into the fruit mixture and mix thoroughly. Turn into the prepared tin (the mixture will only come half-way up the tin) and level the surface.

Bake in the pre-heated oven for about 1–1¼ hours or until well risen and firm. A fine skewer inserted into the centre should come out clean. Loosely cover the teabread with foil towards the end of cooking if it is becoming too brown. Allow to cool in the tin for about 10 minutes, then turn out and leave to cool completely on a wire rack. Serve sliced and buttered.

Walnut Teabread

Makes 1 × 2 lb (900 g) Loaf

This teabread freezes well. It's delicious spread with good butter, and I like coming across the walnuts in the bread – they give an interesting texture. (See photograph on page 143.)

4 oz (100 g) granulated sugar
6 oz (175 g) golden syrup
7 fl oz (200 ml) milk
2 oz (50 g) sultanas
8 oz (225 g) self-raising flour
1 teaspoon baking powder
2 oz (50 g) walnuts, roughly chopped
1 egg, beaten

Pre-heat the oven to 180°C/350°F/Gas 4. Lightly grease and base line a 2 lb (900 g) loaf tin with greased greaseproof paper.

Measure the sugar, syrup, milk and sultanas into a pan and heat gently until the sugar has dissolved. Leave to cool.

Measure the flour and baking powder into a bowl and add the roughly chopped walnuts. Add the cooled syrup mixture to the dry ingredients with the beaten egg and stir well until the mixture is smooth. Pour into the prepared tin.

Bake in the pre-heated oven for about 50–60 minutes or until firm to the touch and a skewer inserted into the centre comes out clean. Cover the top of the cake loosely with foil towards the end of the cooking time if the cake is becoming too brown. Leave to cool in the tin for about 10 minutes, then turn out and leave to cool completely on a wire rack. Serve buttered.

Secrets of Success

To break up walnuts, or pulverize biscuits or cornflakes, put in a strong polythene bag and crush with a rolling pin.

Banana and Honey Teabread

MAKES 1 × 2 LB (900 G) LOAF

THIS TEABREAD HAS quite a pale colour even when cooked, due to the thick pale honey used. It is a very good way of using up over-ripe bananas.

8 oz (225 g) self-raising flour
¼ teaspoon freshly grated nutmeg
4 oz (100 g) margarine
8 oz (225 g) bananas
4 oz (100 g) caster sugar
grated rind of 1 lemon
2 extra large eggs
6 tablespoons thick honey

FOR THE TOPPING

2 tablespoons thick honey
nibbed sugar or crushed sugar cubes for sprinkling

Pre-heat the oven to 180°C/350°F/Gas 4. Lightly grease and base line a 2 lb (900 g) loaf tin with greased greaseproof paper.

Measure the flour and nutmeg into a large bowl and rub in the fat using the fingertips until the mixture resembles fine breadcrumbs.

Peel and mash the bananas and stir into the flour mixture with the sugar, lemon rind, eggs and honey. Beat well until evenly mixed, then turn into the prepared tin and level the surface.

Bake in the pre-heated oven for about 1¼ hours or until a fine skewer inserted into the centre comes out clean. Cover the teabread loosely with foil during the end of the cooking time if it is browning too much. Allow the teabread to cool slightly in the tin, then turn out on to a wire rack and leave to cool completely.

For the topping, gently warm the honey in a small pan, then brush over the top of the teabread. Sprinkle with the nibbed sugar.

(Top right) Banana and Honey Teabread, (bottom right) Walnut Teabread (page 141)

Chapter 7

Biscuits and Shortbread

People often appear apologetic when they offer biscuits instead of cakes, and I cannot understand this. A genuine home-made biscuit is very special and much lighter than a wedge of cake. They beat bought ones any day, they are quick to make, and they retain their flavour well if kept in an airtight tin. However, as the contents of the tin seem to disappear in a flash, I now freeze most of my biscuits!

The prerequisites of good home-made biscuits are a reliable recipe and the best ingredients. I don't always use butter, though, only if there is no masking flavour like spices or ginger; margarine is fine in a more intensely flavoured mixture. And don't add too much egg or liquid to a biscuit mix or the biscuits will become hard and tough.

Thereafter, it all depends on you. There's no necessity for you to expend as much energy in the creaming and mixing process as there is with cakes; you only need to soften the fat and sugar sufficiently to allow them to absorb the dry ingredients. You can make the biscuits any size or shape you like: large for hungry school children, small for *petits fours*. Just remember to space them well apart on the baking trays as they will spread during baking, and adjust the cooking time accordingly. If you're rolling biscuits, do make them of even thickness, otherwise thin ones will burn.

Ovens vary so enormously that my baking instructions might not quite suit your particular one. If a biscuit took longer to reach the perfect pale caramel biscuit colour, write a note to that effect on the recipe itself, or attach a little yellow sticker. You may need to rotate the baking trays, for instance, if the heat is fiercer at the back of the oven. Remember to note this down as well.

Even here, though, biscuits are easy. If a shortbread, say, is done at the sides, but not in the middle, you can put it back in the oven for a few minutes. None of the sinking fears attached to cake making are relevant to biscuits. And if the biscuits, once baked, lose their crispness, all you have to do is pop them back into a medium oven to refresh them and crisp them up again.

The Very Best Shortbread

MAKES 8 WEDGES

FOR A REALLY GOOD shortbread it is essential to use butter, not margarine. Cornflour or ground rice can replace the semolina. You can make a larger thinner circle if you like thin shortbread. Remember the cooking time will be shorter.
Glacé cherries, dried apricots and sultanas make delicious additions to shortbread, but the biscuits then need to be eaten on the day of making as they soon become soggy with the moisture from the fruit. *(See photograph on pages 146–7.)*

4 oz (100 g) plain flour
2 oz (50 g) semolina
4 oz (100 g) butter
2 oz (50 g) caster sugar
1 oz (25 g) flaked almonds (optional)
a little caster or demerara sugar for dusting

Pre-heat the oven to 160°C/325°F/Gas 3. Lightly grease a baking tray.

Mix the flour with the semolina in a bowl or food processor. Add the butter and sugar and rub together with the fingertips, or process in the food processor, until the mixture is just beginning to bind together. Knead lightly until the mixture forms a smooth dough.

Place the dough on to the prepared baking tray and roll out to a 7 in (18 cm) circle. Crimp the edges to decorate and prick all over with a fork. Mark into 8 wedges, sprinkle over the flaked almonds if used, and chill until firm.

Bake in the pre-heated oven for about 35 minutes or until a very pale golden brown. Re-mark the sections, dust with the caster sugar and leave to cool on the baking tray for about 5 minutes. Carefully lift off with a palette knife and finish cooling on a wire rack.

Alternatively, press the dough out into a greased 7 in (18 cm) sandwich tin, bake as before and then mark into 8 wedges. Leave to cool in the tin and sprinkle with caster sugar.

SECRETS OF SUCCESS

Shortbread, traditionally eaten at Christmas and New Year, can be decoratively shaped in wooden or earthenware moulds. Lightly flour the mould, press the shortbread dough into the patterned depression, level with a rolling pin, then turn out on to a baking tray, patterned side up, to bake.

New wooden moulds will need to be seasoned a couple of times before use: rub with a little flavourless salad oil.

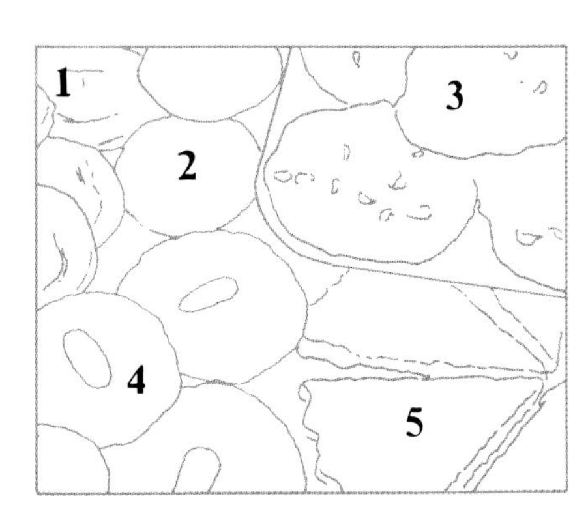

Biscuits and Shortbread

1 *Refrigerator Cookies (page 153)*

2 *Cornish Fairings (page 156)*

3 *Mega Chocolate Chip Cookies (page 151)*

4 *Macaroons (page 157)*

5 *The Very Best Shortbread (page 145)*

Millionaires' Shortbread

MAKES ABOUT 24 SQUARES

CUT INTO SMALL SQUARES or bars, this shortbread is always popular. The different textures are the principal appeal – the crunch of the shortbread base, the caramel in the middle, and the cold, crisp chocolate on top.

Do make sure you stir the caramel mixture continuously. If you leave it for even a second it will catch on the bottom of the pan and burn. *(See photograph on pages 154–5.)*

FOR THE SHORTBREAD

9 oz (250 g) plain flour

3 oz (75 g) caster sugar

6 oz (175 g) butter, softened

FOR THE CARAMEL

4 oz (100 g) butter or margarine

4 oz (100 g) light muscovado sugar

2 × 14 oz (397 g) cans condensed milk

FOR THE TOPPING

7 oz (200 g) plain or milk chocolate, broken into pieces

Pre-heat the oven to 180°C/350°F/Gas 4. Lightly grease a 13 × 9 in (33 × 23 cm) Swiss roll tin.

To make the shortbread, mix the flour and caster sugar in a bowl. Rub in the butter until the mixture resembles fine breadcrumbs. Knead the mixture together until it forms a dough, then press into the base of the prepared tin. Prick the shortbread lightly with a fork and bake in the pre-heated oven for about 20 minutes or until firm to the touch and very lightly browned. Cool in the tin.

To make the caramel, measure the butter, sugar and condensed milk into a pan and heat gently until the sugar has dissolved. Bring to the boil, stirring all the time, then reduce the heat and simmer very gently, stirring continuously, for about 5 minutes or until the mixture has thickened slightly. Pour over the shortbread and leave to cool.

For the topping, melt the chocolate slowly in a bowl over a pan of hot water. Pour over the cold caramel and leave to set. Cut into squares or bars.

SECRETS OF SUCCESS

You could use chocolate-flavoured cake covering instead of chocolate; this will set more quickly.

A marbled chocolate top looks stunning. Simply melt just over 2 oz (50 g) each of plain, milk and white chocolate in separate bowls. Place the chocolate in spoonfuls over the set caramel, alternating the 3 types. Use a skewer to marble the edges of the chocolate together, then leave to set.

Easter Biscuits

Makes about 24 Biscuits

Bought Easter biscuits are usually larger than these. If you like them that way, simply use a larger cutter. (See photograph on pages 154–5.)

4 oz (100 g) butter, softened
3 oz (75 g) caster sugar
1 egg, separated
7 oz (200 g) plain flour
½ teaspoon mixed spice
½ teaspoon ground cinnamon
2 oz (50 g) currants
1 oz (25 g) mixed candied peel, chopped
1–2 tablespoons milk
caster sugar for sprinkling

Pre-heat the oven to 200°C/400°F/ Gas 6. Lightly grease 3 baking trays.

Measure the butter and sugar into a bowl and cream together until light and fluffy. Beat in the egg yolk. Sift in the flour and spices and mix well. Add the currants and mixed peel and enough milk to give a fairly soft dough.

Knead the mixture lightly on a lightly floured surface and roll out to a thickness of ¼ in (5 mm). Cut into rounds using a 2½ in (6 cm) fluted cutter. Place on the prepared baking trays.

Bake in the pre-heated oven for about 8–10 minutes. Remove from the oven, brush the biscuits with the lightly beaten egg white, sprinkle with a little caster sugar and return to the oven for another 4–5 minutes or until pale golden brown. Lift on to a wire rack to cool. Store in an airtight container.

Secrets of Success

If bought or home-made biscuits have gone a little soft, place on a baking tray and crisp in a moderate oven for a few minutes.

Shrewsbury Biscuits

Makes about 24 Biscuits

These biscuits have a delicate lemony flavour.

4 oz (100 g) butter, softened
3 oz (75 g) caster sugar
1 egg, separated
7 oz (200 g) plain flour
grated rind of 1 lemon
2 oz (50 g) currants
1–2 tablespoons milk
caster sugar for sprinkling

Pre-heat the oven to 200°C/400°F/Gas 6. Lightly grease 3 baking trays.

Measure the butter and sugar into a bowl and cream together until light and fluffy. Beat in the egg yolk. Sift in the flour and lemon rind and mix well. Add the currants and enough milk to give a fairly soft dough.

Knead the mixture lightly on a lightly floured surface and roll out to a thickness of $\frac{1}{4}$ in (5 mm). Cut into rounds using a $2\frac{1}{2}$ in (6 cm) fluted cutter. Place on the prepared baking trays.

Bake in the pre-heated oven for about 8–10 minutes. Remove from the oven, brush the biscuits with the lightly beaten egg white, sprinkle with a little caster sugar and return to the oven for another 4–5 minutes or until pale golden brown. Lift on to a wire rack to cool. Store in an airtight container.

Melting Moments

Makes about 36 Biscuits

These old-fashioned biscuits are very short in texture. They are best eaten within a couple of days of making. (See photograph on pages 6–7.)

8 oz (225 g) soft margarine
6 oz (175 g) golden caster sugar
2 egg yolks
a few drops of vanilla essence
10 oz (275 g) self-raising flour
2 oz (50 g) rolled oats
12 glacé cherries, quartered (optional)

Pre-heat the oven to 190°C/375°F/Gas 5. Lightly grease 2 baking trays.

Measure the margarine, sugar, egg yolks, vanilla essence and flour into a mixing bowl. Mix together to form a soft dough.

Divide the mixture into about 36 portions. Form each piece into a ball and roll in the oats to cover. Flatten each ball slightly and top each with a quartered glacé cherry, if liked. Place on the prepared baking trays. Bake in the pre-heated oven for about 20 minutes or until golden. Allow to cool slightly on the baking trays for a few moments before lifting on to a wire rack to cool.

Mega Chocolate Chip Cookies

Makes about 24 Biscuits

Roughly chop plain chocolate if you don't have any chocolate chips. These cookies are not quite as crisp as a biscuit; and they won't keep for long, a couple of days at the most. *(See photograph on pages 146–7.)*

6 oz (175 g) soft margarine

8 oz (225 g) caster sugar

2 eggs

12 oz (350 g) self-raising flour

4 oz (100 g) plain chocolate chips

Pre-heat the oven to 180°C/350°F/Gas 4. Lightly grease 3 baking trays.

Measure all the ingredients into a medium bowl and mix thoroughly until a smooth biscuit dough is formed.

Place large spoonfuls of the mixture well apart on the prepared baking trays and flatten slightly using the back of a spoon.

Bake in the pre-heated oven for about 15–20 minutes or until golden brown and just firm to the touch. Cool on a wire rack, then store in an airtight container.

Secrets of Success

Run a knife under biscuits on the tray to see if they are done. If outside ones are browned, remove to a cooling rack and return the others to the oven.

Viennese Fingers

MAKES ABOUT 20 BISCUITS

THESE BISCUITS MUST BE made with butter. The mixture holds its shape beautifully for piping, so use for all shapes of piped biscuits. *(See photograph on pages 154–5.)*

4 oz (100 g) butter, softened
1 oz (25 g) icing sugar
4 oz (100 g) plain flour
¼ teaspoon baking powder
2 oz (50 g) plain chocolate, broken into pieces

Pre-heat the oven to 190°C/375°F/Gas 5. Lightly grease 2 baking trays. Fit a nylon piping bag with a medium star nozzle.

Measure the butter and icing sugar into a bowl and beat well until pale and fluffy. Sift in the flour and baking power. Beat well until thoroughly mixed.

Spoon into the piping bag and pipe out finger shapes about 3 in (7.5 cm) long, spacing them well apart.

Bake in the pre-heated oven for 10–15 minutes or until a pale golden brown. Lift off and cool on a wire rack.

Melt the chocolate slowly in a bowl over a pan of hot water. Dip both ends of the biscuits into the chocolate and leave to set on the wire rack.

Fast Flapjacks

MAKES ABOUT 24 FLAPJACKS

CRUNCHY AND TRADITIONAL, BUT take care not to overbake them, as they become hard and dark. *(See photograph on pages 6–7.)*

8 oz (225 g) margarine
8 oz (225 g) demerara sugar
2 tablespoons golden syrup
10 oz (275 g) rolled oats

Pre-heat the oven to 160°C/325°F/Gas 3. Lightly grease a 12 × 9 in (30 × 23 cm) roasting tin.

Melt the margarine in a large pan with the sugar and syrup and then stir in the oats. Mix well and then turn into the prepared tin and press flat with a palette knife or the back of a spoon.

Bake in the pre-heated oven for about 35 minutes or until pale golden brown. Remove from the oven and then leave to cool for 10 minutes. Mark into 24 squares and leave to finish cooling in the tin.

Refrigerator Cookies

Makes about 32 Biscuits

The dough for these biscuits can be kept in the refrigerator and baked when required. Vary the flavour by substituting orange rind for the lemon, or omit the lemon and add a teaspoon of vanilla essence. If you like you could roll the 'sausage' of biscuit dough in mixed chopped nuts or demerara sugar before slicing. *(See photograph on pages 146–7.)*

5 oz (150 g) butter, softened

5 oz (150 g) caster sugar

grated rind of 1 lemon

1 egg, beaten

8 oz (225 g) plain flour

Lightly grease 2 baking trays.

Measure the butter, sugar, lemon rind, egg and flour into a bowl and mix together until a smooth dough is formed. Lightly knead, then wrap in greaseproof paper and chill in the refrigerator for about 30 minutes.

Roll the dough into a sausage shape about 2 in (5 cm) in diameter and 8 in (20 cm) long. Wrap in greaseproof paper and chill again for about 30 minutes or until firm enough to slice.

Pre-heat the oven to 190°C/375°F/Gas 5. Unwrap the dough, then cut into $\frac{1}{4}$ in (5 mm) slices. Place on the prepared baking trays and bake in the pre-heated oven for about 12–15 minutes or until golden. Lift off and cool on a wire rack.

Secrets of Success

Some biscuit doughs can be rolled into a sausage shape, wrapped in cling film, then chilled for an hour or so until firm. Slice into thin circles and bake in the usual way.

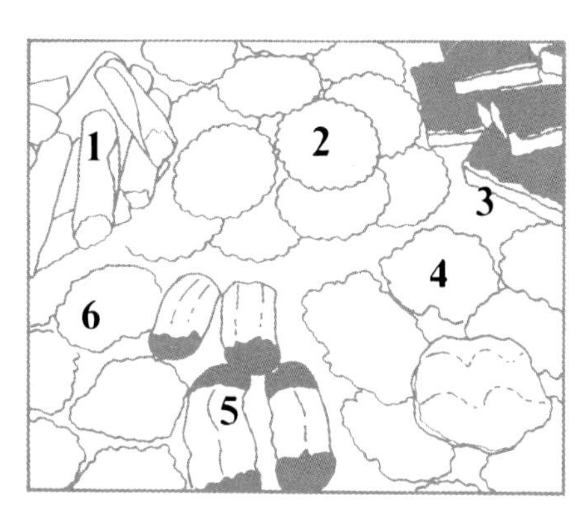

Biscuits and Shortbread

1 *Brandy Snaps (page 159)*

2 *Easter Biscuits (page 149)*

3 *Millionaires' Shortbread (page 148)*

4 *Florentines (page 158)*

5 *Viennese Fingers (page 152)*

6 *Anzac Biscuits (page 156)*

Anzac Biscuits

Makes about 36 Biscuits

Another very traditional biscuit recipe which is simplicity itself to make. (See photograph on pages 154–5.)

5 oz (150 g) soft margarine	**3 oz (75 g) self-rasing flour**
1 rounded tablespoon golden syrup	**3 oz (75 g) desiccated coconut**
6 oz (175 g) granulated sugar	**4 oz (100 g) porridge oats**

Pre-heat the oven to 180°C/350°F/Gas 4. Lightly grease 2 baking trays.

Measure the margarine, syrup and sugar into a pan and heat gently until melted. Stir in the remaining ingredients. Mix well until blended then spoon about 36 slightly flattened mounds well apart on the prepared baking trays.

Bake in the pre-heated oven for about 10 minutes until they have spread out flat and are lightly browned at the edges. Leave to cool on the trays for a few moments. Carefully lift off with a palette knife and finish cooling on a wire rack.

Cornish Fairings

Makes about 24 Biscuits

Take care not to bake these too long as they become hard and too crisp. Banging the baking tray part way through cooking makes the mixture crack and flatten. (See photograph on pages 146–7.)

4 oz (100 g) plain flour	**½ teaspoon bicarbonate of soda**
¼ teaspoon ground ginger	**2 oz (50 g) soft margarine**
¼ teaspoon mixed spice	**2 oz (50 g) caster sugar**
¼ teaspoon ground cinnamon	**2 tablespoons golden syrup**

Pre-heat the oven to 180°C/350°F/Gas 4. Lightly grease 2 baking trays.

Measure the flour, spices and bicarbonate of soda into a bowl. Rub the margarine into the flour until the mixture is like fine breadcrumbs. Mix in the sugar.

Gently melt the syrup and stir into the mixture to make a soft dough.

Roll the mixture into balls about the size of a cherry and place on the prepared baking trays, allowing room for them to spread. Bake in the pre-heated oven for 10 minutes then take the baking trays out of the oven and hit on a solid surface to make the biscuits crack and spread. Bake for a further 5 minutes until a good even brown. Cool on a wire rack.

Secrets of Success

Ground spices quickly lose their colour and flavour. Store them in the dark. Use ground within a year; whole spices last longer.

Macaroons

Makes about 16 Macaroons

Traditionally macaroons were always made on rice paper but as this is not always easy to get hold of I've used non-stick baking paper. (See photograph on pages 146–7.)

2 egg whites
8 whole blanched almonds, halved
4 oz (100 g) ground almonds
6 oz (175 g) caster sugar
1 oz (25 g) ground rice or semolina
a few drops of almond essence

Pre-heat the oven to 150°C/300°F/Gas 2. Line 2 baking trays with non-stick baking paper.

Put the egg whites into a bowl, dip in the blanched almonds and put on one side. Whisk the egg whites with an electric whisk until they form soft peaks. Gently fold in the ground almonds, sugar, ground rice or semolina and almond essence.

Spoon the mixture in teaspoonfuls on to the lined baking trays, and smooth out with the back of a spoon to form circles. Place an almond half in the centre of each.

Bake in the pre-heated oven for about 20–25 minutes or until a pale golden brown. Leave to cool on the trays for a few moments, then lift off and allow to cool completely on a wire rack.

Florentines

Makes about 20 Florentines

Using non-stick baking paper makes it so much simpler to get the biscuits off the baking trays. You can simply use a well greased baking tray, but be careful not to leave the florentines for too long or they will harden before you have a chance to lift them off. *(See photograph on pages 154–5.)*

2 oz (50 g) butter

2 oz (50 g) demerara sugar

2 oz (50 g) golden syrup

2 oz (50 g) plain flour

4 glacé cherries, finely chopped

2 oz (50 g) mixed candied peel, finely chopped

2 oz (50 g) mixed almonds and walnuts, finely chopped

6 oz (175 g) plain chocolate, broken into pieces

Pre-heat the oven to 180°C/350°F/Gas 4. Line 3 baking trays with non-stick baking paper.

Measure the butter, sugar and syrup into a small pan and heat gently until the butter has melted. Remove from the heat and add the flour, chopped cherries, candied peel and nuts to the pan and stir well to mix. Spoon teaspoonfuls of the mixture on to the prepared baking trays, leaving plenty of room for them to spread.

Bake in the pre-heated oven for about 8–10 minutes or until golden brown. Allow the florentines to cool on the paper before lifting on to a cooling rack with a palette knife. (If the florentines have been baked on greased baking trays, then allow them to harden for a few moments only before lifting on to cooling racks to cool completely. If the florentines do become too hard to remove, then pop them back into the oven for a few moments to allow them to soften.)

Melt the chocolate in a bowl placed over a pan of hot water. Spread a little melted chocolate over the flat base of each florentine, mark a zig-zag in the chocolate with a fork and leave to set, chocolate side up, on the cooling rack. Store in an airtight container.

Secrets of Success

These are very luxurious biscuits, but you do need patience and accurate scales to make them.

Brandy Snaps

Makes about 24 Biscuits

I must confess that I rarely make these myself as it is so easy to buy good ones. Serve plain with ice-cream or mousses, or fill with whipped cream and serve with fruit. If you want to make basket shapes, just mould them over greased cups. For cornet shapes, mould round greased metal cornet moulds. *(See photograph on pages 154–5.)*

2 oz (50 g) butter
2 oz (50 g) demerara sugar
2 oz (50 g) golden syrup
2 oz (50 g) plain flour
½ teaspoon ground ginger
½ teaspoon lemon juice

Pre-heat the oven to 160°C/325°F/Gas 3. Line 2 baking trays with non-stick baking paper, and oil the handles of 4 wooden spoons.

Measure the butter, sugar and syrup into a small pan and heat gently until the butter and sugar have dissolved. Allow the mixture to cool slightly and then sift in the flour and the ginger. Add the lemon juice and stir well to mix thoroughly. Place teaspoons of the mixture on to the prepared baking trays, at least 4 in (10 cm) apart, and only 4 teaspoons at a time.

Bake in the pre-heated oven for about 8 minutes or until the mixture is well spread out and a dark golden colour. Remove from the oven and leave for a few minutes to firm, then lift from the paper using a fish slice. Turn over and roll around the handle of the wooden spoons. Leave to set on a wire rack and then slip out the spoons.

Repeat until all the mixture has been used. When cold, store in an airtight tin.

Chapter 8

Continental Cakes

On the Continent, there is a long and famous tradition of rich cakes and pastries. This flowered from about the middle of the eighteenth century, when many countries became more affluent, when special cake ingredients such as fine flour became more widely available, and when cooking was elevated to an art. To show off their skills, pastry cooks vied with each other to produce even more elaborate confections; they also opened shops in which to sell their wares in all of the European capitals, particularly Paris, Vienna and Budapest. Famous Continental cakes such as *Gâteau Saint Honoré*, *Doboz Torte* and *Tarte Tatin* all date from this time.

This rich cake-making tradition still flourishes on the Continent, as do the shops in which they are sold. Have you never stood outside some *pâtisserie* in France, and wondered at the colourful and mouth-watering displays of cakes large and small, tarts glistening with fruit, and caramel-brown, light, flaky pastries. Very few cakes on the Continent are actually made at home, because the *pâtissier* is there with his wares ready to be packaged in boxes and taken home. We have nothing like the same tradition in Britain. The best baking in Britain has always been home-baking, using the finest ingredients for our traditional recipes.

Each country seems to have its own specialty, and I've selected a few for this chapter (although, of course, a few appear elsewhere as well). Most are rather more complicated to make than the other cakes in the book, but they are all delicious, just right for a special occasion – a special tea, or the finale of a dinner party. Most should be baked and eaten on the same day, although individual *elements* of some may be frozen, and the decoration done on the day.

Bring a little bit of Continental excitement into your life, and try at least one or two of the cakes in this chapter!

Nusskuchen

Serves 6

Nusskuchen comes in many forms, but always contains hazelnuts. This one is filled with a delicious apple mixture and topped with melted chocolate.

1½ oz (40 g) hazelnuts
4 oz (100 g) butter, softened
4 oz (100 g) caster sugar
2 eggs, separated
1 teaspoon instant coffee
1 tablespoon warm milk
4 oz (100 g) self-raising flour

For the Filling

1 lb (450 g) dessert apples, such as Cox's, peeled, cored and sliced
2 tablespoons apricot jam
grated rind and juice of ½ lemon

To Finish

2 oz (50 g) plain chocolate, broken into pieces

Pre-heat the oven to 190°C/375°F/Gas 5. Grease and base line an 8 in (20 cm) deep round cake tin with greased greaseproof paper.

First prepare the hazelnuts: place them on a baking tray and put into the oven for about 10 minutes. Tip on to a clean tea towel and rub the nuts well together to remove the skins. (Some stubborn ones may need to go back into the oven but don't worry about getting every last bit of skin off, it's not necessary.) Place the nuts into a food processor or blender and grind.

Measure the softened butter and the sugar into a bowl and beat together until light and fluffy. Gradually beat in the egg yolks and stir in the prepared nuts. Dissolve the coffee in the warm milk then stir it into the mixture. Carefully fold in the flour.

In a separate bowl, whisk the egg whites until they form soft peaks and then gently fold into the mixture. Turn the cake mixture into the prepared tin.

Bake in the pre-heated oven for about 25 minutes until the cake is firm to the touch and has shrunk slightly from the sides of the tin. Allow to cool in the tin for a few minutes, then turn out, remove the paper and leave to cool on a wire rack.

Meanwhile, prepare the filling. Peel, core and slice the apples and place in a pan with the apricot jam, lemon juice and rind. Cover and cook very gently until the apples are soft but still retain their shape. Leave to cool.

Split the cake in half horizontally and fill with the cooled apple mixture. Melt the chocolate slowly in a bowl over a pan of hot water. Spread over the top of the cake and leave to set. Serve with cream or *crème fraîche*.

Gâteau Moka aux Amandes

SERVES ABOUT 8

THIS IS ONE OF MY favourite coffee cakes, and it looks spectacular, too. Add a little brandy to the filling, if you like.

3 extra large eggs
4 oz (100 g) caster sugar
3 oz (75 g) self-raising flour

FOR THE *CRÈME AU BEURRE MOKA*

3 oz (75 g) caster sugar
4 tablespoons water
2 egg yolks
6 oz (175 g) butter, softened
1–2 tablespoons coffee essence

TO FINISH

6 oz (175 g) blanched almonds, shredded and toasted
icing sugar for dusting (optional)

Pre-heat the oven to 190°C/375°F/Gas 5. Grease and base line a 9 in (23 cm) deep round cake tin with greased greaseproof paper.

Measure the eggs and sugar into a large bowl and whisk at full speed with an electric whisk until the mixture is pale in colour and thick enough to just leave a trail when the whisk is lifted. Sift the flour over the surface of the mixture and gently fold in with a metal spoon or spatula. Turn into the prepared tin.

Bake in the pre-heated oven for about 30 minutes until well risen and golden brown. Turn out and leave to cool on a wire rack.

To make the *crème au beurre moka* (coffee butter cream), measure the sugar and water into a small heavy-based pan. Heat very gently until the sugar has dissolved. Bring to the boil and boil steadily for 2–3 minutes until a temperature of 107°C (225°F) on a sugar thermometer is reached, or until the syrup will form a slim thread when pulled apart between 2 teaspoons. Place the egg yolks into a bowl and give them a quick stir to break them up. Pour the syrup in a thin stream on to the egg yolks, whisking all the time. Continue to whisk until the mixture is thick and cold. In another bowl, cream the butter until very soft and gradually beat in the egg yolk mixture. Stir in the coffee essence to flavour.

Cut the cake in half horizontally and sandwich with a thin layer of the coffee butter cream. Spread the butter cream over the top and sides of the cake as well, and then press the toasted almonds all over the cake. Dredge lightly with icing sugar and decorate with rosettes of butter cream on each portion, if liked.

Gâteau Moka aux Amandes

Chocolatines

Makes 9 Chocolatines

These very small cakes are fiddly to make, but are delicious, made with a sponge that is moist and light due to the added butter. They are the sort of cake that would be on sale in the very best of French pâtisseries.

For the Genoese Sponge

1½ oz (40 g) butter

3 extra large eggs

3 oz (75 g) caster sugar

2½ oz (65 g) self-raising flour

1 tablespoon cornflour

For the *Crème au beurre Chocolat*

2 oz (50 g) granulated sugar

4 tablespoons water

2 egg yolks

6 oz (175 g) unsalted butter, softened

4 oz (100 g) plain chocolate, melted

To Finish

3 oz (75 g) chopped mixed nuts, toasted

Pre-heat the oven to 180°C/350°F/Gas 4. Grease and base line a shallow 7 in (18 cm) square cake tin with greased greaseproof paper.

For the sponge, gently melt the butter in a pan. Leave on one side to cool slightly.

Measure the eggs and sugar into a large bowl and whisk at full speed with an electric whisk until the mixture is pale and mousse-like, and thick enough so that a trail is left when the whisk is lifted from the mixture. Sift the flours together into a bowl. Fold half the flour carefully into the egg mixture. Gently pour half the cooled butter around the edge of the mixture and gently fold in. Repeat with the remaining flour and butter. Pour the mixture into the prepared tin.

Bake in the pre-heated oven for about 35–40 minutes until the cake is well risen, firm to the touch and beginning to shrink away from the sides of the tin. Leave the cake to cool in the tin for a few minutes, then turn out and leave to cool completely on a wire rack.

To make the *crème au beurre chocolat* (chocolate butter cream), measure the sugar and water into a small heavy-based pan. Heat very gently until the sugar has dissolved. Bring to the boil and boil steadily for 2–3 minutes until a temperature of 107°C (225°F) on a sugar thermometer is reached or until the syrup will form a slim thread when pulled apart between 2 teaspoons. Place the egg yolks into a bowl and give them a quick stir to break them up. Pour the syrup in a thin stream on to the egg yolks, whisking all the time. Continue to whisk until the mixture is thick and cold. In another bowl, cream the butter until very soft and gradually beat in the egg yolk mixture. Stir in the cooled, melted chocolate to flavour.

Split the cold sponge in half horizontally and sandwich with a thin layer of the chocolate butter cream. Re-shape the cake, then trim and cut neatly into 2 in (5 cm) squares. Spread the top and sides of each cake with most of the remaining chocolate butter cream and press the chopped, toasted nuts around the sides. Finish the tops of the cakes by piping with tiny rosettes of the remaining chocolate butter cream.

Secrets of Success

Left-over egg whites can be stored in a covered container in the fridge for up to three weeks, or frozen for up to six months.

Mokatines

MAKES 8 MOKATINES

THESE ARE A coffee-flavoured variation of Chocolatines. I've often seen them in smart Parisian pâtisseries.

FOR THE GENOESE SPONGE

1½ oz (40 g) butter

3 extra large eggs

3 oz (75 g) caster sugar

2½ oz (65 g) self-raising flour

1 tablespoon cornflour

FOR THE *CRÈME AU BEURRE MOKA*

1½ oz (40 g) caster sugar

2 tablespoons water

1 egg yolk

3 oz (75 g) butter, softened

1 tablespoon coffee essence

TO FINISH

about 3 tablespoons apricot jam

FOR THE SOFT COFFEE ICING

2 oz (50 g) butter

3 tablespoons milk

1 tablespoon instant coffee

8 oz (225 g) icing sugar, sifted

Pre-heat the oven to 180°C/350°F/Gas 4. Grease and base line a shallow 7 in (18 cm) square cake tin with greased greaseproof paper.

For the sponge, gently melt the butter in a pan. Leave on one side to cool slightly.

Measure the eggs and sugar into a large bowl and whisk at full speed with an electric whisk until the mixture is pale and mousse-like, and thick enough so that a trail is left when the whisk is lifted from the mixture. Sift the flours together into a bowl. Fold half the flour carefully into the egg mixture. Gently pour half the cooled butter around the edge of the mixture and gently fold in. Repeat with the remaining flour and butter. Pour the mixture into the prepared tin.

Bake in the pre-heated oven for about 35–40 minutes until the cake is well risen, firm to the touch and beginning to shrink away from the sides of the tin. Leave the cake to cool in the tin for a few minutes, then turn out and leave to cool completely on a wire rack.

To make the *crème au beurre moka* (coffee butter cream), measure the sugar and water into a small heavy-based pan. Heat very gently until the sugar has dissolved. Bring to the boil and boil steadily for 2–3 minutes until a temperature of 107°C (225°F) on a sugar thermometer is reached or until the syrup will form a slim thread when pulled apart between 2 teaspoons. Place the egg yolk into a bowl and give it a quick stir to break it up. Pour the syrup in a thin stream on to the egg yolk, whisking all the time. Continue to whisk until the mixture is thick and cold. In another bowl, cream the butter until very soft and gradually beat in the egg yolk mixture. Stir in the coffee essence to flavour.

Split the cold cake in half horizontally and sandwich with a thin layer of the coffee butter cream. Re-shape the cake, trim and then neatly cut in half, and then each half into 4 to give 8 oblongs.

Sieve the apricot jam into a small pan and warm gently. Brush the top and sides of the cakes with the hot apricot jam.

For the coffee icing, measure the butter, milk and coffee into a small pan and heat gently until the butter has melted. Add the sifted icing sugar and beat until smooth and glossy. Leave to thicken slightly, then pour over each cake, smoothing the sides quickly if necessary. Leave to set and then decorate with the remaining piped coffee butter cream.

Secrets of Success

Store eggs in a cool place, larder or refrigerator, pointed end down, and away from strong-smelling foods such as fish or melon. Let them reach room temperature before using.

Doboz Torte

Serves 8

From Austria, this is not the quickest of cakes to make but it does look spectacular when finished. Make the cake layers ahead and freeze them. It is worth making a 'proper' butter cream for this, but it is possible to make a quick butter cream so long as you use butter and not margarine!

The caramel topping will eventually soften due to the moisture from the cake, so serve within 12 hours. (See photograph on pages 170–71.)

For the Sponge Layers

4 eggs

6 oz (175 g) caster sugar

5 oz (150 g) self-raising flour, sifted

For the Butter Cream

2 egg whites

4 oz (100 g) icing sugar

8 oz (225 g) unsalted butter, softened

4 oz (100 g) plain chocolate, broken into pieces

For the Caramel

6 oz (175 g) granulated or caster sugar

5 tablespoons water

Pre-heat the oven to 220°C/425°F/Gas 7. Mark an 8 in (20 cm) circle on 6 pieces of non-stick baking paper and lay these on baking trays.

To make the sponge layers, break the eggs into a large bowl and add the sugar. Whisk at full speed with an electric whisk until the mixture is light and foamy and the whisk just leaves a trail when lifted out of the mixture. Lightly fold in the flour, a little at a time. Divide the mixture between the 6 marked circles, spreading the mixture out evenly. Bake 2 or 3 at a time if you have room, for about 6–8 minutes until pale golden and springy to the touch. With a sharp knife, trim the circles. Peel off the paper and leave the sponge discs to cool on a wire rack.

To make the butter cream, whisk the egg whites and icing sugar in a bowl over a pan of simmering water until the mixture holds its shape. Cream the butter until really soft then add the meringue mixture to it a little at a time. Melt the chocolate slowly in a bowl over a pan of hot water. Cool slightly then add to the butter cream and mix well until evenly blended.

Take one of the discs of sponge and place it on a sheet of non-stick baking paper, ready to be topped with caramel. Lay out another sheet of non-stick baking paper ready for the left-over caramel which will be crushed once set.

For the caramel, dissolve the sugar in the water over a low heat, then increase the heat and boil the syrup until it reaches a deep straw colour. Allow it to cool slightly then pour just over half of it over the disc of sponge. Pour the remainder on to the second sheet of paper. When the caramel on top of the sponge is just beginning to set, mark it and then cut into 8 portions with an oiled knife. Once the caramel on the second sheet of paper is completely set, crush it up with a rolling pin.

Sandwich the sponge layers together with the butter cream. Spread butter cream around the sides, leaving some for piping, and press the crushed caramel on to the sides to decorate. Pipe a rosette of the chocolate butter cream onto each portion and place a caramel topped wedge of cake at an angle on top of the rosettes to form the top layer.

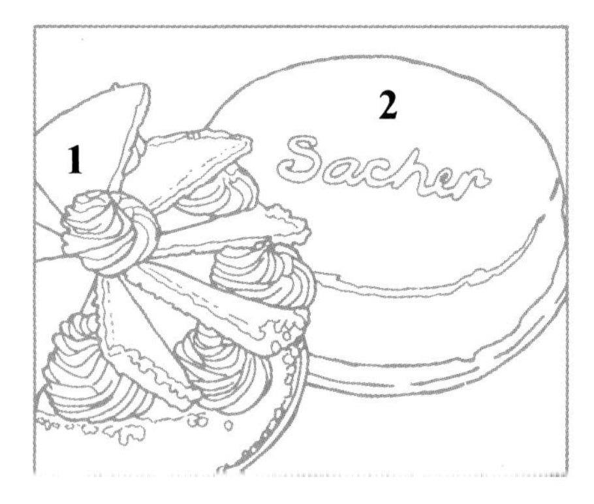

Continental Cakes

1 Doboz Torte (page 168)

2 Sachertorte (page 172)

Sacher

Sachertorte

Serves 12

This special chocolate cake is said to have been invented in Vienna by the chef Franz Sacher in 1832. It improves if left a day or two before cutting. It is quite dense and rich, so serve small wedges only, with coffee or tea. *(See photograph on pages 170–71.)*

5 oz (150 g) plain chocolate, broken into pieces

5 oz (150 g) unsalted butter, softened

4 oz (100 g) caster sugar

½ teaspoon vanilla essence

5 extra large eggs separated

3 oz (75 g) ground almonds

1½ oz (40 g) plain flour

For the Topping and Icing

about 6 tablespoons apricot jam

5 oz (150 g) plain chocolate, broken into pieces

7 fl oz (200 ml) double cream

1 oz (25 g) milk chocolate, broken into pieces

Pre-heat the oven to 180°C/350°F/Gas 4. Grease and base line a 9 in (23 cm) deep round cake tin with greased greaseproof paper.

Melt the chocolate slowly in a bowl over a pan of hot water, then cool slightly.

Beat the butter until really soft and gradually beat in the sugar until the mixture is light and fluffy. Add the cooled chocolate and the vanilla essence and mix well. Add the egg yolks to the mixture, mixing well between each addition, and then stir in the ground almonds and the flour. The mixture will be quite thick at this stage.

In a separate bowl, whisk the egg whites until they are stiff but not dry. Add about one-third to the chocolate mixture and stir in vigorously. Gently fold in the remaining egg whites. Pour the mixture into the prepared tin and level the surface.

Bake in the pre-heated oven for about 45–50 minutes or until the cake is well risen and firm to the touch. Leave the cake to cool in the tin for a few minutes before turning out and leaving to cool completely on a wire rack.

For the topping, heat the apricot jam in a small pan and then brush evenly over the top and sides of the cake. Allow to set.

For the icing, melt the plain chocolate slowly in a small bowl, with the double cream, over a pan of hot water, stirring occasionally. Allow to cool for a couple of minutes to thicken slightly, then pour the icing into the centre of the cake. Spread it gently over the top and down the sides, and leave to set.

For the icing 'writing', melt the milk chocolate slowly in a bowl over a pan of hot water. Spoon into a small paper icing bag or polythene bag and snip off the corner. Pipe 'Sacher' across the cake and leave to set.

Frangipane Tartlets

MAKES 12 TARTLETS

PÂTE SUCRÉE *is the classic French sweet pastry. I make mine in the food processor, or in a bowl, which is easier than the traditional way: where the flour is sifted on to a work surface, and the other ingredients are placed into a well in the flour and worked together to a paste before the flour is gently worked in.*

FOR THE *PÂTE SUCRÉE*

4 oz (100 g) plain flour

2 oz (50 g) butter, softened

2 oz (50 g) caster sugar

2 egg yolks

FOR THE FRANGIPANE

2 oz (50 g) butter, softened

2 oz (50 g) caster sugar

1 egg, beaten

2 oz (50 g) ground almonds

½ oz (15 g) plain flour

a few drops of almond essence

2 oz (50 g) flaked almonds

TO FINISH

about 3 tablespoons apricot jam

about 2 tablespoons ground almonds

First make the *pâte sucrée*. Measure the flour into a bowl. Rub in the butter with the fingertips until the mixture resembles fine breadcrumbs. Stir in the sugar, then add the egg yolks and mix until the ingredients come together to form a dough. Knead the mixture gently until smooth. Wrap the dough in cling film and leave to rest in the fridge for about 30 minutes. (Or process the flour, butter and sugar briefly in the food processor, add the egg yolks and process until *just* blended. Knead and wrap as before.)

Pre-heat the oven to 190°C/375°F/Gas 5.

Roll out the pastry on a lightly floured work surface and cut out about 12 rounds using a 3 in (7.5 cm) plain pastry cutter. Re-roll the trimmings once only. Ease the pastry rounds into the patty tins and prick lightly with a fork. Chill while you are making the frangipane.

For the frangipane, measure the butter and sugar into a bowl and beat well together until light and fluffy. Gradually beat in the egg, then stir in the ground almonds, flour and almond essence. Fill the chilled tartlet cases with the frangipane and scatter the flaked almonds on top.

Bake in the pre-heated oven for about 15 minutes until the frangipane is golden and firm to the touch. Ease the tartlets out of the tin and on to a wire rack to cool.

Sieve the apricot jam into a small pan and warm gently. Brush the tartlets with the apricot glaze and decorate the outside edge with a thin line of ground almonds. Leave the tartlets to cool completely.

Swiss Wild Strawberry and Walnut Cake

Serves 8

This is served on the Continent as a cake cum pudding. It's a light walnut sponge filled with wild strawberries and cream. For a lighter filling, you can use crème fraîche.

3 extra large eggs

4 oz (100 g) caster sugar

3 oz (75 g) self-raising flour

2 oz (50 g) walnut pieces, roughly chopped

For the Filling and Topping

10 fl oz (300 ml) double cream, whipped

1 lb (450 g) fresh Alpine or wild strawberries

extra strawberries for decoration

Pre-heat the oven to 180°C/350°F/Gas 4. Grease and base line an 8 in (20 cm) deep round cake tin with greased greaseproof paper.

Measure the eggs and sugar into a large bowl and whisk at full speed with an electric whisk until the mixture is thick and mousse-like and leaves a trail when the whisk is lifted out of the mixture. Sift the flour on to the mixture and lightly fold in with the chopped walnuts. Turn into the prepared cake tin.

Bake in the pre-heated oven for about 40–45 minutes until well risen, golden and firm to the touch. Allow the cake to cool in the tin for a few minutes, then turn out and leave to cool completely on a wire rack.

When cold, cut the cake into 3 horizontally. Fill lavishly with the whipped cream and strawberries. Spread the remaining cream over the top and the sides of the cake and decorate with the reserved strawberries.

(Right) Swiss Wild Strawberry and Walnut Cake

Glazed Fruit Tartlets

MAKES 12 TARTLETS

THESE LITTLE TARTS look best if each one is filled with all one type of fruit. Use redcurrant glaze for red fruits, and apricot glaze for orange or green fruits such as green grapes and kiwi fruit. Fill at the last moment as they soften quickly.

FOR THE *PÂTE SUCRÉE*

4 oz (100 g) plain flour

2 oz (50 g) butter, softened

2 oz (50 g) caster sugar

2 egg yolks

FOR THE FILLING AND GLAZE

5 fl oz (150 ml) double cream

8 oz (225 g) fresh fruits (strawberries, raspberries, grapes)

about 4 tablespoons redcurrant jelly (or apricot jam)

First make the *pâte sucrée.* Measure the flour into a bowl. Rub in the butter with the fingertips until the mixture resembles fine breadcrumbs. Stir in the sugar, then add the egg yolks and mix until the ingredients come together to form a dough. Knead the mixture gently until smooth. Wrap the dough in cling film and leave to rest in the fridge for about 30 minutes. (Or process the flour, butter and sugar briefly in the food processor, add the egg yolks and process until *just* blended. Knead and wrap as before.)

Pre-heat the oven to 190°C/375°F/Gas 5.

Roll out the pastry on a lightly floured work surface and cut out about 12 rounds using a 3 in (7.5 cm) fluted pastry cutter. Re-roll the trimmings once only. Ease the pastry rounds into the patty tins and prick lightly with a fork. Place small pieces of greaseproof paper or foil into each pastry case and fill with baking beans.

Bake the pastry cases in the pre-heated oven for about 15 minutes or until golden brown. Turn out on to a wire rack, remove the paper and baking beans, and leave to cool.

Whip the cream until it forms soft peaks and spoon a little into each tartlet case. Arrange the fruits on top. Warm the redcurrant jelly or apricot jam in a small pan and brush liberally over the fruits to glaze.

Glazed Lemon Tart

Serves 6

A classic French tart with a crisp sweet pastry case and a sharp lemon filling, the sliced lemon topping is optional, but it does make it special.

For the *Pâte Sucrée*

6 oz (175 g) plain flour

3 oz (75 g) butter, softened

3 oz (75 g) caster sugar

3 egg yolks

For the Filling

2 extra large eggs

3½ oz (90 g) caster sugar

5 oz (150 g) ground almonds

3½ fl oz (85 ml) whipping cream

4 lemons

To Finish

5 oz (150 g) caster sugar

4½ fl oz (135 ml) water

2 lemons

about 6 tablespoons apricot jam

First make the *pâte sucrée*. Measure the flour into a bowl. Rub in the butter with the fingertips until the mixture resembles fine breadcrumbs. Stir in the sugar, then add the egg yolks and mix until the ingredients come together to form a dough. Knead the mixture gently until smooth. Wrap the dough in cling film and leave to rest in the fridge for about 30 minutes. (Or process the flour, butter and sugar briefly in the food processor, add the egg yolks and process until *just* blended. Knead and wrap as before.)

Pre-heat the oven to 180°C/350°F/Gas 4.

Roll out the pastry on a lightly floured work surface and use to line a 9 in (23 cm) loose-bottomed flan tin. Prick the pastry all over with a fork. Chill whilst preparing the filling.

For the filling, beat together the eggs, sugar, ground almonds and cream. Add the finely grated rind of all 4 lemons and the juice of 2. Pour the filling into the pastry case and bake in the pre-heated oven for about 30–35 minutes until the filling is golden and firm to the touch.

Meanwhile prepare the lemon slices to finish the top of the tart. Measure the sugar and water into a pan and heat gently until the sugar dissolves, then boil for 1 minute. Slice the lemons thinly, discard any pips, and place into the hot syrup. Bring the syrup back to the boil, then remove the pan from the heat, pour into a bowl and leave to soak for at least 2 hours.

Drain the lemon slices and arrange overlapping on the tart. Sieve the apricot jam into a small pan and heat until boiling. Brush liberally over the tart and leave to set.

Lemon Griesstorte

Serves 6

Made without flour, this cake has a lovely light but 'short' texture. It keeps better than an ordinary sponge cake, and is delicious with different fruits. For an even more luscious cake, fill and top with cream and lemon curd.

3 eggs, separated

4 oz (100 g) caster sugar

grated rind and juice of ½ lemon

2 oz (50 g) fine semolina

½ oz (15 g) ground almonds

For the Filling

5 fl oz (150 ml) whipping cream

about 4 tablespoons lemon curd

4 oz (100 g) fresh raspberries (optional)

To Finish

icing sugar

Pre-heat the oven to 180°C/350°F/Gas 4. Grease and line an 8 in (20 cm) deep round cake tin with greased greaseproof paper.

Measure the egg yolks and sugar into a bowl and whisk on full speed with an electric whisk until pale and light in texture. Add the lemon juice and continue to whisk until the mixture is thick. Fold in the grated lemon rind, semolina and ground almonds.

Whisk the egg whites in a separate bowl until they form soft peaks, then fold into the mixture until evenly blended. Turn into the prepared tin.

Bake in the pre-heated oven for about 30–35 minutes until well risen and pale golden brown. Leave in the tin for a few minutes then turn out, remove the paper and leave to cool completely on a wire rack.

Cut the cake in half horizontally. Whisk the cream until it holds its shape, then fold in the lemon curd. Sandwich the cake together with the lemon cream and raspberries, if liked, and dust the top with icing sugar to serve.

Secrets of Success

Flours, porridge oats and semolina should all be used within four months once the bags or packets have been opened.

Lemon Griesstorte

Almond Tuiles

Makes about 20 Biscuits

These slim, crisp, curled biscuits are wonderful with light mousses, ice-cream and fruit salads. They keep well in an airtight tin or, if made a long way in advance, in the freezer. Store in a rigid box or tin so they cannot be broken.

3 oz (75 g) butter, softened

3 oz (75 g) caster sugar

2 oz (50 g) plain flour

3 oz (75 g) blanched, shredded almonds

icing sugar to finish

Pre-heat the oven to 200°C/400°F/Gas 6. Lightly grease 2 baking trays.

Measure the butter and sugar into a bowl and beat well together until pale and fluffy. Sift in the flour and stir into the mixture with the almonds.

Place teaspoons of the mixture on to the prepared baking trays, about 4 at a time, leaving ample room for the biscuits to spread.

Bake in the pre-heated oven for about 6–8 minutes until they are browned around the edge but not in the middle. Remove from the oven and leave to stand for a second or two, then remove from the tray with a palette knife and curl over a rolling pin until set.

When cool, store in an airtight container. Serve with a dusting of icing sugar.

Gâteau Saint Honoré

Serves 6

A Parisian speciality, this gâteau was named in honour of Saint Honoré, the patron saint of bakers. The different stages (but not the caramel and spun sugar) can be made ahead of time, and the gâteau assembled about two hours before serving. *(See photograph on page 182.)*

For the *Pâte Sucrée*

- *4 oz (100 g) plain flour*
- *2 oz (50 g) butter, softened*
- *2 oz (50 g) caster sugar*
- *2 egg yolks*

For the Choux Pastry

- *2 oz (50 g) butter or margarine*
- *5 fl oz (150 ml) water*
- *2½ oz (65 g) plain flour*
- *2 eggs, beaten*

For the *Crème Pâtissière*

- *1 pint (600 ml) milk*
- *1 vanilla pod*
- *4 eggs*
- *4 oz (100 g) caster sugar*
- *2 oz (50 g) plain flour*
- *5 fl oz (150 ml) double cream, whipped*

For the Caramel

- *8 oz (225 g) granulated sugar*
- *3 fl oz (75 ml) water*

For the Spun Sugar (optional)

- *4 oz (100 g) granulated sugar*
- *2 fl oz (50 ml) water*
- *2 tablespoons liquid glucose*

Pre-heat the oven to 190°C/375°F/Gas 5. Lightly grease 3 baking trays.

First make the *pâte sucrée*. Measure the flour into a bowl and rub in the butter with the fingertips until the mixture resembles fine breadcrumbs. Stir in the sugar, then add the egg yolks and mix until the ingredients come together to form a dough. Knead the mixture gently until smooth. Wrap the dough in cling film and leave to rest in the fridge

for about 30 minutes. (Or process the flour, butter and sugar briefly in the food processor, add the egg yolks and process until *just* blended. Knead and wrap as before.)

Roll out the *pâte sucrée* on a lightly floured work surface to a 7 in (18 cm) round. Place on one of the prepared baking trays, crimp the edges and prick all over with a fork.

Bake in the pre-heated oven for about 15–20 minutes or until the pastry is a pale golden brown.

Increase the oven temperature to 220°C/425°F/Gas 7. Next make the choux pastry. Measure the butter or margarine and water into a medium pan, allow to melt and then bring slowly to the boil. Remove the pan from the heat, add the flour all at once and beat until the mixture forms a soft ball. Allow the flour mixture to cool slightly, then gradually beat in the eggs, beating well between each addition to give a smooth shiny paste.

Spoon the choux pastry dough into a piping bag fitted with a ½ in (1 cm) plain nozzle (see *figure 26*). Pipe a 7 in (18 cm) ring of choux pastry on to a second baking tray and pipe the remaining choux pastry into pieces about the size of a walnut (see *figure 27*).

Bake in the pre-heated oven for about 10 minutes, then reduce the temperature to 190°C/375°F/Gas 5 and cook for a further 20 minutes until well risen, golden brown and crisp. Remove from the oven and pierce the choux ring and the buns at intervals underneath, to allow the steam to escape. Return to the oven for about 5 minutes to dry out completely. Cool on a wire rack.

To make the *crème pâtissière*, measure the milk into a small pan and add the vanilla pod. Bring to just below boiling point then turn off the heat and leave to infuse for about 10 minutes. Strain and discard the vanilla pod. In a bowl, beat the eggs, sugar and flour together with a little of the strained milk. Pour the remaining milk on to the egg mixture, stir and then pour back into the pan. Cook the custard over a gentle heat, stirring all the time until thickened. Pour into a clean bowl and cover the surface tightly with cling film to prevent a skin forming. Allow to cool, stirring occasionally.

Whip the cream until it forms soft peaks. Whisk the cooled custard until smooth and fold in the cream. Cover tightly with cling film and chill thoroughly before using.

Pipe or spoon a little of the *crème pâtissière* into the choux ring and the buns, through the hole which was made in the bases to allow the steam to escape. Leave in a cool place while making the caramel.

For the caramel, measure the sugar and water into a heavy-based pan. Heat gently until the sugar has dissolved, brushing down the sides of the pan with hot water from time to time. Bring to the boil and boil the syrup until it turns a golden caramel colour. Immediately plunge the base of the pan into cold water to stop the caramel darkening further. Place the pan in a large bowl and fill the bowl with boiling water; this will keep the caramel fluid.

Place the *pâte sucrée* base on a plate and position the choux ring on top. One by one, dip the base of each choux bun in the caramel and place on the choux ring, holding it in place for a few seconds to secure. Continue with the remaining choux buns, placing

(Left) Gâteau Saint Honoré (page 181)

them close together to form a ring. Spoon a little caramel over the top of each choux bun.

For the spun sugar, cover your working area with sheets of oiled foil and also cover a rolling pin with foil and oil it lightly. Have ready 2 forks taped together back to back. Measure the sugar and water into a small heavy-based pan and heat gently until melted. Bring to the boil, then add the glucose. Half cover the pan and boil to 152°C (305°F) on a sugar thermometer. Immediately dip the base of the pan into cold water and cool for 30 seconds only. Dip the prongs of the forks in the syrup and, holding the covered rolling pin in the other hand, flick the forks backwards and forwards over the rolling pin to form long strands of sugar (see *figure 28*). Repeat with the remaining syrup, then place on an oiled baking sheet until needed.

Spoon the remaining *crème pâtissière* into the choux case and decorate with the spun sugar if using. Serve the gâteau within the hour if decorating with spun sugar as the sugar will gradually start to disintegrate due to the moisture.

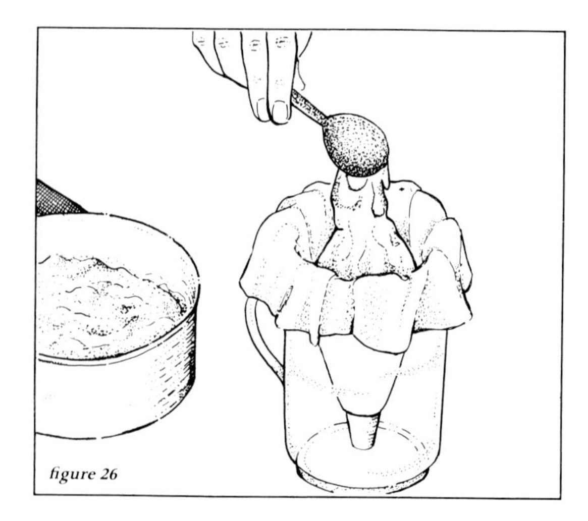

figure 26

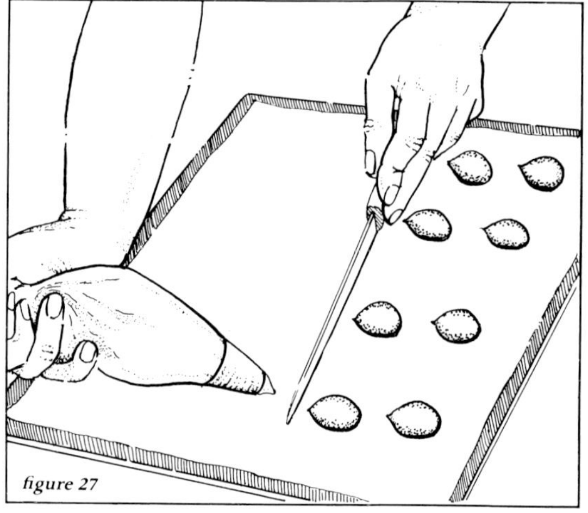

figure 27

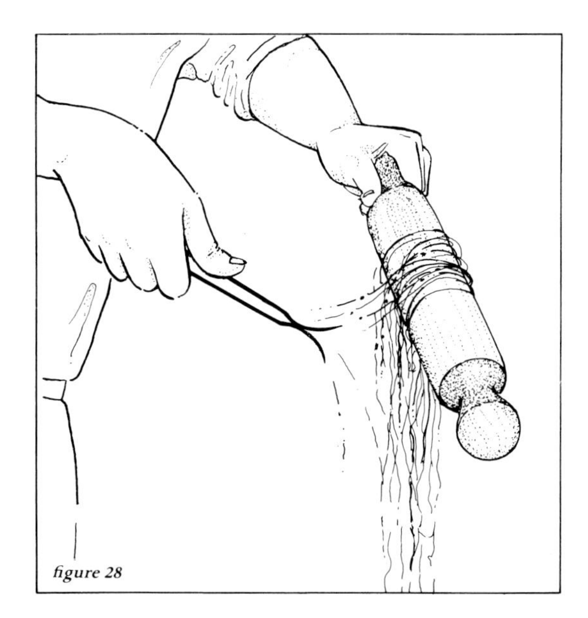
figure 28

Warning

Sugar syrups, whether in the form of caramel or spun sugar, can easily burn the skin. Please take extra care when handling them, particularly if you have children in the house at the time.

Tarte Tatin

Serves 6

Tarte tatin is a classic 'upside-down' French tart, which should be served as a pudding rather than as a cake.

For the Pastry

4 oz (100 g) self-raising flour
2 oz (50 g) butter, cubed
1 tablespoon icing sugar, sifted
1 egg yolk
scant tablespoon cold water

For the Topping

3 oz (75 g) butter
3 oz (75 g) demerara sugar
2 lb (900 g) Cox's dessert apples, or similar
Finely grated rind and juice of 1 lemon

To Finish

2 tablespoons demerara sugar (optional)

First prepare the pastry. Measure the flour, butter and icing sugar into a bowl and rub in the butter until the mixture resembles fine breadcrumbs. Add the egg yolk and enough water to bring the mixture together to a firm but not sticky dough. Knead lightly, wrap in cling film and chill for about 30 minutes.

Pre-heat the oven to 200°C/400°F/Gas 6.

To prepare the top, measure the butter and sugar into a small pan and heat gently until both have melted. Pour into the base of a 9 in (23 cm) sandwich cake tin. Peel, core and thinly slice the apples and sprinkle over the lemon juice and rind. Arrange a single layer of the best apples in a circular pattern over the sugar and butter. Cover with the remainder of the apple.

Roll out the chilled pastry and use to cover the apples. Bake in the pre-heated oven for about 20 minutes or until the pastry is crisp and golden brown. (When cooked, the pastry will have shrunk a little.)

Tip the juices from the cake tin into a small pan. Turn the tart out on to a plate with the pastry on the bottom. Boil the juices to reduce to a syrupy caramel and pour over the apple. If there is very little juice – the amount will depend on the apples – add 2 tablespoons of demerara sugar, dissolve in the pan with the juices and cook until syrupy. Serve warm with cream, *crème fraîche* or yoghurt.

(Right) Tarte Tatin

Danish Pastries

Makes 16 Pastries

Made in various traditional shapes, these are fiddly and time-consuming, but better than any you can buy! They are best eaten on the day of making. The basic recipe filling is almond paste, but do try one of the alternative fillings on pages 190–91.

For the Pastry Dough

- ***1 lb (450 g) strong plain flour***
- ***½ teaspoon salt***
- ***12 oz (350 g) butter, softened***
- ***1 sachet easy-blend dried yeast***
- ***2 oz (50 g) caster sugar***
- ***10 tablespoons warm milk***
- ***2 eggs, beaten***
- ***a little beaten egg to glaze***

For the Filling and Topping

- ***8 oz (225 g) almond paste, bought or home-made (see page 93)***
- ***a little glacé icing made with 4 oz (100 g) icing sugar and 1–2 tablespoons warm water***
- ***2 oz (50 g) flaked almonds, toasted***
- ***2 oz (50 g) glacé cherries, washed, dried and chopped***

Lightly grease 3 baking trays.

Measure the flour and salt into a bowl and rub in 2 oz (50 g) of the butter. Add the yeast and sugar and stir to mix. Make a well in the centre, add the warm milk and eggs, and mix to a soft dough. Knead the dough until smooth, then put it into a clean bowl, cover with cling film and leave to rise in a warm place for about 1 hour or until the dough has doubled in bulk. Punch down the dough, knead until smooth and then roll out to an oblong about 14 × 8 in (35 × 20 cm). Cover the top two-thirds of the dough with half the remaining butter, dotting it over the dough in pieces as you would for flaky pastry. Fold the bottom third of dough up and the top third down to form a parcel. Seal the edges then give the dough a quarter turn so that the folded side is to the left. Roll out to the same sized oblong as before. Dot over the remaining butter in the same way and fold the dough as before. Wrap the dough in cling film at this stage and leave to rest in the fridge for about 15 minutes. Turn the dough so that the fold is on the left again and roll and fold the dough, with no butter, twice more. Wrap the dough in cling film and leave to rest for another 15 minutes in the fridge. The dough is now ready for shaping: divide into 4 equal pieces.

For Crescents

Take one-quarter of the dough and roll out to a 9 in (23 cm) circle. Divide the circle into 4 equal wedges (see *figure 29*). Place a small sausage of almond paste at the wide end of each wedge and roll up loosely towards the point (see *figure 30*). Bend them round to form a crescent (see *figure 31*).

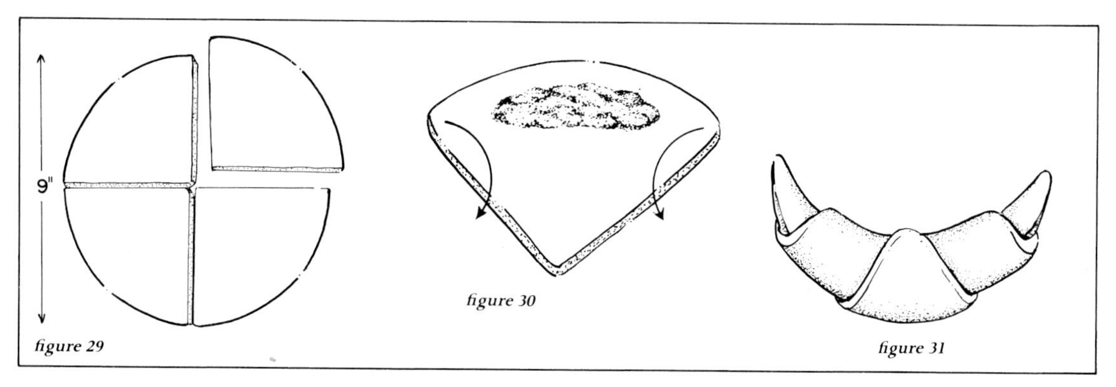

figure 29

figure 30

figure 31

For Pinwheels

Roll out another quarter of the dough to form an 8 in (20 cm) square. Cut the square into 4. Place a small amount of almond paste in the centre of each square. Make cuts from each corner almost to the centre and fold 4 alternate points to the centre, pressing them down firmly (see *figures 32* and *33*).

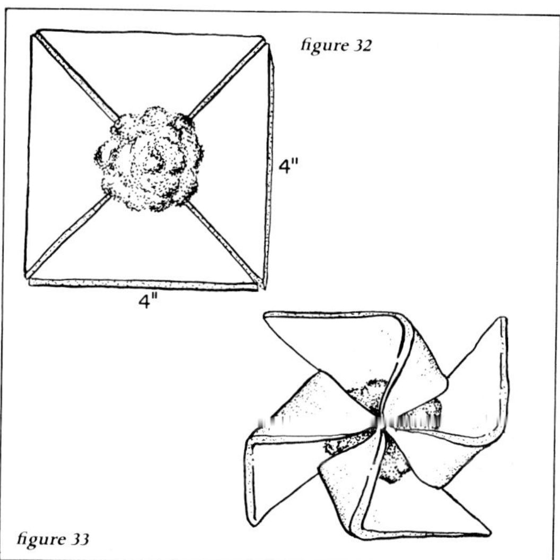

figure 32

figure 33

For Kite Shapes

Roll out another quarter of the dough thinly to form an 8 in (20 cm) square. Cut the square into 4. Place a small piece of almond paste in the centre of each square. Cut from A to B, and from C to D (see *figure 34*) – then lift both corner strips and cross them over the almond paste in the centre (see *figure 35*).

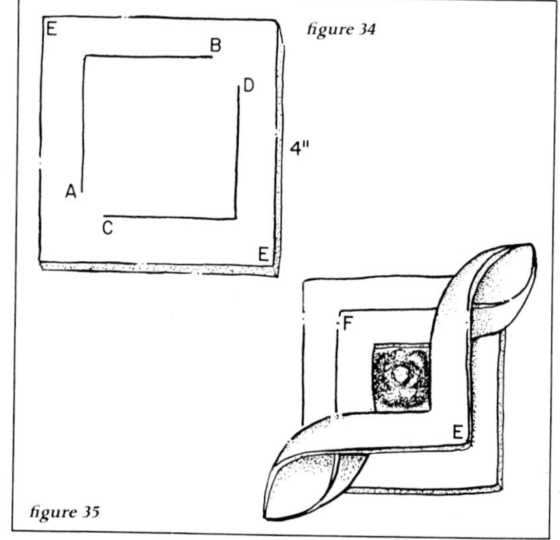

figure 34

figure 35

For Envelopes
Roll out the remaining dough thinly and cut into 4 in (10 cm) squares (see *figure 36*). Place a piece of almond paste into the centre and fold 2 opposite corners (see *figure 37*) or all 4 corners (see *figure 38*) into the middle. Press the edges down lightly. (These are especially good filled with vanilla cream or the apple mixture, see *opposite*.)

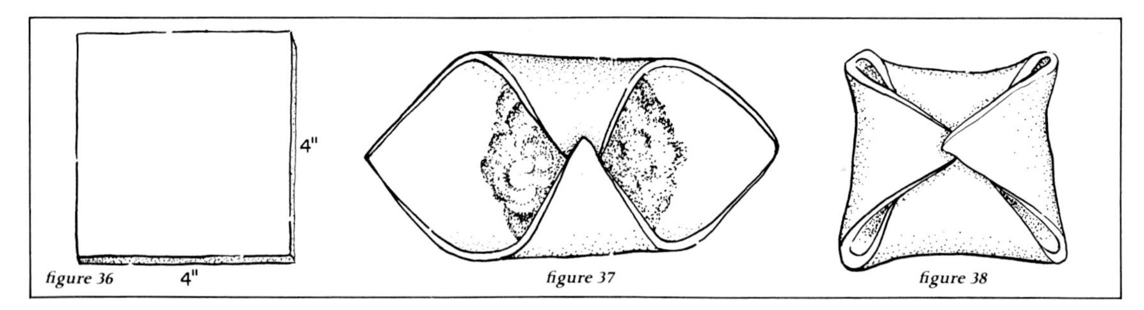

figure 36 *figure 37* *figure 38*

For Cartwheels
Roll out the dough thinly, spread with a thin layer of almond filling and sprinkle with a handful of raisins. Roll up the dough like a Swiss roll and cut into $\frac{1}{4}$ in (5 mm) slices. Place, cut side down, on to the prepared baking trays.

After shaping, arrange the pastries on the prepared baking trays, cover with oiled cling film or put the trays inside oiled polythene bags, and leave to prove for about 20 minutes in a warm place, until they are beginning to look puffy.

Pre-heat the oven to 220°C/425°F/Gas 7. Brush each pastry with beaten egg and bake in the oven for about 15 minutes until golden brown. Lift on to a wire rack to cool.

Make up the glacé icing by putting the icing sugar in a bowl and gradually mixing in the water. Spoon a little icing over each pastry while they are still warm. Sprinkle some with toasted flaked almonds and some with small pieces of glacé cherry.

ALTERNATIVE DANISH PASTRY FILLINGS

Almond Filling

THIS IS SOFTER AND moister than prepared almond paste. Use it in any of the pastry shapes.

4 oz (100 g) ground almonds
4 oz (100 g) caster sugar
a little beaten egg

Mix the almonds and sugar together and bind with enough egg to form a soft paste.

Vanilla Cream

THIS IS PARTICULARLY good in the 'envelopes'.

1 tablespoon flour

1 teaspoon cornflour

1 egg yolk

1 tablespoon caster sugar

5 fl oz (150 ml) milk

2–3 drops vanilla essence

Mix together the flours, egg yolk and sugar, and blend with a little of the milk. Bring the remaining milk to the boil, pour on to the flour mixture, blend and then return to the pan. Heat gently, stirring, until boiling. Allow to cool then flavour with a few drops of vanilla essence.

Apple Filling

USE THIS FILLING for any of the pastry shapes.

1 lb (450 g) cooking apples

½ oz (15 g) butter

grated rind and juice of ½ lemon

4 tablespoons light muscovado sugar

3 oz (75 g) sultanas (optional)

Wipe, quarter and core the apples (no need to peel) and put into a pan with the butter, lemon rind and juice. Cover and cook until soft. Rub the apples through a nylon sieve, return to the rinsed out pan and add the sugar. Cook until the sugar has dissolved and the apple mixture is thick. Add the sultanas, if liked. Leave until cold before using.

Chapter 9

Family Cakes

Family cakes can be defined, I suppose, as those one might expect to find in the cake tin. None of the recipes here is too elaborate, and they can all be made with a minimum of fuss and effort. Most use the all-in-one method – where everything is mixed together at the same time – so are simplicity itself. All of them keep for a few days, some better than others, so are ideal for making on Friday to be eaten at Saturday or Sunday tea in front of the fire after those long bracing walks so many of us indulge in at the weekend!

Most of the cakes here are fairly traditional to Britain, a lot dating from Victorian times. Queen Victoria is said to have popularized the cream-and-jam filled sponge cake, which was named after her, and a fruit cake of some sort – often made with fresh or glacé cherries – was a favourite on nineteenth-century tea tables. At this time cake was also often eaten with a sweet wine such as Madeira, thus Madeira cake – a habit that could be interesting to re-establish. A few years ago we stayed in Madeira, and tucked down the hill near our hotel was a bar that did just that – Madeira and coffee at about 11.30. Parkins and gingerbreads are from an older tradition, and are more regional in origin, both from Northern England. The only cake which is not so obviously British is Swiss roll; it is said that at the turn of the century British enthusiasts of the new sport, skiing, persuaded a St Moritz *pâtissier* to part with the recipe, and thus it became a stalwart of the British tea tradition!

When my children were living at home, there would be nothing left of cake at the end of the weekend. Now, when they come home, I send them back with remnants of cake wrapped in foil. If you are left with some, serve to the children in their lunchboxes, or when they come home from school, or offer as a pudding on Monday with some cream. Wedges of sponge and fruit cake freeze well, so can be enjoyed at another time.

Large All-in-one Victoria Sandwich

MAKES 1 × 8 IN (20 CM) CAKE

THIS MUST BE THE BEST known and loved of all family cakes. The all-in-one method takes away all the hassle of creaming, and ensures success every time. (See photograph on page 194.)

8 oz (225 g) soft margarine

8 oz (225 g) caster sugar

4 eggs

8 oz (225 g) self-raising flour

2 teaspoons baking powder

FOR THE FILLING AND TOPPING

about 4 tablespoons raspberry or strawberry jam

a little caster sugar

Pre-heat the oven to 180°C/350°F/Gas 4. Grease and base line 2 × 8 in (20 cm) sandwich tins with greased greaseproof paper.

Measure the margarine, sugar, eggs, flour and baking powder into a large bowl and beat well until thoroughly blended. Divide the mixture evenly between the tins and level out.

Bake in the pre-heated oven for about 25 minutes or until well risen and the tops of the cakes spring back when lightly pressed with a finger. Leave to cool in the tins for a few moments then turn out, peel off the paper and finish cooling on a wire rack.

When completely cold, sandwich the cakes together with the jam. Sprinkle with caster sugar to serve.

Large All-in-one Victoria Sandwich (page 193)

Orange Victoria Sandwich

Makes 1 × 8 in (20 cm) Cake

You can make a lemon sandwich in the same way by substituting a lemon for the orange in the cake mixture and sandwiching the cakes together with lemon curd.

8 oz (225 g) soft margarine

8 oz (225 g) caster sugar

4 eggs

8 oz (225 g) self-raising flour

2 teaspoons baking powder

finely grated rind of 1 orange

For the Filling and Topping

about 4 tablespoons orange marmalade

a little caster sugar

Pre-heat the oven to 180°C/350°F/Gas 4. Grease and base line 2 × 8 in (20 cm) sandwich tins with greased greaseproof paper.

Measure all the ingredients into a large bowl and beat well until thoroughly blended. Divide the mixture evenly between the tins and level out.

Bake in the pre-heated oven for about 25 minutes or until well risen and the tops of the cakes spring back when lightly pressed with a finger. Leave to cool in the tins for a while then turn out, peel off the paper and finish cooling on a wire rack.

When completely cold, sandwich the cakes together with the marmalade. Sprinkle with caster sugar to serve.

Coffee Victoria Sandwich

Makes 1 × 8 in (20 cm) Cake

Instead of the coffee essence in the icing, you can use 1 heaped teaspoon of instant coffee dissolved in 1 tablespoon of hot water.

4 eggs, beaten

2 heaped teaspoons instant coffee

8 oz (225 g) soft margarine

8 oz (225 g) caster sugar

8 oz (225 g) self-raising flour

2 teaspoons baking powder

For the Filling and Topping

2 oz (50 g) soft margarine

6 oz (175 g) icing sugar, sifted

1 tablespoon coffee essence

1 tablespoon milk (optional)

Pre-heat the oven to 180°C/350°F/Gas 4. Grease and base line 2 × 8 in (20 cm) sandwich tins with greased greaseproof paper.

Place the eggs in a bowl and stir in the coffee until dissolved. Add the remaining ingredients and beat well until thoroughly blended. Divide the mixture evenly between the tins and level out.

Bake in the pre-heated oven for about 25 minutes or until well risen and the tops of the cakes spring back when lightly pressed with a finger. Leave to cool in the tins for a few moments then turn out, peel off the paper and finish cooling on a wire rack.

To make the butter cream, blend together the margarine, icing sugar and coffee essence until smooth, adding the milk if necessary. Use half the butter cream to sandwich the cakes together. Spread the remaining butter cream on top.

SECRETS OF SUCCESS

When making an all-in-one mixture in a food mixer, cover the front end of the machine and the bowl with a tea towel to prevent flour scattering over the floor. (Watch carefully that the towel doesn't slip and get caught in the spindle.) The newest mixing machines have a rigid plastic cover to clip over the mixing bowl instead of a tea towel.

Chocolate Victoria Sandwich

MAKES 1 × 8 IN (20 CM) CAKE

THIS LIGHT CHOCOLATE cake is sandwiched together with a white butter cream and looks as good as it tastes.

2 tablespoons cocoa
3 tablespoons boiling water
8 oz (225 g) soft margarine
8 oz (225 g) caster sugar
4 eggs
8 oz (225 g) self-raising flour
2 teaspoons baking powder

FOR THE FILLING AND TOPPING

2 oz (50 g) soft margarine
6 oz (175 g) icing sugar, sifted
1 tablespoon milk
coarsely grated chocolate to decorate

Pre-heat the oven to 180°C/350°F/Gas 4. Grease and base line 2 × 8 in (20 cm) sandwich tins with greased greaseproof paper.

Blend the cocoa and water in a mixing bowl then leave to cool slightly. Measure all the remaining ingredients into the bowl and beat well until thoroughly blended. Divide the mixture evenly between the tins and level out.

Bake in the pre-heated oven for about 25 minutes or until well risen and the tops of the cakes spring back when lightly pressed with a finger. Leave to cool in the tins for a few moments then turn out, peel off the paper and finish cooling on a wire rack.

To make the butter cream, blend together the margarine, icing sugar and milk until smooth. Use half the butter cream to sandwich the cakes together. Spread the remaining butter cream on top and decorate with the grated chocolate.

Small All-in-one Victoria Sandwich

MAKES 1 × 7 IN (18 CM) CAKE

HERE IS THE RECIPE for a smaller cake so that you don't have to calculate the quantities if you use smaller tins.

6 oz (175 g) soft margarine

6 oz (175 g) caster sugar

3 eggs

6 oz (175 g) self-raising flour

$1\frac{1}{2}$ teaspoons baking powder

FOR THE FILLING AND TOPPING

about 4 tablespoons raspberry or strawberry jam

a little caster sugar

Pre-heat the oven to 180°C/350°F/Gas 4. Grease and base line 2 × 7 in (18 cm) sandwich tins with greased greaseproof paper.

Measure all the ingredients into a large bowl and beat well until thoroughly blended. Divide the mixture evenly between the tins and level out.

Bake in the pre-heated oven for about 25 minutes or until well risen and the tops of the cakes spring back when lightly pressed with a finger. Leave to cool in the tins for a few moments then turn out, peel off the paper and finish cooling on a wire rack.

When completely cold, sandwich the cakes together with the jam. Sprinkle with caster sugar to serve.

SECRETS OF SUCCESS

For a 6 in (15 cm) Victoria sandwich cake, use 2 eggs, 4 oz (100 g) of soft margarine, 4 oz (100 g) of caster sugar, 4 oz (100 g) of self-raising flour and 1 teaspoon of baking powder. Bake in 2 × 6 in (15 cm) sandwich tins for about 20 minutes.

Crunchy Top Lemon Cake

Makes 1 × 7 in (18 cm) Cake

The same crunchy topping can be used on traybakes and teabreads. The secret is to pour the crunchy topping over the cake while it is still warm so that the lemon soaks in and the sugar stays on top.

4 oz (100 g) soft margarine

6 oz (175 g) caster sugar

6 oz (175 g) self-raising flour

1 teaspoon baking powder

2 extra large eggs

4 tablespoons milk

finely grated rind of 1 lemon

For the Crunchy Topping

juice of 1 lemon

4 oz (100 g) caster or granulated sugar

Pre-heat the oven to 180°C/350°F/Gas 4. Lightly grease and base line a 7 in (18 cm) deep round cake tin with greased greaseproof paper.

Measure all the ingredients for the cake into a large bowl and beat well for about 2 minutes until smooth and well blended. Turn the mixture into the prepared tin and level the surface.

Bake in the pre-heated oven for about 35–40 minutes or until the cake has shrunk slightly from the sides of the tin and springs back when lightly pressed with a finger.

Whilst the cake is baking, make the crunchy topping. Measure the lemon juice and sugar into a bowl and stir until blended. When the cake comes out of the oven, spread the lemon paste over the top whilst the cake is still hot. Leave in the tin until cold, then turn out and remove the paper.

Secrets of Success

If a soft cake has sunk disastrously in the middle, cut this out, fill with soft fruits and whipped cream, and serve as a dessert.

(Right) Crunchy Top Lemon Cake

Madeira Cake

Makes 1 × 7 in (18 cm) Cake

It is essential that the butter is of a creamy spreading consistency before mixing the ingredients together in the usual all-in-one way.

6 oz (175 g) butter, softened

6 oz (175 g) caster sugar

8 oz (225 g) self-raising flour

2 oz (50 g) ground almonds

3 extra large eggs

finely grated rind of 1 lemon

a thin slice of citron peel

Pre-heat the oven to 180°C/350°F/Gas 4. Lightly grease and base line a 7 in (18 cm) deep round cake tin with greased greaseproof paper.

Measure the butter, sugar, flour, ground almonds, eggs and grated lemon rind into a large bowl. Beat well for 1 minute to mix thoroughly. Turn into the prepared tin.

Bake in the pre-heated oven for 30 minutes. Place the slice of citron peel on top of the cake and continue cooking for a further 30–45 minutes or until a warm skewer inserted into the centre comes out clean. Leave to cool in the tin for 10 minutes then turn out and finish cooling on a wire rack.

Secrets of Success

If a fruit or Madeira cake has a slight dip in the centre when it comes out of the oven, turn on to greaseproof paper on a cooling rack upside down. *The action of gravity and the weight of the cake will level the top while it cools. A bit of a cheat, but it works!*

English Cherry Cake

Makes 1 × 8 in (20 cm) Cake

Wash and dry the quartered cherries thoroughly before adding to the cake mixture; this prevents them from sinking to the bottom during baking. *(See photograph on pages 6–7.)*

7 oz (200 g) glacé cherries

10 oz (275 g) self-raising flour

3 oz (75 g) ground almonds

2 teaspoons baking powder

8 oz (225 g) soft margarine

8 oz (225 g) caster sugar

4 eggs

Pre-heat the oven to 160°C/325°F/Gas 3. Lightly grease and base line an 8 in (20 cm) deep round cake tin with greased greaseproof paper.

Cut each cherry into quarters, put in a sieve and rinse under running water. Drain well then dry thoroughly on kitchen paper.

Measure all the remaining ingredients into a large bowl and beat well for 1 minute to mix thoroughly. Lightly fold in the cherries. Turn into the prepared tin and level the surface.

Bake in the pre-heated oven for about $1\frac{1}{2}$–$1\frac{3}{4}$ hours or until a skewer inserted into the centre of the cake comes out clean. Leave the cake to cool in the tin for 10 minutes then turn out and leave to cool on a wire rack.

Double Orange Cake

Makes 1 × 8 in (20 cm) Cake

A lovely light sponge cake, this is always popular with the family – young or old – and is especially good on the day it's made. *(See photograph on pages 2–3.)*

6 oz (175 g) soft margarine

6 oz (175 g) caster sugar

3 eggs

6 oz (175 g) self-raising flour

1½ teaspoons baking powder

grated rind and juice of 1 large orange

To Finish

about 2 tablespoons apricot jam

4 oz (100 g) icing sugar

finely shredded rind and juice of ½ orange

Pre-heat the oven to 180°C/350°F/Gas 4. Lightly grease and base line an 8 in (20 cm) deep round cake tin with greased greaseproof paper.

Measure all the ingredients for the cake into a large bowl and beat well until thoroughly blended. Turn into the prepared cake tin and level the surface.

Bake in the pre-heated oven for about 35 minutes until well risen and springy to the touch. Turn out on to a cooling rack and leave to cool.

Measure the apricot jam into a small pan and gently warm through. Brush over the top of the cake. Sift the icing sugar into a bowl and mix in the orange juice. Pour over the top of the cake and gently spread out with a small palette or round bladed knife. Leave to set and then decorate with fine shreds of orange rind.

Swiss Roll

MAKES 1 × 9 IN (23 CM) SWISS ROLL

TO MAKE A SMALLER Swiss Roll, use 3 eggs and 3 oz (75 g) each of sugar and flour. Bake in an 11 × 7 in (28 × 18 cm) Swiss roll tin.

4 extra large eggs, at room temperature

4 oz (100 g) caster sugar

4 oz (100 g) self-raising flour

FOR THE FILLING

about 4 tablespoons strawberry or raspberry jam

Pre-heat the oven to 220°C/425°F/Gas 7. Grease and line a 13 × 9 in (33 × 23 cm) Swiss roll tin with greased greaseproof paper.

Whisk the eggs and sugar together in a large bowl until the mixture is light and frothy and the whisk leaves a trail when lifted out. Sift the flour into the mixture, carefully folding at the same time. Turn the mixture into the prepared tin and give it a gentle shake so that the mixture finds its own level, making sure that it spreads evenly into the corners.

Bake in the pre-heated oven for about 10 minutes or until the sponge is golden brown and begins to shrink from the edges of the tin.

While the cake is cooking, place a piece of non-stick baking paper a little bigger than the size of the tin on to a work surface and sprinkle it with caster sugar.

Invert the cake on to the sugared paper. Quickly loosen the paper on the bottom of the cake and peel it off. Trim the edges of the sponge with a sharp knife and make a score mark 1 in (2.5 cm) in from one shorter edge, being careful not to cut right through.

Leave to cool slightly, then spread with the jam. If the cake is too hot the jam will soak straight into the sponge. Roll up the cake firmly from the cut end.

Lemon Swiss Roll

You can make an orange Swiss roll by substituting an orange for the lemon and orange marmalade for the lemon curd.

4 eggs, extra large, at room temperature

4 oz (100 g) caster sugar

finely grated rind of 1 lemon

4 oz (100 g) self-raising flour

For the Filling

about 4 tablespoons lemon curd

Pre-heat the oven to 220°C/425°F/Gas 7. Grease and line a 13 × 9 in (33 × 23 cm) Swiss roll tin with greased greaseproof paper.

Whisk the eggs, sugar and lemon rind in a large bowl until the mixture is light and frothy and the whisk leaves a trail when lifted out. Sift the flour into the mixture, carefully folding at the same time. Turn the mixture into the prepared tin and give it a gentle shake so that the mixture finds its own level, making sure that it spreads evenly into the corners.

Bake in the pre-heated oven for about 10 minutes or until the sponge is golden brown and begins to shrink from the edges of the tin.

While the cake is cooking, place a piece of non-stick baking paper a little bigger than the size of the tin on to a work surface and sprinkle it with caster sugar.

Invert the cake on to the sugared paper. Quickly loosen the paper on the bottom of the cake and peel it off. Trim the edges of the sponge with a sharp knife and make a score mark 1 in (2.5 cm) in from one shorter edge, being careful not to cut right through.

Leave to cool slightly, then spread with the lemon curd. If the cake is too hot the lemon curd will soak straight into the sponge. Roll up the cake firmly from the cut end.

Chocolate Swiss Roll

MAKES 1 × 9 IN (23 CM) SWISS ROLL

A FAMILY CLASSIC, you can butter ice this roll to use for a Christmas log.

4 extra large eggs, at room temperature

4 oz (100 g) caster sugar

$2\frac{1}{2}$ oz (65 g) self-raising flour

$1\frac{1}{2}$ oz (40 g) cocoa

FOR THE FILLING

2 tablespoons strawberry jam

10 fl oz (300 ml) whipping cream, whipped

Pre-heat the oven to 220°C/425°F/Gas 7. Grease and line a 13 × 9 in (33 × 23 cm) Swiss roll tin with greased greaseproof paper.

Whisk the eggs and sugar in a large bowl until the mixture is light and frothy and the whisk leaves a trail when lifted out. Sift the flour and cocoa into the mixture, carefully folding at the same time. Turn the mixture into the prepared tin and give it a gentle shake so that the mixture finds its own level, making sure that it spreads evenly into the corners.

Bake in the pre-heated oven for about 10 minutes or until the sponge begins to shrink from the edges of the tin.

While the cake is cooking, place a piece of non-stick baking paper a little bigger than the size of the tin on to a work surface and sprinkle it with caster sugar.

Invert the cake on to the sugared paper. Quickly loosen the paper on the bottom of the cake and peel it off. Trim the edges of the sponge with a sharp knife and make a score mark 1 in (2.5 cm) in from one shorter edge, being careful not to cut right through. Roll up the cake firmly from the cut end, with the paper inside, and leave to cool.

Warm the jam gently in a small pan until it is of a consistency that is easy to spread; if it is too warm it will soak straight into the sponge. Carefully unroll the cooled cake. Remove the paper, spread with jam and whipped cream and re-roll.

Frosted Walnut Layer Cake

CUTS INTO 12 GENEROUS WEDGES

SOME OF US MIGHT remember Fuller's tea shops, and their walnut cake. This is very similar and tastes wonderful.

8 oz (225 g) soft margarine
8 oz (225 g) caster sugar
4 eggs
8 oz (225 g) self-raising flour
2 teaspoons baking powder
4 oz (100 g) walnuts, finely chopped

FOR THE FROSTING

2 egg whites
12 oz (350 g) caster sugar
4 tablespoons water
¼ teaspoon cream of tartar

TO DECORATE

walnut halves

Pre-heat the oven to 160°C/325°F/Gas 3. Lightly grease and base line 3 × 8 in (20 cm) sandwich tins with greased greaseproof paper.

Measure all the ingredients for the cake into a large bowl and beat together until thoroughly blended. Divide equally between the tins and level the surface.

Bake in the pre-heated oven for about 25–30 minutes until the cakes are golden and springy to the touch. Turn out and leave to cool on a wire rack.

For the frosting, measure all the ingredients into a bowl over a pan of hot water and whisk, using an electric or rotary whisk, for 10–12 minutes until thick. Sandwich the cake layers together with a little of the frosting, then use the remainder to cover the top and sides of the cake, swirling the icing to form soft peaks. Decorate with the walnut halves.

SECRETS OF SUCCESS

In the all-in-one method, self-raising flour and baking powder are used together to give the cake the necessary lift. The quickness of the method means that less air is beaten into the mixture than if making the cake the traditional way. Don't be tempted to use more baking powder than specified or the cake will rise up and then sink back again.

(Right) Frosted Walnut Layer Cake

Marmalade Cake

Makes 1 × 2 lb (900 g) Cake

Don't overdo the marmalade or the fruit will sink to the bottom of the cake. Too much marmalade alters the sugar proportion of the recipe, but also slackens the mixture, which causes the fruit to drop.

1½ oz (40 g) glacé cherries, quartered
4 oz (100 g) soft margarine
4 oz (100 g) caster sugar
4 oz (100 g) sultanas
4 oz (100 g) currants
2 extra large eggs
6 oz (175 g) self-raising flour
1 rounded tablespoon chunky marmalade, chopped

To Finish

about 1 tablespoon chunky marmalade, chopped
or caster sugar for sprinkling

Pre-heat the oven to 160°C/325°F/Gas 3. Lightly grease and base line a 2 lb (900 g) loaf tin with greased greaseproof paper.

Place the cherries in a sieve and rinse under running water. Drain well then dry thoroughly on kitchen paper.

Measure all the remaining ingredients together into a large bowl, add the cherries and mix well until blended. Turn into the prepared tin and level the top.

Bake in the pre-heated oven for about 1½ hours or until a skewer inserted into the centre of the cake comes out clean. Allow the cake to cool in the tin for 10 minutes then turn out and leave to cool completely on a wire rack.

To finish, warm the chopped marmalade in a small pan and then spoon over the top of the cake and leave to set. Or simply sprinkle the top of the cake with caster sugar before serving.

Secrets of Success

Store dried fruits in the freezer, well wrapped, and use within two years.

Quick Boiled Fruit Cake

MAKES 1 × 7 IN (18 CM) CAKE

A MOIST FRUIT CAKE which keeps well, this is a recipe that was popular after the Second World War. I'm often asked for the boiled fruit cake with condensed milk and no fat that Granny used to make – and this is it – although here I do use fat because it is tastier.

1 × 14 oz (397 g) can condensed milk

5 oz (150 g) margarine

8 oz (225 g) raisins

8 oz (225 g) sultanas

6 oz (175 g) currants

6 oz (175 g) glacé cherries, roughly chopped

8 oz (225 g) self-raising flour

2 teaspoons mixed spice

1 teaspoon ground cinnamon

2 eggs

Pre-heat the oven to 150°C/300°F/Gas 2. Lightly grease and line a 7 in (18 cm) deep round cake tin with greased greaseproof paper.

Pour the condensed milk into a heavy-based pan and add the margarine, fruit and glacé cherries. Place over a low heat until the condensed milk and margarine have melted. Stir well, then simmer gently for 5 minutes. Remove from the heat and leave on one side to cool for about 10 minutes, stirring occasionally.

Measure the flour and spices into a large bowl and make a well in the centre. Add the eggs and the cooled fruit mixture and quickly mix together until well blended. Turn into the prepared tin.

Bake in the pre-heated oven for about 1¾–2 hours or until the cake is well risen, golden brown and the top feels firm. A skewer inserted into the centre should come out clean. Leave the cake to cool in the tin for about 10 minutes, then turn out and leave to cool completely on a wire rack.

Battenburg Cake

Makes 1 × 7 in (18 cm) Cake

Use home-made or bought almond paste for this famous chequerboard cake.

4 oz (100 g) soft margarine
4 oz (100 g) caster sugar
2 extra large eggs
2 oz (50 g) ground rice
4 oz (100 g) self-raising flour
½ teaspoon baking powder
a few drops of almond essence
red food colouring

To Finish

about 3–4 tablespoons apricot jam
8 oz (225 g) almond paste (see page 93)

Pre-heat the oven to 160°C/325°F/Gas 3. Grease and base line a 7 in (18 cm) shallow square cake tin with greased greaseproof paper.

Measure the margarine, sugar, eggs, ground rice, flour, baking powder and almond essence into a large bowl and beat well for about 2 minutes until smooth.

Spoon half the mixture into one half of the prepared tin as neatly as possible. Add a few drops of red food colouring to the remaining mixture to turn it a deep pink colour, then spoon this into the other half of the tin. Try to get the join between the 2 mixtures as neat as possible. Smooth the surface.

Bake in the pre-heated oven for about 35–40 minutes or until the cake is well risen, springy to the touch and has shrunk slightly from the sides of the tin. Turn out and leave to cool on a wire rack.

Trim the edges of the cake and then cut into 4 equal strips down the length of the colours. Gently heat the apricot jam in a small pan and stick the strips of cake together, one plain piece next to one coloured piece, and then vice-versa to make a chequerboard effect. Brush the top of the assembled cake with apricot jam.

Roll out the almond paste into an oblong the length of the cake and sufficiently wide to wrap around the cake. Invert the cake on to the almond paste, then brush the remaining 3 sides with apricot jam. Press the almond paste neatly around the cake, arranging the join in one corner. Score the top of the cake with a criss-cross pattern and crimp the edges with your fingers to decorate.

Battenburg Cake

Pound Cake

MAKES 1 × 8 IN (20 CM) CAKE

IN VICTORIAN TIMES, cakes were made larger than they are now, and so one pound quantities – hence the name – would have been used. Here the main ingredients are in half-pound proportions.

8 oz (225 g) soft margarine

8 oz (225 g) light muscovado sugar

4 eggs

8 oz (225 g) self-raising flour

8 oz (225 g) raisins

8 oz (225 g) sultanas

4 oz (100 g) glacé cherries quartered, washed and dried

½ teaspoon mixed spice

1 tablespoon brandy

Pre-heat the oven to 150°C/300°F/Gas 2. Lightly grease and line an 8 in (20 cm) deep round cake tin with greased greaseproof paper.

Measure all the ingredients into a large bowl and beat well together until thoroughly combined. Turn the mixture into the prepared tin and level the surface.

Bake in the pre-heated oven for about 2–2¼ hours, covering the top with paper after an hour to prevent the cake becoming too brown. When cooked the cake should be firm to the touch, and a skewer inserted into the centre will come out clean. Leave the cake to cool in the tin for about 30 minutes, then turn out and leave to cool completely on a wire rack.

Carrot and Orange Loaf

Makes 1 × 2 lb (900 g) Cake

This is a moist loaf which needs no buttering. Store it in the fridge if you want to keep it for any length of time.

1 orange

5 oz (150 g) soft margarine

5 oz (150 g) light muscovado sugar

6 oz (175 g) carrots, peeled and grated

2 eggs, beaten

7 oz (200 g) self-raising flour

1 teaspoon baking powder

½ teaspoon mixed spice

about 1 tablespoon milk

To Finish

about 2 tablespoons clear honey

Pre-heat the oven to 180°C/350°F/Gas 4. Lightly grease and base line a 2 lb (900 g) loaf tin with greased greaseproof paper.

Finely grate the orange rind, cut away the pith and slice the orange thinly. Place the rind in a large bowl and add the margarine, sugar, carrots, eggs, flour, baking powder and spice and mix well until thoroughly blended. Add the tablespoon of milk if necessary to give a dropping consistency. Spoon into the prepared tin.

Bake in the pre-heated oven for about 1 hour or until just firm to the touch. Remove the cake from the oven and arrange the thin slices of orange over the top. Brush with the honey and return the cake to the oven for a further 15 minutes or until a skewer inserted into the centre of the cake comes out clean. Leave to cool in the tin for a few minutes then turn out and leave to cool completely on a wire rack.

Traditional Parkin

Cuts into 16 Squares

This is an old-fashioned parkin, using black treacle. Parkin definitely improves with keeping, so try to store it for a week before cutting.

6 oz (175 g) black treacle
5 oz (150 g) margarine
4 oz (100 g) dark muscovado sugar
6 oz (175 g) plain flour
2 teaspoons ground ginger
1 teaspoon ground cinnamon
1 teaspoon freshly grated nutmeg
10 oz (275 g) medium oatmeal
1 egg
5 fl oz (150 ml) milk
1 teaspoon bicarbonate of soda

Pre-heat the oven to 180°C/350°F/Gas 4. Lightly grease and base line a 7 in (18 cm) deep square cake tin with greased greaseproof paper.

Measure the treacle, margarine and sugar into a medium pan and heat gently until the margarine and sugar have melted. Allow to cool slightly.

Sift the flour and spices into a large bowl and add the oatmeal. Mix together the egg and milk and stir in the bicarbonate of soda. Add to the dry ingredients with the treacle mixture and stir well to mix. Pour into the prepared tin.

Bake in the pre-heated oven for about 1 hour or until firm to the touch. Allow to cool in the tin for about 10 minutes then turn out and leave to cool completely on a wire rack.

Wrap the cold parkin in greaseproof paper and store in a cake tin for a week before cutting.

Iced Gingerbread with Stem Ginger

Cuts into 16 Squares

Gingerbread is said to be one of the oldest forms of cake in the world. Most European countries have their own version; the British one seems to be more popular in the north. One of the major advantages of home-made gingerbread is that it improves with keeping.

4 oz (100 g) margarine
4 oz (100 g) light muscovado sugar
2 eggs
5 oz (150 g) black treacle
5 oz (150 g) golden syrup
8 oz (225 g) plain flour
1 teaspoon ground ginger
1 teaspoon mixed spice
½ teaspoon bicarbonate of soda
2 tablespoons milk

For the Icing

6 oz (175 g) icing sugar
3 tablespoons stem ginger syrup
3–4 teaspoons water
1 × 1 in (2.5 cm) piece stem ginger

Pre-heat the oven to 160°C/325°F/Gas 3. Lightly grease and base line a 7 in (18 cm) deep square cake tin with greased greaseproof paper.

Measure the margarine, sugar, eggs, treacle and syrup into a bowl and whisk together until thoroughly mixed. Sift the flour with the spices and fold into the mixture. Add the bicarbonate of soda to the milk and then stir this into the mixture. Pour into the prepared tin.

Bake in the pre-heated oven for 1 hour. Reduce the oven temperature to 150°C/300°F/Gas 2 and bake for a further 15–30 minutes until well risen and firm to the touch. Allow the cake to cool in the tin for about 10 minutes, then turn out and leave to cool completely on a wire rack.

For the icing, sift the icing sugar into a bowl and add the stem ginger syrup and the water. Mix to give a smooth icing. Thinly shred the stem ginger and add to the icing. Pour the icing over the cake and leave to set before cutting into squares.

Chapter 10

Little Cakes, Rock Cakes and Yeasted Buns

Individual little cakes, such as those in this chapter, are one of the quickest forms of baking. Apart from the fact that they take less time to cook, their preparation can also be speeded up because, for quite a few of them, you can use paper cases instead of going through all the business of greasing and lining tins. For others, however, like English or French madeleines, you do need to use the special tins. These can be quite expensive to buy but they can be used again and again, and they make such wonderful and sophisticated shapes.

I love the *variety* of little cakes. They include pastry tarts such as Eccles cakes, and little tarts with a base of crumbly shortbread. These are ideal for afternoon tea – they're so easy to eat – as are fairy cakes, which can be made in a number of different flavours. These are particularly popular with the children. Traditional rock cakes are a favourite with almost everyone. They are always best made on the day of eating and they're ideal for a lunchbox or for taking on a picnic.

The classic English muffin is raised with yeast, but the American version – which uses self-raising flour and baking powder – has become hugely popular and very widespread in Britain. With added flavourings or fruit – blueberries seem to be the most favoured – they are a sort of cross between a scone and a cake. Served warm, they are ideal, delicious and generous fare for breakfast or for brunch.

Although I haven't included much yeast cookery in this book, I have included Bath buns. They're fun to make, and wonderful served hot and fresh, even though they may take longer because of the rising times involved.

One of the main advantages of small cakes as far as I am concerned, is that they can be frozen. If you have a small family, then you can make one or two batches, and then freeze half of either or both. In this way you can control the rate at which small cakes disappear – you can't really do this with a whole, large cake – and you will always have something in the freezer as a stand-by for an emergency.

Traditional Rock Cakes

MAKES 12 CAKES

THESE ARE VERY TRADITIONAL English cakes, probably the first things most of us made at school. They're inexpensive, can be large or tiny, and need no special equipment. They are best eaten on the day of making. (See photograph on pages 6–7.) See Wholewheat Sultana and Apricot Rock Cakes on page 290 for a more unusual version.

8 oz (225 g) self-raising flour
2 teaspoons baking powder
4 oz (100 g) soft margarine
2 oz (50 g) granulated sugar
4 oz (100 g) mixed dried fruit
2 oz (50 g) currants
1 egg
about 1 tablespoon milk

TO FINISH

demerara sugar

Pre-heat the oven to 200°C/400°F/Gas 6. Lightly grease 2 baking trays.

Measure the flour and baking powder into a large bowl, add the margarine and rub in with the fingertips until the mixture resembles fine breadcrumbs. Stir in the sugar and fruit. Add the egg and milk and mix to a stiff mixture. If dry, add a little more milk. Using 2 teaspoons, shape the mixture into about 12 rough mounds on the prepared baking trays. Sprinkle generously with demerara sugar.

Bake in the pre-heated oven for about 15 minutes or until a pale golden brown at the edges. Cool on a wire rack.

SECRETS OF SUCCESS

Use wholemeal self-raising flour if you like, although you may need a little more milk to mix.

Apricot Swiss Cakes

Makes about 18 Cakes

Traditionally a red jam is used for the centre of these cakes, which are buttery and very delicious.

8 oz (225 g) butter
3 oz (75 g) icing sugar, sifted
7 oz (200 g) self-raising flour
2 oz (50 g) cornflour

To Finish

a little apricot jam
icing sugar

Pre-heat the oven to 180°C/350°F/Gas 4. Place paper cake cases into about 18 bun tins.

Soften the butter in a large bowl. Add the icing sugar and beat well until really soft and fluffy. Stir in the flours and mix until smooth.

Spoon the mixture into a large piping bag fitted with a large star nozzle. Pipe circles of the mixture into the base of each paper case until all the mixture is used up.

Bake the cakes in the pre-heated oven for about 15–20 minutes or until pale golden brown. Leave to cool in the paper cases then put a small amount of apricot jam on to the centre of each cake. Dust lightly with sifted icing sugar.

Apricot Swiss Cakes

Fairy Cakes

Makes about 18 Cakes

These are made from a Victoria sponge mixture, but baked in paper cake cases. Children like to make them: use petits fours *paper cases for tiny cakes.*

4 oz (100 g) soft margarine
4 oz (100 g) caster sugar
2 eggs
4 oz (100 g) self-raising flour
1 teaspoon baking powder

Pre-heat the oven to 200°C/400°F/Gas 6. Place about 18 paper cake cases in bun tins.

Measure all the ingredients into a large bowl and beat well for 2–3 minutes until the mixture is well blended and smooth. Half fill the paper cases with the mixture.

Bake in the pre-heated oven for about 15–20 minutes until the cakes are well risen and golden brown. Lift the cakes out of the bun tins and cool on a wire rack.

Queen Cakes

Makes about 18 Cakes

You can vary a simple fairy cake recipe by adding store-cupboard ingredients.

4 oz (100 g) soft margarine
4 oz (100 g) caster sugar
2 eggs
4 oz (100 g) self-raising flour
1 teaspoon baking powder
25 g (1 oz) currants

Pre-heat the oven to 200°C/400°F/Gas 6. Place about 18 paper cake cases in bun tins.

Measure all the ingredients into a large bowl and beat well for 2–3 minutes until the mixture is well blended and smooth. Half fill the paper cases with the mixture.

Bake in the pre-heated oven for about 15–20 minutes until the cakes are well risen and golden brown. Lift the cakes out of the bun tins and cool on a wire rack.

Iced Fairy Cakes

Makes about 18 Cakes

This makes special little cakes, ideal for parties or visiting children.

4 oz (100 g) soft margarine
4 oz (100 g) caster sugar
2 eggs
4 oz (100 g) self-raising flour
1 teaspoon baking powder

For the Icing

8 oz (225 g) icing sugar, sifted
2–3 tablespoons warm water
fancy sweets to decorate

Pre-heat the oven to 200°C/400°F/Gas 6. Place about 18 paper cake cases in bun tins.

Measure all the ingredients into a large bowl and beat well for 2–3 minutes until the mixture is well blended and smooth. Half fill the paper cases with the mixture.

Bake in the pre-heated oven for about 15–20 minutes until the cakes are well risen and golden brown. Lift the cakes out of the bun tins and cool on a wire rack.

Place the icing sugar in a bowl and gradually blend in the water until you have a fairly stiff icing. Spoon over the top of the cakes and decorate with fancy sweets.

Chocolate Fairy Cakes

Makes about 18 Cakes

Chocolate cakes of any size are always popular with children.

4 oz (100 g) soft margarine
4 oz (100 g) caster sugar
2 eggs
3 oz (75 g) self-raising flour
1 oz (25 g) cocoa, sifted
1 teaspoon baking powder

Pre-heat the oven to 200°C/400°F/Gas 6. Place about 18 paper cake cases in bun tins.

Measure all the ingredients into a large bowl and beat well for 2–3 minutes until the mixture is well blended and smooth. Spoon the mixture into the paper cases to half-fill.

Bake in the pre-heated oven for about 15–20 minutes until the cakes are well risen and spring back when pressed lightly with a finger. Lift the cakes out of the bun tins and cool on a wire rack.

Butterfly Cakes

Butterfly Cakes

Makes about 18 Cakes

Butterfly cakes are quick and easy to make and very effective for a children's party.

4 oz (100 g) soft margarine
4 oz (100 g) caster sugar
2 eggs
4 oz (100 g) self-raising flour
1 teaspoon baking powder

For the Icing

6 oz (175 g) butter, softened
12 oz (350 g) icing sugar, sifted
icing sugar, sifted

Pre-heat the oven to 200°C/400°F/Gas 6. Place about 18 paper cake cases in bun tins.

Measure all the ingredients into a large bowl and beat well for 2–3 minutes until the mixture is well blended and smooth. Half fill the paper cases with the mixture.

Bake in the pre-heated oven for about 15–20 minutes until the cakes are well risen and golden brown. Lift the cakes out of the bun tins and cool on a wire rack.

To make the icing, beat the butter and icing sugar until well blended.

Cut a slice from the top of each cake and cut this slice in half. Pipe a swirl of butter cream into the centre of each cake and place the half slices of cake into the butter cream at an angle to resemble butterfly wings. Dust the cakes with icing sugar to finish.

Chocolate Butterfly Cakes

Makes about 18 Cakes

Chocolate butter cream looks very attractive on a plain fairy cake, or you can replace 1 oz (25 g) of the flour for the cakes with cocoa to make the cakes chocolate too. Make orange or lemon butterfly cakes by using grated orange or lemon rind and icing them with a butter cream made with butter, icing sugar and orange or lemon juice.

4 oz (100 g) soft margarine
4 oz (100 g) caster sugar
2 eggs
4 oz (100 g) self-raising flour
1 teaspoon baking powder

For the Icing

2 tablespoons cocoa
3 tablespoons hot water
6 oz (175 g) butter, softened
12 oz (350 g) icing sugar, sifted
icing sugar, sifted

Pre-heat the oven to 200°C/400°F/Gas 6. Place about 18 paper cake cases in bun tins.

Measure all the ingredients into a large bowl and beat well for 2–3 minutes until the mixture is well blended and smooth. Spoon the mixture into the paper cases to half-fill.

Bake in the pre-heated oven for about 15–20 minutes until the cakes are well risen and golden brown. Lift the cakes out of the bun tins and cool on a wire rack.

To make the icing, blend the cocoa and hot water then allow it to cool slightly. Beat in the butter and icing sugar until well blended.

Cut a slice from the top of each cake and cut this slice in half. Pipe a swirl of butter cream into the centre of each cake and place the half slices of cake into the butter cream at an angle to resemble butterfly wings. Dust the cakes with icing sugar to finish.

Secrets of Success

Icing sugar must be sifted when no heat is involved, otherwise it can be very lumpy. If cocoa is used dry, it can cake together if not sifted first.

Orange Fairy Cakes

Makes about 18 Cakes

You can make lemon fairy cakes by substituting lemon rind for the orange rind in the cake mixture and using lemon juice to make the glacé icing.

- *4 oz (100 g) soft margarine*
- *4 oz (100 g) caster sugar*
- *2 eggs*
- *4 oz (100 g) self-raising flour*
- *1 teaspoon baking powder*
- *grated rind of 1 orange*

For the Icing

- *8 oz (225 g) icing sugar, sifted*
- *juice of 1 orange*

Pre-heat the oven to 200°C/400°F/Gas 6. Place about 18 paper cake cases in bun tins.

Measure all the ingredients into a large bowl and beat well for 2–3 minutes until the mixture is well blended and smooth. Spoon the mixture into the paper cases to half-fill.

Bake in the pre-heated oven for about 15–20 minutes until the cakes are well risen and golden brown. Lift the cakes out of the bun tins and cool on a wire rack.

Place the icing sugar in a bowl and gradually blend in the orange juice until you have a fairly stiff icing. Spoon over the top of the cakes.

Makes 16 Doughnuts

Excellent for hungry teenagers, these are best eaten as fresh as possible.

1 lb (450 g) plain white flour
1 sachet easy-blend dried yeast
1 oz (25 g) butter or margarine
3 oz (75 g) caster sugar
2 eggs, beaten
6 tablespoons tepid milk
6 tablespoons tepid water
light vegetable oil for deep-frying

For the Filling

raspberry jam

For the Coating

4 oz (100 g) caster sugar
2 teaspoons ground cinnamon

Lightly grease and flour 3 baking trays.

Measure the flour into a large bowl and stir in the yeast. Rub in the butter with the fingertips until the mixture resembles fine breadcrumbs, then stir in the sugar. Make a well in the centre of the dry ingredients and pour in the eggs, milk and water. Mix to a smooth dough.

Turn out on to a lightly floured work surface and knead for about 5 minutes until the dough is smooth and elastic. Return it to the bowl, cover with oiled cling film and leave to rise until doubled in size, about 1–1½ hours in a warm room.

Turn the risen dough out of the bowl and knead to knock out the air until the dough is smooth and elastic once more. Divide into 16 equal pieces and shape each into a ball. Flatten each ball, then place a small teaspoon of jam in the centre of each piece. Gather the edges together over the jam and pinch firmly to seal. Place well apart on the prepared baking trays, then cover with oiled cling film or put the trays inside large polythene bags and leave to prove for about 30 minutes, until they have doubled in size.

Heat the oil in a deep-fat fryer to 170°C (340°F), and fry the doughnuts a few at a time, turning them once, until they are golden brown all over. This will take about 5 minutes. Lift out with a slotted spoon and drain well on kitchen paper.

Put the sugar and cinnamon into a large polythene bag and shake to mix. Then toss the doughnuts, a few at a time, in the sugar mixture until each is well coated. Serve freshly made.

English Madeleines

Makes 10 Madeleines

For these you will need dariole moulds, which are available from specialist cook shops or department stores. Cook in two batches if you don't have enough moulds.

4 oz (100 g) soft margarine
4 oz (100 g) caster sugar
2 eggs
4 oz (100 g) self-raising flour
1 teaspoon baking powder
2–3 drops of vanilla essence

To Finish

about 4 tablespoons raspberry or strawberry jam, sieved
2 oz (50 g) desiccated coconut
5 glacé cherries, halved

Pre-heat the oven to 180°C/350°F/Gas 4. Lightly grease 10 dariole moulds and place small circles of greaseproof paper in the bases. Stand the tins on a baking tray.

Measure the cake ingredients into a large bowl and beat for about 2 minutes until the mixture is well blended and smooth. Spoon the mixture into the dariole moulds, filling them about half full.

Bake in the pre-heated oven for about 20 minutes until well risen and firm to the touch. Leave to cool for about 5 minutes, then turn out on to a wire rack.

When the cakes are cool, trim the bases so that they stand firmly. Warm the sieved jam in a small pan and spread the coconut out on a large plate. Use a fork to spear the bases of the cakes to hold them. Brush them with the warm jam, then roll in the coconut to coat. Decorate each madeleine with a halved glacé cherry.

French Madeleines

Makes about 30 Madeleines

These shell-shaped cakes do need a madeleine tin, available from specialist kitchen shops (see page 304). It is worth greasing and flouring the tins well so that the madeleines come out cleanly. They don't keep particularly well and, unlikely as it may seem, in France they are traditionally dipped into tea to eat! They are best on the day of making.

5 oz (150 g) butter
3 extra large eggs
5 oz (150 g) caster sugar
5 oz (150 g) self-raising flour
$\frac{1}{2}$ teaspoon baking powder
grated rind of 1 lemon

(Above) English Madeleines, (top) French Madeleines

Pre-heat the oven to 220°C/425°F/Gas 7. Lightly grease a madeleine tray, dust with flour and shake off any excess.

Melt the butter in a small pan and allow to cool slightly. Measure the eggs and sugar into a large bowl and whisk until pale and thick. Sift in half the flour with the baking powder and fold in gently with the lemon rind. Pour in half of the melted butter around the edge of the bowl and fold in. Repeat using the remaining flour and butter. Spoon the mixture into the prepared moulds so that it is just about level with the tops.

Bake in the pre-heated oven for about 8–10 minutes until well risen, golden and springy to the touch. Ease out of the tins with a small palette knife and cool on a wire rack. Re-grease and flour the tins and repeat until all the mixture has been used up.

Makes about 8 Cakes

Not surprisingly, these spicy little currant cakes, enclosed in a flaky pastry, come from the north of England.

For the Flaky Pastry

- ***8 oz (225 g) plain flour***
- ***6 oz (175 g) butter***
- ***a squeeze of lemon juice***
- ***about 8 tablespoons cold water***

For the Filling

- ***2 oz (50 g) butter, softened***
- ***2 oz (50 g) light muscovado sugar***
- ***½ teaspoon ground mixed spice***
- ***2 oz (50 g) mixed candied peel, chopped***
- ***4 oz (100 g) currants***

To Finish

- ***1 egg white, beaten***
- ***caster sugar***

First make the flaky pastry. Measure the flour into a bowl. Divide the butter into 4 equal portions and rub one-quarter of it into the flour, using the fingertips, until the mixture resembles fine breadcrumbs. Add the lemon juice and water to the flour and mix with a round-bladed knife to form a soft dough.

On a lightly floured work surface, gently knead the dough until smooth. Roll out into an oblong three times as long as it is wide (see *figure 39*). Dot a second quarter of the butter in small pieces over the top two-thirds of the pastry (see *figure 40*). Fold the bottom third of the pastry up over the middle third (see *figure 41*), and the top third down (see *figure 42*), then seal the edges well with the edge of your hand (see *figure 43*). Wrap the pastry in cling film and put into the fridge to relax for about 15 minutes.

Re-roll the pastry as before, always starting with the folds of the dough to the left, until the 2 remaining quarters of fat have been used up. Wrap the pastry again in cling film and leave in the fridge for at least 30 minutes before using.

Make the filling by mixing the butter, sugar, spice, mixed peel and currants together.

Pre-heat the oven to 220°C/425°F/Gas 7.

Roll out the pastry thinly and cut into rounds about 6 in (15 cm) in diameter (use a saucer as a guide). Place a good tablespoon of the filling into the centre of each round, dampen the pastry edges with water and then draw together to enclose the filling. Turn the pastry over and flatten gently with the rolling pin so that the currants just show through. Re-shape to a round with the hands if necessary. Make 3 small cuts in the top of each cake, brush with the beaten egg white, and sprinkle with caster sugar. Place on a baking tray.

Bake in the pre-heated oven for about 10–15 minutes until golden. Leave to cool on the baking tray for a few minutes before lifting them on to a wire rack to cool completely.

SECRETS OF SUCCESS

For light pastry, incorporate as much air as possible by sifting flour from a height, cutting in small pieces of fat with a knife, and lifting your hands well above the bowl when rubbing in.

If you are in a hurry for your Eccles Cakes you can use frozen puff pastry for this recipe, but remember to roll it out very thinly otherwise it'll be too thick when cooked.

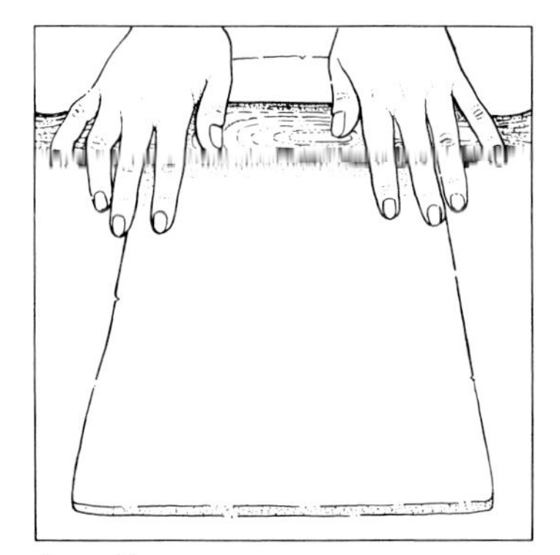

figure 39

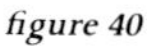

figure 40

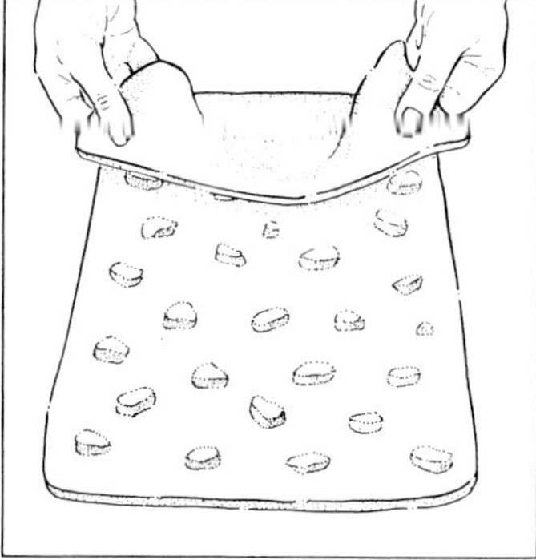

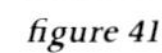

figure 41

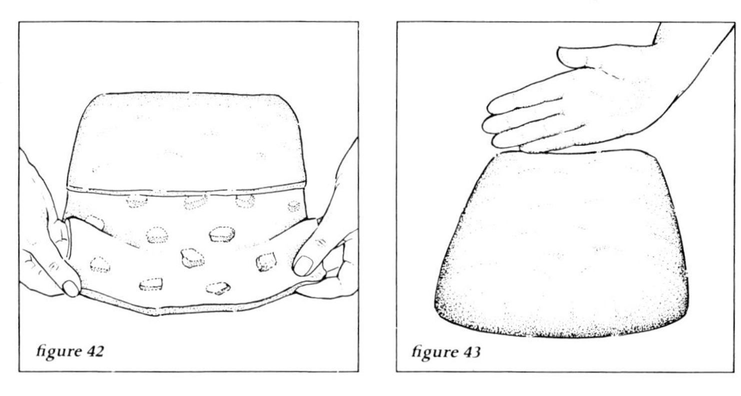

figure 42

figure 43

Lemon Cream Fruit Tarts

Makes about 10 Tarts

These lovely little shortbread cases can actually be filled with anything you like – a good way of spinning out a small amount of fruit, like the first strawberries, for instance. They're quite crumbly to eat.

For the Shortbread

4 oz (100 g) butter, softened

2 oz (50 g) caster sugar

2 oz (50 g) semolina

4 oz (100 g) plain flour

For the Filling

about 3 tablespoons good lemon curd

5 fl oz (150 ml) double cream, whipped

a few fresh strawberries, sliced

First make the shortbread. Soften the butter in a bowl, add the sugar, semolina and flour and work together to form a smooth dough. Wrap in cling film and chill the dough in the refrigerator for about 15 minutes.

Pre-heat the oven to 150°C/300°F/Gas 2.

On a lightly floured work surface, roll out the shortbread to just under $\frac{1}{4}$ in (5 mm) in thickness. Cut out circles using a 3 in (7.5 cm) fluted cutter, then ease the circles into a bun tin tray. Prick the bases well.

Bake in the pre-heated oven for about 20–25 minutes or until firm and golden. Leave the shortbread in the tins to harden slightly then ease out of the tins and leave to cool completely on a wire rack.

For the filling, mix together the lemon curd and the whipped cream. Just before serving, spoon a little of the filling into each shortbread case and top with sliced strawberries.

Secrets of Success

The shortbread cases can be made ahead, and they can be frozen. Once filled, however, they go soft very quickly, so serve and eat straightaway.

(Right) Lemon Cream Fruit Tarts

Bath Buns

MAKES 18 BUNS

THE SPA TOWN OF BATH is famous for its buns, distinguished by the coarse sugar topping. They are said to have been created in the eighteenth century.

1 lb (450 g) strong plain flour
1 sachet easy-blend dried yeast
1 teaspoon salt
2 oz (50 g) caster sugar
2 oz (50 g) butter, melted and cooled
2 eggs, beaten
5 fl oz (150 ml) tepid milk
6 oz (175 g) sultanas
2 oz (50 g) mixed candied peel, chopped

TO FINISH

1 egg to glaze
nibbed sugar or coarsely crushed sugar cubes

Lightly grease 2 baking trays.

Measure the flour, yeast, salt and caster sugar into a large bowl and mix well. Make a well in the centre and pour in the melted, cooled butter, eggs and milk, adding the sultanas and mixed peel last. Mix to a smooth, soft dough.

Turn the dough out on to a lightly floured work surface and knead for about 5 minutes or until smooth and elastic. Place in an oiled bowl and cover with oiled cling film, or put the bowl inside a large polythene bag. Leave to rise until doubled in size, about 1 hour in a warm room.

Turn the risen dough out of the bowl and knead well until the dough is again smooth and elastic. Divide into 18 equal pieces. Shape each piece of dough into a bun and place on the prepared baking trays. Cover again with oiled cling film and leave in a warm place until doubled in size, about 30 minutes.

Pre-heat the oven to 190°C/375°F/Gas 5.

Brush the buns with the beaten egg and sprinkle with the nibbed sugar. Bake in the pre-heated oven for about 15 minutes or until golden brown and hollow-sounding when tapped. Lift on to a wire rack to cool. Serve buttered.

SECRETS OF SUCCESS

Always cover a yeast-raised dough well when it is rising or proving to prevent a skin forming on the surface. Use an oiled polythene bag or cling film.

Hot Cross Buns

Makes 12 Buns

This used to be baked as one large bun; today it is usual to have individual buns. For a more definite cross on the top of the buns, make up 2 oz (50 g) of shortcrust pastry (using 2 oz (50 g) of plain flour, 1 tablespoon of butter and 1 tablespoon of lard), cut it into thin strips and lay over the top of the buns before baking. *(See photograph on page 234.)*

1 lb (450 g) strong plain flour
1 teaspoon salt
1 teaspoon mixed spice
1 teaspoon ground cinnamon
½ teaspoon freshly grated nutmeg
1 sachet easy-blend dried yeast
2 oz (50 g) caster sugar
2 oz (50 g) butter, melted and cooled
5 fl oz (150 ml) tepid milk
5 tablespoons tepid water
1 egg, beaten
3 oz (75 g) currants
2 oz (50 g) chopped mixed peel

To Glaze

2 tablespoons granulated sugar
2 tablespoons water

Lightly grease 2 baking trays.

Measure the flour, salt, spices, yeast and sugar into a large bowl and stir to mix. Make a well in the centre and pour in the melted, cooled butter, milk, water and egg, adding the currants and mixed peel to the mixture last. Mix to a soft dough, then turn out on to a lightly floured work surface and knead for about 10 minutes until smooth and elastic. Cover the bowl with oiled cling film and leave to rise until the dough has doubled in size, about 1½ hours in a warm room.

Turn the risen dough out on to a lightly floured work surface again and knead for 2–3 minutes. Divide the dough into 12 equal pieces and shape each one into a round bun. Make a cross in the top of each bun with a knife, then place on to the prepared baking trays and cover with oiled cling film. Leave to rise again in a warm place until doubled in size, about 30 minutes.

Pre-heat the oven to 220°C/425°F/Gas 7.

Bake the buns in the pre-heated oven for about 15 minutes until brown and hollow-sounding when tapped. While the buns are baking, dissolve the sugar in the water over a gentle heat. As soon as the buns come out of the oven, brush them with the syrup to give a sticky glaze.

Secrets of Success

Because this is an enriched dough, it will take longer to rise than plain doughs.

MAKES ABOUT 12 MUFFINS

THE AMERICAN MUFFIN HAS increased in popularity in Britain. A cross between a scone and a fairy cake, but bigger, American muffins are best served warm, traditionally at breakfast time. Muffiin paper cases are now much more widely available.

9 oz (250 g) self-raising flour

1 teaspoon baking powder

2 oz (50 g) soft margarine

3 oz (75 g) caster sugar

6 oz (175 g) fresh blueberries

grated rind of 1 lemon

2 extra large eggs

8 fl oz (250 ml) milk

Pre-heat the oven to 200°C/400°F/Gas 6. Lightly grease 12 deep muffin tins if you are using ordinary fairy cake paper cases, as the mixture will rise well above the paper cases, and place the paper cases in the tin. You do not need to grease the tins if muffin paper cases are used.

Measure the flour and baking powder into a large bowl. Rub in the margarine with the fingertips until the mixture resembles fine breadcrumbs. Stir in the sugar, blueberries and the grated lemon rind. Mix together the eggs and milk, then pour the mixture all in one go into the dry ingredients. Mix quickly to blend. The mixture should have a lumpy consistency. Spoon the mixture into the prepared tins or paper cases, filling almost to the top.

Bake in the pre-heated oven for about 20–25 minutes until well risen, golden and firm to the touch. Leave the muffins to cool for a few minutes in the tray, then lift out and cool for a little longer on a wire rack. Serve warm.

(Top left) Hot Cross buns (page 233), (bottom left) Blueberry Muffins

Chapter 11

Bazaars and Fêtes

If it is known that you are a keen baker, you will undoubtedly be asked to contribute something to be sold at a fund-raising bazaar or fête in aid of the local church, hospital or school, for a charity, or for a bring-and-buy sale. I've been doing this for years, and I still enjoy it: it's a fun way of donating, and people love home-baked goods so much, they always make a beeline for my stall!

Whether you're an expert or not, I think it's always best to stick to the recipes that you're good at and familiar with. This is not the time for something too exotic or something too fragile. Don't forget the traybakes in Chapter 3, but here there are loaf cakes and biscuits which I consider best for these sorts of occasions – but if your *pièce de résistance* is a sponge cake, make that instead. However, that sponge would probably be better baked as a traybake: you can cook more than one at a time; it's quicker to bake; it will transport better; and you can get more money-making portions from it. There are also lots of other suitable recipes throughout the book.

If you're short of time, bake things that can be done in advance, such as biscuits, shortbreads and some loaf cakes. You can freeze cakes, obviously, and then thaw and ice them on the day but, although there is no danger in possible re-freezing, I think the potential customer should know: mention this on the wrapping in some way.

If you're short of money, choose cakes using less expensive ingredients such as scones and drop scones. You can economize in other ways, too. Try to make full use of the oven when baking, placing tins side by side, and allowing a little longer baking time. Use a less expensive jam for spreading on cakes; warming it first makes it go even further. If you have free produce from the garden, use that – apples, soft fruit and, although outside the scope of this book, a glut of something like onions would make wonderful tarts for any home-baking stall.

Once you've been asked, or once you've decided to contribute, do sit down and think about what you've got and what you would like to use and make. And even if you've no time at all to bake for such a good cause, you can still contribute: offer the ingredients, windfalls, or the cost of the ingredients to someone else who has more time and who enjoys baking at home.

Presentation is all. The stall must look good for a start, if that's part of your responsibility. For one school fête recently, we adopted a Scottish theme: a tartan rug covered the table, and little sprigs of heather were interspersed among Scottish goodies such as shortbread and tartan-ribboned jars of marmalade.

The cakes and biscuits themselves must be packaged attractively, too. Cover cardboard with foil for give-away cakeboards. Wrap cakes in cellophane and tie with colourful ribbons. Package biscuits, six at a time, on paper plates with cling film; or present in a big coffee jar. Loaf and round cakes can be baked in bought greaseproof cases – perfect packaging for a stall – as can smaller cakes. Cut traybakes and loaf cakes into pieces and slices respectively; wrap the former individually in cling film, butter the latter if appropriate, and present a few on a paper plate under cling film.

The children can help you with all this: they could also decorate and write out labels. Get them to emphasize the most attractive selling points such as 'Freshly Baked Scones' or 'Real Butter Shortbread'.

To price goods, add up the cost of the ingredients, add on a little for fuel and time, and double it! It is obviously better if the final figure is less than the equivalent in the shops, although people will usually pay a little more for home-made freshness and, of course, for a good cause.

Finally, take along some supermarket bags; potential buyers almost always forget to bring anything with them in which to carry their booty home.

Orange Wholemeal Victoria Loaf

Makes 1 × 2 lb (900 g) Loaf

Loaf tin liners are perfect when used for cakes to be sold at a fête or bazaar. They are available by mail order from Lakeland Ltd *(see page 304)*.

4 oz (100 g) soft margarine

4 oz (100 g) light muscovado sugar

2 eggs

2 oz (50 g) self-raising brown flour

2 oz (50 g) self-raising white flour

grated rind of 1 orange

For the Topping

1 oz (25 g) soft margarine

3 oz (75 g) icing sugar, sieved

1 tablespoon fine-cut marmalade

Pre-heat the oven to 180°C/350°F/Gas 4. Lightly grease and base line a 2 lb (900 g) loaf tin with greased greaseproof paper, or use a 2 lb (900 g) loaf tin liner.

Measure all the cake ingredients into a large bowl and beat well for about 2 minutes until smooth and blended. Turn into the prepared tin and level the surface – don't expect the mixture to fill the tin.

Bake in the pre-heated oven for about 40 minutes or until well risen, golden and shrinking slightly from the sides of the tin. Turn out on to a wire rack to cool.

To make the topping, measure all the topping ingredients into a bowl and blend together until smooth. Spoon on top of the cake and swirl the top with a small palette knife to decorate.

Orange Wholemeal Victoria Loaf

Crunchy Lemon Syrup Loaves

Makes 2 × 1 lb (450 g) Loaves

I've seen these for sale in Wycombe market. They may not look madly exciting, but they are very popular, and delicious to eat.

4 oz (100 g) soft margarine
6 oz (175 g) self-raising flour
1 teaspoon baking powder
6 oz (175 g) caster sugar
2 eggs
4 tablespoons milk
finely grated rind of 1 lemon

For the Topping

juice of 1 lemon
4 oz (100 g) granulated sugar

Pre-heat the oven to 180°C/350°F/Gas 4. Lightly grease and base line 2 × 1 lb (450 g) loaf tins with greased greaseproof paper.

Measure all the cake ingredients into a large bowl and beat well for about 2 minutes. Divide the mixture evenly between the tins and level the surface of each.

Bake in the pre-heated oven for about 30 minutes or until the cakes spring back when the surface is lightly pressed with the finger and have shrunk slightly from the sides of the tins.

Whilst the cakes are baking, make the crunchy topping. Measure the lemon juice and sugar into a small bowl and stir to mix. Spread the lemon mixture over the baked loaves whilst they are still hot, and then leave to cool completely in the tins. Turn out and remove the paper once cold.

Sultana Malt Loaves

MAKES 2 × 1 LB (450 G) LOAVES

THESE CAN BE MADE well ahead as they keep very well. If you're busy baking for a fête, you can freeze them, but if selling whole, the label ought to say that they've been frozen. If selling in slices, butter the slices.

8 oz (225 g) plain flour

½ teaspoon bicarbonate of soda

1 teaspoon baking powder

8 oz (225 g) sultanas

2 oz (50 g) demerara sugar

6 oz (175 g) malt extract

1 tablespoon black treacle

2 eggs, beaten

5 fl oz (150 ml) strained cold black tea

Pre-heat the oven to 150°C/300°F/Gas 2. Grease and base line 2 × 1 lb (450 g) loaf tins with greased greaseproof paper.

Measure the flour, bicarbonate of soda and baking powder into a bowl. Stir in the sultanas.

Gently heat the sugar, malt extract and black treacle together. Pour on to the dry ingredients with the beaten eggs and the tea. Beat well until smooth. Pour into the prepared tins.

Bake in the pre-heated oven for about 1 hour or until well risen and firm to the touch. Allow to cool for 10 minutes in the tins before turning out on to a wire rack to cool. These loaves are best kept for 2 days before eating.

SECRETS OF SUCCESS

Freeze cakes as soon as they are cold. Some icings often lose their sheen in the freezer, so it's usually best to freeze the cake by itself, and ice later. Buttercream icing is an exception.

Iced Apricot Fruit Loaf

Makes 1 × 2 lb (900 g) Loaf

Like any fruit loaf, this is easy to make, and easy to sell, both whole, and in slices.

3 oz (75 g) glacé cherries

3 extra large eggs

6 oz (175 g) self-raising flour

4 oz (100 g) soft margarine

4 oz (100 g) light muscovado sugar

4 oz (100 g) ready-to-eat dried apricots, chopped

5 oz (150 g) sultanas

For the Icing

4 oz (100 g) icing sugar, sifted

1 tablespoon apricot jam

1 tablespoon water

2 ready-to-eat dried apricots, chopped

Pre-heat the oven to 160°C/325°F/Gas 3. Lightly grease and base line a 2 lb (900 g) loaf tin with greased greaseproof paper.

First prepare the cherries. Quarter, wash and thoroughly dry on kitchen paper.

Break the eggs into a large bowl and then measure in the remaining cake ingredients including the cherries. Beat well until the mixture is smooth. Turn into the prepared tin and level the top.

Bake in the pre-heated oven for about 1 hour 10 minutes or until the cake is golden brown, firm to the touch and shrinking away from the sides of the tin. A fine skewer inserted into the centre of the cake should come out clean. Allow the cake to cool in the tin for about 10 minutes then turn out, remove the paper and leave to cool completely on a wire rack.

For the icing, measure the sifted icing sugar into a bowl. Heat the apricot jam and water together until the jam melts then pour on to the icing sugar. Mix to a smooth spreading consistency, then spoon over the top of the cake. Decorate the cake by sprinkling the chopped apricots down the centre of the cake.

(Right) Iced Apricot Fruit Loaf

Chocolate Chip Flapjacks

MAKES 24 SQUARES

DO MAKE SURE THAT the flapjack mixture is quite cool before you add the chocolate chips or they will simply melt into the mixture instead of staying whole. *(See photograph on page 247.)*

8 oz (225 g) margarine

8 oz (225 g) demerara sugar

2 tablespoons golden syrup

10 oz (275 g) rolled oats

4 oz (100 g) plain chocolate chips

Pre-heat the oven to 160°C/325°F/Gas 3. Lightly grease a 12 × 9 in (30 × 23 cm) roasting tin.

Melt the margarine in a pan with the sugar and syrup and then stir in the oats. Mix well and then leave to cool before stirring in the chocolate chips. Turn into the prepared tin and press flat with a palette knife or the back of a spoon.

Bake in the pre-heated oven for about 35 minutes or until pale golden brown. Remove from the oven and then leave to cool for about 10 minutes. Mark into 24 squares and leave to finish cooling in the tin.

Muesli Flapjacks

MAKES 16 FLAPJACKS

THE GREAT THING ABOUT these flapjacks is that they will turn out differently each time, depending upon the type of muesli used. If you like a lot of raisins, add 1–2 oz (25–50 g) to taste. Be careful not to overcook the flapjacks or they become impossible to get out of the tin and are very hard to eat. *(See photograph on page 247.)*

8 oz (225 g) margarine

8 oz (225 g) demerara sugar

2 tablespoons golden syrup

6 oz (175 g) muesli

4 oz (100 g) rolled oats

Pre-heat the oven to 160°C/325°F/Gas 3. Lightly grease a 12 × 9 in (30 × 23 cm) roasting tin.

Melt the margarine in a pan with the sugar and the golden syrup and then stir in the muesli and the oats. Mix well, then turn into the prepared tin and press flat with a palette knife or the back of a spoon.

Bake in the pre-heated oven for about 35 minutes or until pale golden brown. Remove from the oven and then leave to cool for about 10 minutes. Mark into 16 fingers and leave to finish cooling in the tin.

Bishop's Shortbread Fingers

Makes 12 Fingers

If you notice that the underside of the shortbread is not pale gold, return to the oven for a further 5–10 minutes. (See photograph opposite.)

4 oz (50 g) plain flour
1 oz (25 g) ground almonds
1 oz (25 g) semolina
4 oz (100 g) butter
2 oz (50 g) caster sugar
a few drops of almond essence
1 oz (25 g) flaked almonds
caster sugar for dusting

Pre-heat the oven to 160°C/325°F/Gas 3. Lightly grease a 7 in (18 cm) shallow square tin.

Mix the flour, ground almonds and semolina in a bowl or food processor. Add the butter, sugar and almond essence and rub together with the fingertips, or process in the food processor, until the mixture is just beginning to bind together. Knead lightly until smooth. Press the dough into the prepared tin and level the surface with the back of a metal spoon or a palette knife. Sprinkle over the flaked almonds.

Bake in the pre-heated oven for about 30–35 minutes or until a very pale golden brown. Mark the shortbread into 12 fingers, sprinkle with caster sugar and leave to cool in the tin. When completely cold, cut into fingers, lift out carefully and store in an airtight tin.

Bazaars and Fêtes

1 Chocolate Fork Biscuits (page 248)
2 Fork Biscuits (page 248)
3 Orange Fork Biscuits (page 249)
4 Chocolate Chip Flapjacks (page 244)
5 Bishop's Shortbread Fingers (above)
6 Muesli Flapjacks (page 245)

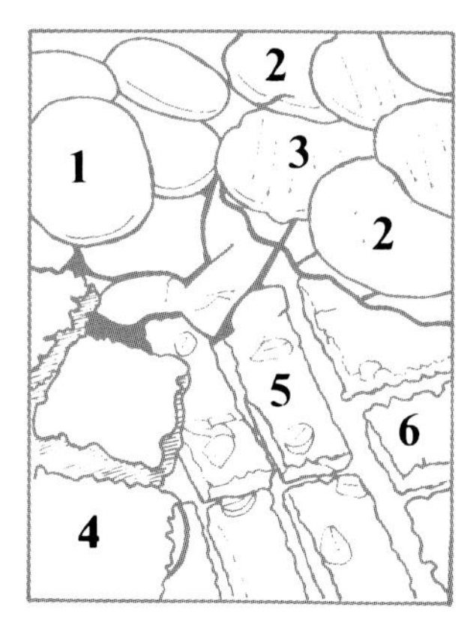

Fork Biscuits

Makes about 16 Biscuits

These biscuits first made their appearance in that famous old red Cordon Bleu book, and I've been making them for years. Perfect for tea or coffee, make them with butter for an even more delicious biscuit. *(See photograph on page 247.)*

4 oz (100 g) butter, softened
2 oz (50 g) caster sugar
5 oz (150 g) self-raising flour

Pre-heat the oven to 180°C/350°F/Gas 4. Lightly grease 2 baking trays.

Measure the butter into a bowl and beat with a wooden spoon. Gradually beat in the sugar and then mix in the flour. Bring the mixture together with your hands to form a dough. Form the dough into balls about the size of a walnut and place well apart on the prepared baking trays. Dip a fork in a little water and use this to flatten the biscuits.

Bake in the pre-heated oven for about 15–20 minutes until a very pale golden. Lift off the baking tray and leave to cool completely on a wire rack.

Chocolate Fork Biscuits

Makes about 16 Biscuits

These make a delicious accompaniment to tea or coffee. *(See photograph on page 247.)*

4 oz (100 g) soft margarine
2 oz (50 g) caster sugar
4½ oz (120 g) self-rasing flour
½ oz (15 g) cocoa

Pre-heat the oven to 180°C/350°F/Gas 4. Lightly grease 2 baking trays.

Measure the margarine into a bowl and soften with a wooden spoon. Gradually beat in the sugar and then mix in the flour and cocoa. Bring the mixture together with your hands to form a dough. Form the dough into balls about the size of a walnut and place well apart on the prepared baking trays. Dip a fork in a little water and use this to flatten the biscuits.

Bake in the pre-heated oven for about 15–20 minutes until browned. Lift off the baking tray and leave to cool completely on a wire rack.

Makes about 16 Biscuits

Make lemon fork biscuits by substituting the grated rind of a lemon for the orange rind. *(See photograph on page 247.)*

4 oz (100 g) butter, softened

2 oz (50 g) caster sugar

grated rind of 1 small orange

5 oz (150 g) self-raising flour

Pre-heat the oven to 180°C/350°F/Gas 4. Lightly grease 2 baking trays.

Measure the butter into a bowl and beat with a wooden spoon. Gradually beat in the sugar and orange rind and then mix in the flour. Bring the mixture together with your hands to form a dough. Form the dough into balls about the size of a walnut and place well apart on the prepared baking trays. Dip a fork in a little water and use this to flatten the biscuits.

Bake in the pre-heated oven for about 15–20 minutes until very pale golden. Lift off the baking tray and leave to cool completely on a wire rack.

French Apple Tart

Serves 6

Although this is very time-consuming to make, it is always good to have something professional-looking to sell. It's an economical choice in the autumn when you can use your own free apples, or get them cheaply from elsewhere.

For the Pastry

6 oz (175 g) plain flour
1½ oz (40 g) butter, diced
1½ oz (40 g) white vegetable fat, diced
1 egg yolk
water, if necessary

For the Filling

2 lb (900 g) cooking apples
2 oz (50 g) butter
2 tablespoons water
4 tablespoons apricot jam
2 oz (50 g) caster sugar
grated rind of ½ lemon
8 oz (225 g) eating apples
1–2 tablespoons lemon juice
about 1 teaspoon caster sugar for sprinkling

For the Glaze

4 tablespoons apricot jam

First make the pastry. Measure the flour into a large bowl, add the fats and rub in with the fingertips until the mixture resembles fine breadcrumbs. Add the egg yolk, stir into the flour mixture with a round-bladed knife, and bring the mixture to a dough, adding a little water if necessary. Knead the pastry very lightly, then wrap and chill in the fridge for about 30 minutes.

Pre-heat the oven to 200°C/400°F/Gas 6.

While the oven is pre-heating and the pastry resting, start to make the apple filling. Cut the cooking apples into quarters, remove the core and chop the apple into chunks (no need to peel). Melt the butter in a large pan and then add the prepared apples and water. Cover and cook very gently for 10–15 minutes until the apples have become soft and mushy.

Rub the apple through a nylon sieve into a clean pan, add the apricot jam, sugar and grated lemon rind. Cook over a high heat for about 10–15 minutes, stirring constantly, until all the excess liquid has evaporated and the apple mixture is thick. Allow to cool.

Roll out the pastry thinly on a lightly floured work surface and use to line an 8 in (20 cm) loose-based fluted flan tin. Cover with greaseproof paper and fill with baking beans. Bake blind in the oven for about 10–15 minutes (see *page 27*), then remove the paper and beans and bake for about another 5 minutes until the pastry at the base of the flan has dried out.

French Apple Tart

Spoon the cooled apple purée into the flan case and level the surface. Peel, quarter and core the eating apples, then slice them very thinly. Arrange in neat overlapping circles all over the apple purée, brush with the lemon juice and sprinkle with the caster sugar. Return the flan to the oven and bake for about a further 25 minutes or until the pastry and the edges of the apples are lightly browned. Allow to cool a little.

For the glaze, sieve the apricot jam into a small pan and heat gently until runny. Brush all over the top of the apples and pastry. Serve warm or cold.

Apple and Cinnamon Cake

Cuts into 8–10 Wedges

This is the sort of cake that you would expect to find in a first-class coffee or tea shop. Sell it in wedges with a pretty ingredients label, and the suggestion to serve it warm with cream.

8 oz (225 g) soft margarine

8 oz (225 g) light muscovado sugar

3 extra large eggs

4 oz (100 g) walnut pieces, chopped

4 oz (100 g) sultanas

8 oz (225 g) self-raising flour

2 teaspoons baking powder

14 oz (400 g) cooking apples, peeled, cored and grated

1 teaspoon ground cinnamon

To Finish

light muscovado sugar for sprinkling

extra chopped walnuts for sprinkling

icing sugar for dusting

Pre-heat the oven to 180°C/350°F/Gas 4. Lightly grease and base line a 9 in (23 cm) deep round cake tin with greased greaseproof paper.

Measure the margarine, sugar, eggs, chopped walnuts, sultanas, flour and baking powder into a large bowl and beat well for about 2 minutes until thoroughly blended. Spoon half the mixture into the prepared tin then spread the grated apple and ground cinnamon in an even layer on top. Spread the remaining cake mixture on top, level the surface then sprinkle generously with light muscovado sugar and walnuts.

Bake in the pre-heated oven for about 1¼ –1½ hours or until the cake is well risen and golden brown. Remove from the oven and leave to cool in the tin for a few minutes before turning out and leaving to cool completely on a wire rack.

Dust with icing sugar to serve.

Chocolate Chip American Muffins

Makes about 12 Muffins

These are large, and look quite impressive. They're best freshly baked on the actual day of the bazaar or fête.

9 oz (250 g) self-raising flour

1 teaspoon baking powder

2 oz (50 g) soft margarine

3 oz (75 g) caster sugar

6 oz (175 g) plain chocolate chips

2 extra large eggs

1 teaspoon vanilla essence

8 fl oz (250 ml) milk

Pre-heat the oven to 200°C/400°F/Gas 6. Lightly grease 12 deep muffin tins if using ordinary fairy cake paper cases in the tins as the mixture will rise above the cases, and place the paper cases in the tin. There is no need to grease the tins if you are using muffin paper cases.

Measure the flour and baking powder into a large bowl, add the margarine, and rub into the flour until the mixture resembles fine breadcrumbs. Stir in the sugar and chocolate chips.

Mix together the eggs, vanilla essence and milk, then pour the mixture all in one go into the dry ingredients. Mix quickly to blend. The mixture should have a lumpy consistency. Spoon the mixture into the prepared tins or paper cases in the tins, filling almost to the top.

Bake in the pre-heated oven for about 20–25 minutes or until well risen and firm to the touch. Leave the muffins to cool for a few minutes in the tray, then lift out and cool for a little longer on a wire rack. Serve warm.

Cheese and Olive Scone Bake

Makes 12 Squares

Making one large scone is fastest of all, as you don't have to roll and cut out the mixture. Break this scone into fours to sell. Shape the dough into an oblong on a baking tray if you don't have a roasting tin.

1 lb (450 g) self-raising flour

2 teaspoons baking powder

1 teaspoon salt

4 oz (100 g) butter

7 oz (200 g) mature Cheddar, grated

4 oz (100 g) pitted black olives, roughly chopped

2 eggs

milk

1 oz (25 g) Parmesan, grated

Pre-heat the oven to 230°C/450°F/Gas 8. Lightly grease a 12 × 9 in (30 × 23 cm) roasting tin.

Measure the flour, baking powder and salt into a large bowl. Add the butter and rub into the flour using the fingertips until the mixture resembles fine breadcrumbs. Stir in the grated Cheddar and the roughly chopped olives. Break the eggs into a measuring jug and make up to 10 fl oz (300 ml) with milk. Add to the flour mixture, mixing to form a soft dough.

Knead the dough quickly and lightly until smooth, then roll out on a lightly floured work surface to an oblong to fit the roasting tin. Mark into 12 squares and brush the top with a little milk.

Bake in the pre-heated oven for about 15 minutes. Sprinkle the top with the Parmesan and bake for a further 5 minutes until the scone is well risen and golden. Turn out on to a wire rack to cool. Break into fours to pack and sell.

Cheese and Olive Scone Bake

Chapter 12

No-bake Cakes and Cakes for Children to Make

A delicious cake made without even turning on the oven has got to be a bonus. Most of the cakes in this chapter simply involve melting ingredients together and setting them in the fridge for an hour or so. The only skill required from small cooks is patience! Some of these cakes do require baking, but so long as you are around, this shouldn't present too much of a problem.

When my children were small, mothers used to make a play dough with flour, water, salt and a little colouring. I always thought this was a waste of time. What was wrong with a *proper* dough, something that they could actually bake and then eat, because children so much enjoy eating what they have made themselves. I used to love doing this with my own children, and found it an effective way of entertaining some of their friends, too. I have wonderful memories of rapt little faces, rolling packet bread dough out into pizza circles then arranging on them a selection of toppings I'd put into small bowls. If you ever have a child who's finicky about food, this is one way of curing them!

I believe that it's never too early to encourage children to know the basics about food and food preparation. But the kitchen is a dangerous place – full of sharp knives and heat – so you must always be on hand to supervise. Your own children may know all about pots on the stove and hot oven doors, but their little guests may not. Hover in a reassuring way, but let them get on with it themselves, and *don't* hurry them. You may want to be getting on with other things, but I'm afraid they do tend to do things slowly.

So far as cakes and biscuits are concerned, children like to make small, colourful things. A cornflake cake in a paper case is a firm favourite. Sweets are another popular item, and are ideal for children to make as birthday or Christmas presents. The best of all, though, are the little iced and sweet-topped cakes and gingerbread men, as there is so much scope for individual creativity.

It is also a good idea to make it quite clear that cleaning up afterwards is an integral part of the whole experience. Children tend to lose interest once the cakes are actually made and baked, but now is a good time for them to learn those basics of cooking as well!

Coconut Pyramids

Makes about 12 Pyramids

The moulds for these easy little cakes can be dariole moulds or egg cups, or you can buy special pyramid moulds for a more pointed shape. *(See photograph on pages 258–9.)*

8 oz (225 g) desiccated coconut

4 oz (100 g) caster sugar

2 eggs, beaten

a little pink food colouring (optional)

Pre-heat the oven to 180°C/350°F/Gas 4. Place non-stick baking paper on to 2 baking trays.

Measure the coconut and sugar into a bowl and mix together. Beat in sufficient egg to bind the mixture together and add a few drops of pink colouring, if liked. Dip each dariole mould or egg cup into cold water and drain it well. Fill with the coconut mixture and press down lightly. Turn the moulded coconut out on to the baking tray. Continue with the remaining mixture.

Bake in the pre-heated oven for about 20 minutes or until the pyramids are tinged a pale golden brown. Lift off the baking tray and leave to cool on a wire rack.

Makes about 32 Tiny Buns

Simplicity itself to make, you can top the buns with any fancy sweets.

$1\frac{1}{2}$ oz (40 g) soft margarine

1 egg

2 oz (50 g) self-raising flour

$\frac{1}{2}$ teaspoon baking powder

$1\frac{1}{2}$ oz (40 g) caster sugar

For the Icing

2 oz (50 g) icing sugar, sifted

about $\frac{1}{2}$ tablespoon water

about 32 fancy chocolate sweets to decorate

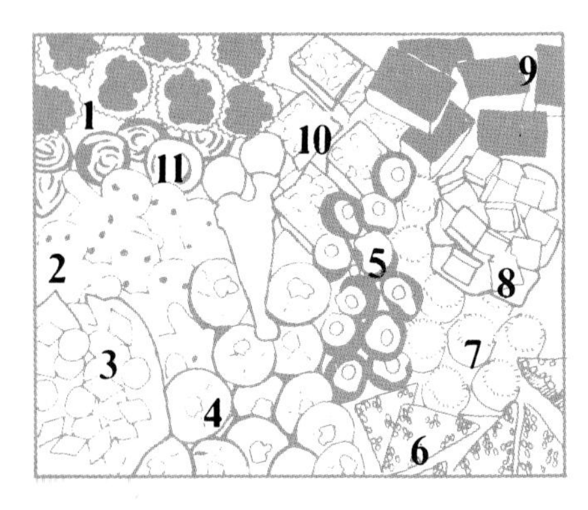

No-bake Cakes and Cakes for Children to Make

1 *Chocolate Cornflake Crunchies (page 264)*

2 *Gingerbread Men (page 263)*

3 *Peppermint Creams (page 265)*

4 *Mini Jammy Buns (page 261)*

5 *Mini Chocolate Buns (page 260)*

6 *Caramel Crunchies (page 263)*

7 *Coconut Pyramids (page 257)*

8 *No-cook Fudge (page 265)*

9 *Date Krispie Slices (page 264)*

10 *Chocolate Nut Tiffin Squares (page 261)*

11 *Chocolate and Vanilla Pinwheel Biscuits (page 262)*

Pre-heat the oven to 180°C/350°F/Gas 4. Arrange about 32 *petits fours* cases on 2 baking trays.

Measure all the cake ingredients into a bowl and beat well until thoroughly blended. Spoon scant teaspoonfuls of the mixture into the cases, being careful not to overfill.

Bake in the pre-heated oven for about 10–15 minutes until well risen and firm to the touch. Cool on a wire rack.

For the icing, measure the icing sugar into a bowl and add sufficient water to give a spreading consistency. Spoon a little on top of each cake and spread out with the back of the teaspoon. When the icing has almost set, top with a sweet.

Mini Chocolate Buns

Makes about 32 Tiny Buns

These are firm favourites with children. *(See photograph on pages 258–9.)*

- ***1½ oz (40 g) soft margarine***
- ***1 egg***
- ***1½ oz (40 g) self-raising flour***
- ***½ oz (15 g) cocoa, sifted***
- ***½ teaspoon baking powder***
- ***1½ oz (40 g) caster sugar***

For the Icing

- ***2 oz (50 g) icing sugar, sifted***
- ***about ½ tablespoon water***
- ***about 32 fancy chocolate sweets to decorate***

Pre-heat the oven to 180°C/350°F/Gas 4. Arrange about 32 *petits fours* cases on 2 baking trays.

Measure all the cake ingredients into a bowl and beat well until thoroughly blended. Spoon scant teaspoonfuls of the mixture into the cases, being careful not to overfill.

Bake in the pre-heated oven for about 10–15 minutes until well risen and firm to the touch. Cool on a wire rack.

For the icing, measure the icing sugar into a bowl and add sufficient water to give a spreading consistency. Spoon a little on top of each cake and spread out with the back of the teaspoon. When the icing has almost set, top with a sweet.

Mini Jammy Buns

Makes about 24 Buns

These are usually made so the jam is enclosed, but here they are left open so that the jam is nice and chewy. They are best served warm. (See photograph on pages 258–9.)

- ***8 oz (225 g) self-raising flour***
- ***$\frac{1}{4}$ teaspoon mixed spice***
- ***2 oz (50 g) soft margarine***
- ***4 oz (100 g) caster sugar***
- ***1 egg, beaten***
- ***about 3–4 tablespoons milk***
- ***a little blackcurrant jam***
- ***a little granulated sugar***

Pre-heat the oven to 200°C/400°F/Gas 6. Lightly grease 2 baking trays.

Measure the flour, spice and margarine into a bowl and rub in the margarine until the mixture resembles fine breadcrumbs. Stir in the sugar.

Mix the egg and milk together and stir into the mixture, adding sufficient of the liquid to make a stiff dough. Divide the mixture into about 24 pieces and roll each piece into a smooth ball. Make a hole in the centre of each ball of dough using the handle of a wooden spoon and put about $\frac{1}{4}$ teaspoon jam into each one. Place the balls of dough as they are jam side up on to the baking trays and sprinkle each one with a little granulated sugar.

Bake in the pre-heated oven for about 10 minutes until they are a pale golden brown. Lift off the tray and allow to cool a little on a wire rack before eating warm.

Chocolate Nut Tiffin Squares

Makes 15 Squares

For a special occasion, spread melted chocolate on top of these. They tend to be a little crumbly and to fall apart, but are quite delicious. (See photograph on pages 258–9.)

- ***4 tablespoons golden syrup***
- ***6 oz (175 g) butter or hard margarine***
- ***4 oz (100 g) plain chocolate, broken into pieces***
- ***8 oz (225 g) digestive biscuits, crushed***
- ***4 oz (100 g) rich tea biscuits, crushed***
- ***4 oz (100 g) walnuts, chopped***
- ***6 oz (175 g) sultanas***

Lightly grease a 12 × 9 in (30 × 23 cm) roasting tin.

Melt the syrup, butter and chocolate together in a heatproof bowl over a pan of hot water. Add the crushed biscuits, walnuts and sultanas and mix well. Spoon into the prepared tin and level the surface. Chill well until set, then cut into 15 squares, and serve from the fridge.

Chocolate and Vanilla Pinwheel Biscuits

Makes about 20 Biscuits

Young children can easily make these – under supervision, of course. They're fun for Bonfire Night. *(See photograph on pages 258–9.)*

For the Vanilla Biscuit Mixture

2 oz (50 g) hard margarine, softened
1 oz (25 g) caster sugar
1 oz (25 g) cornflour
2 oz (50 g) plain flour
a few drops of vanilla essence

For the Chocolate Biscuit Mixture

2 oz (50 g) hard margarine, softened
1 oz (25 g) caster sugar
1 oz (25 g) cornflour
$1\frac{1}{2}$ oz (40 g) plain flour
$\frac{1}{2}$ oz (15 g) cocoa

Lightly grease 2 baking trays.

Measure all the ingredients for the vanilla biscuit mixture into a bowl and mix to form a dough. Knead lightly then wrap in cling film and chill in the fridge for about 30 minutes.

Make the chocolate biscuit mixture in the same way, wrapping and chilling as before.

On a lightly floured surface, roll out both pieces of dough to oblongs about 10 × 7 in (25 × 18 cm). Place the vanilla biscuit dough on top of the chocolate and then roll up the two together from the narrow edge. Wrap in cling film and chill again for about 30 minutes.

Pre-heat the oven to 180°C/350°F/Gas 4.

Cut the roll into about 20 slices using a sharp knife and place on the prepared baking trays. Bake in the pre-heated oven for about 20 minutes until the vanilla biscuit is golden in colour. Lift on to a wire rack and leave to cool.

Gingerbread Men

MAKES ABOUT 20 BISCUITS

I USED A $5\frac{1}{2}$ IN (13.5 CM) gingerbread man cutter to obtain twenty men from this mixture. *(See photograph on pages 258–9.)*

- ***12 oz (350 g) plain flour***
- ***1 teaspoon bicarbonate of soda***
- ***2 teaspoons ground ginger***
- ***4 oz (100 g) margarine***
- ***6 oz (175 g) light muscovado sugar***
- ***4 tablespoons golden syrup***
- ***1 egg, beaten***
- ***currants to decorate***

Pre-heat the oven to 190°C/375°F/Gas 5. Lightly grease 3 baking trays.

Measure the flour, bicarbonate of soda and ginger into a bowl. Rub in the margarine until the mixture resembles fine breadcrumbs, then stir in the sugar. Add the syrup and beaten egg to the flour mixture and mix to form a smooth dough, kneading lightly with the hands towards the end.

Divide the dough in half and roll out one half on a lightly floured surface to a thickness of about $\frac{1}{4}$ in (5 mm). Cut out gingerbread men using a gingerbread man cutter, and place them on to the prepared baking trays. Use the currants for eyes and buttons. Repeat with remaining dough.

Bake in the pre-heated oven for about 10–12 minutes until a slightly darker shade. Cool slightly then lift on to a wire rack and leave to cool completely.

Caramel Crunchies

MAKES ABOUT 24 CRUNCHIES

USE PLAIN, FAIRLY soft toffees or caramels for this recipe. *(See photograph on pages 258–9.)*

- ***4 oz (100 g) hard margarine***
- ***4 oz (100 g) marshmallows***
- ***4 oz (100 g) caramels (toffees)***
- ***7 oz (200 g) rice krispies***

Measure the margarine, marshmallows and caramels into a large heavy-based pan and heat gently until the mixture is melted and smooth. Be patient, this will take about 5 minutes. Stir in the rice krispies and mix well to coat evenly.

Spoon into a 12 × 9 in (30 × 23 cm) roasting tin and level the surface with a palette knife. Leave in a cool place until set and then cut into about 24 triangles.

Date Krispie Slices

Makes 21 Bars

A favourite of my friend Fiona since her first cookery classes at school. (See photograph on pages 258–9.)

4 oz (100 g) caster sugar
4 oz (100 g) margarine
6 oz (175 g) dates, chopped
1 oz (25 g) glacé cherries, quartered
4 oz (100 g) rice krispies
about 7 oz (200 g) milk chocolate, broken into pieces

Lightly grease a 12 × 9 in (30 × 23 cm) roasting tin.

Measure the sugar and margarine into a heavy-based pan and heat gently until melted. Increase the heat and bring the mixture up to the boil. Add the dates and continue to cook for 2 minutes. Stir in the cherries and rice krispies and stir until evenly mixed. Spoon into the prepared tin and level the surface with a palette knife.

Melt the chocolate slowly in a bowl over a pan of hot water. Spread the chocolate over the krispie mixture and leave to set. When set cut into 21 bars.

Chocolate Cornflake Crunchies

These can be made with other breakfast cereals such as rice krispies or bran flakes, just use what you have in the cupboard. Eat on the day of making. (See photograph on pages 258–9.)

2 oz (50 g) margarine
2 tablespoons drinking chocolate
1 rounded tablespoon golden syrup
$2\frac{1}{2}$ oz (65 g) cornflakes

Arrange about 15 paper cases on a baking sheet.

Measure the margarine into a saucepan and heat gently to melt. Stir in the drinking chocolate and golden syrup and mix well. Remove from the heat and add the cornflakes. Stir gently but thoroughly to coat the cornflakes evenly with the chocolate mixture. Using 2 spoons, pile the mixture into the paper cases and leave to set in a cool place for about 30 minutes.

No-cook Fudge

Makes about 36 Squares

This is very easy and safe for children to make. *(See photograph on pages 258–9.)*

6 oz (175 g) butter, softened

$\frac{1}{2}$ × 14 oz (397 g) can condensed milk

$1\frac{3}{4}$ lb (800 g) icing sugar, sifted

Measure the butter into a bowl and beat with a wooden spoon until very soft. Stir in the condensed milk. Gradually add the sifted icing sugar, working it into the butter and milk with a spoon and then your fingertips.

Turn on to a work surface which has been lightly sprinkled with sifted icing sugar and knead until smooth. Roll out to a thickness of $\frac{1}{2}$ in (1 cm) and cut into neat squares. Place on to greaseproof paper and allow to harden overnight.

Peppermint Creams

makes about 30 Sweets

These are good for children to make for Christmas presents. *(See photograph on pages 258–9.)*

1 egg white

$\frac{1}{2}$ teaspoon peppermint essence

12 oz (350 g) icing sugar, sifted

about 4 oz (100 g) plain chocolate (optional)

Whisk the egg white and peppermint essence together with a fork in a medium bowl until frothy. Gradually add the sifted icing sugar and work into the egg white, using the fingertips to knead in the last of the sugar.

Turn out on to a work surface which has been lightly dusted with sifted icing sugar and knead until smooth. Roll out to a thickness of $\frac{1}{4}$ in (5 mm) and cut into rounds or shapes using small cutters. Or use the base of a large piping nozzle or an upturned sherry glass. Place the shapes on greaseproof paper to dry, turning them over once the top side is dry.

If you like, break the chocolate into pieces, and melt in a bowl over a pan of hot water. Dip in the dry peppermint creams to half cover. Allow to set.

Chapter 13

Cakes and Biscuits for Presents

Whether it's a box of simple biscuits or an elaborately iced cake, a food present that you have made yourself is always welcome. For a start it shows that you have spent your valuable time preparing something for that special friend, or indeed maybe a good cause, instead of just money.

With food presents such as cakes and biscuits, you can also give something that you know is particularly liked. In fact, I always make a note of anything that a relative, friend or guest has especially appreciated or praised. For them, to have their tastes remembered virtually doubles the value of the gift.

Food presents are traditional at festivals such as Christmas and Easter. If you are having a festive lunch or dinner with someone, do let the hostess know what you are bringing in advance, be it a jar of brandy butter or your special turkey stuffing; then she can cross that off her lengthy list. And let her know, too, if it is to be a Christmas or Simnel cake – then the household won't be *over*-supplied, and have too much of a good thing as so often happens these days!

However, I also give presents for birthdays or anniversaries, when someone has come out of hospital, or when I go to stay somewhere for a weekend. A special fruit cake, wrapped in cellophane with a large bow, is a wonderful advance 'thank you'. Food presents are ideal for children to give, too; they will have much more of a sense of personal involvement and achievement if they have made it by themselves.

Presentation is important here as well, and wrapping home-made goodies is fun and inexpensive on the whole. Foil is always useful, as is cling film, and for celebratory presents, colourful ribbons will complete the picture. Cellophane boxes, available from many department stores, are ideal for displaying biscuits or cakes. To save money, keep any small boxes and chocolate boxes for this purpose. You can cover them with colourful paper, or paint them. Keep your eyes peeled in junk shops and car-boot sales for unusual decorative jars or baskets which will outlast their contents – a pretty plate spread with delicate chocolates or sweets and covered with cling film, or a chunky jar or collectable old tin for small biscuits. 'Double' the present's value in other ways, too: bake a cake in a new cake tin and make that part of the present; offer very small sweets or biscuits – even cheese straws – in a special wine or brandy glass or a beer mug (cover the top with cling film and tie a ribbon round the stem or handle).

Labelling is important, too, if the recipient needs to know some specific details about storage – such as keeping the cake in the fridge, or eating biscuits within a few days etc. Don't wrap anything, though, until the last minute, as a soggy or stale present is not at all welcome!

Whether large or small – a luscious treacle tart or a little box of *petits fours* – home-made food presents are fun to produce and lovely to receive!

Makes 1 × 2 lb (900 g) Cake

This cake would be a lovely present for someone with a sweet tooth. Remember that it is important to keep it in the fridge as it is very moist, and could go mouldy if left in a tin in a warm kitchen. (See photograph on pages 270–71.)

- ***1 × 8 oz (227 g) can pineapple rings or chunks in fruit juice***
- ***6 oz (175 g) glacé cherries***
- ***5 oz (150 g) soft margarine***
- ***4 oz (100 g) light muscovado sugar***
- ***2 extra large eggs beaten***
- ***7 oz (200 g) self-raising flour***
- ***8 oz (225 g) sultanas***

Pre-heat the oven to 160°C/325°F/Gas 3. Lightly grease and base line a 2 lb (900 g) loaf tin with greased greaseproof paper.

Drain the pineapple, reserving 2 tablespoons of the juice. Dry the pineapple very thoroughly on kitchen paper then chop finely. Quarter the cherries then wash and dry thoroughly.

Measure the margarine, sugar, eggs and flour into a large mixing bowl and beat for about 2 minutes until smooth and well blended. Fold in the sultanas, pineapple and cherries with the reserved pineapple juice. Turn into the prepared loaf tin.

Bake in the pre-heated oven for about $1\frac{1}{4}-1\frac{1}{2}$ hours or until the cake is well risen, golden brown and is shrinking slightly from the sides of the tin. Leave to cool slightly in the tin, then remove the paper and leave to cool completely on a wire rack. Store in an airtight container in the fridge.

Special Fruit Cake

Makes 1 × 6 in (15 cm) Cake

A fruit cake is always a welcome present. Try to plan this one ahead so that you have time to feed it with brandy. *(See photograph on pages 270–71.)*

- *4 oz (100 g) raisins*
- *4 oz (100 g) sultanas*
- *4 oz (100 g) currants*
- *2 oz (50 g) ready-to-eat dried apricots*
- *3 oz (75 g) glacé cherries, quartered*
- *1 oz (25 g) mixed candied peel, chopped*
- *1 tablespoon brandy, rum or sherry*
- *1 oz (25 g) blanched almonds, chopped*
- *grated rind of ½ lemon*
- *6 oz (175 g) plain flour*
- *1 teaspoon mixed spice*
- *1 oz (25 g) ground almonds*
- *4 oz (100 g) dark muscovado sugar*
- *4 oz (100 g) soft margarine*
- *½ tablespoon black treacle*
- *2 eggs*
- *a handful of flaked almonds*
- *brandy, rum or sherry for feeding*

Measure all the dried fruits into a large bowl, add the brandy, rum or sherry, cover the bowl tightly and leave overnight.

Pre-heat the oven to 140°C/275°F/Gas 1. Line the base and sides of a 6 in (15 cm) deep round cake tin with a double layer of greased greaseproof paper.

Measure the almonds, lemon rind, flour, mixed spice, ground almonds, sugar, margarine, treacle and eggs into another large bowl and mix together. Beat thoroughly for about 2–3 minutes until the mixture is smooth. Add the soaked fruit and any liquid to the bowl and stir to mix in thoroughly. Spoon the mixture into the prepared tin, spreading it into the corners. Level the surface and then sprinkle with flaked almonds.

Bake in the pre-heated oven for about 2¼–2½ hours or until a fine skewer inserted into the centre comes out clean. Allow the cake to cool in the tin.

Remove the cake from the tin and pierce the top of the cake in several places with a skewer and spoon in a little brandy, rum or sherry. Replace the bottom lining paper as this helps to keep the cake moist. Wrap in more greaseproof paper and then foil and store in a cool place. Feed at intervals with the alcohol, alternating feeding the top and then the bottom of the cake.

To give as a gift, wrap in cellophane with a generous bow on top.

Tiny Fruit Cakes

Makes 3 × 8 oz (225 g) Cakes

Individual Christmas cakes are particularly welcome for those who live on their own or have small appetites. Baked bean tins are an ideal size, but you can also use muffin rings with a paper collar or small foil pudding containers.

2 oz (50 g) raisins
2 oz (50 g) sultanas
2 oz (50 g) currants
1 oz (25 g) ready-to-eat dried apricots
1½ oz (40 g) glacé cherries, quartered
½ oz (15 g) mixed candied peel, chopped
10 ml (2 tsp) brandy, rum or sherry
½ oz (15 g) blanched almonds, chopped
grated rind of ¼ lemon
3 oz (75 g) plain flour
½ teaspoon mixed spice
½ oz (15 g) ground almonds
2 oz (50 g) dark muscovado sugar
2 oz (50 g) soft margarine
2 teaspoons black treacle
1 egg
1 tablespoon flaked almonds
brandy, rum or sherry for feeding

For the Icing

3 tablespoons apricot jam
8 oz (225 g) almond paste (see page 93)
8 oz (225 g) fondant icing (see page 95)

Measure all the dried fruits into a large bowl, add the brandy, rum or sherry, cover the bowl tightly and leave overnight.

Pre-heat the oven to 160°C/325°F/Gas 3. Remove the labels, wash and thoroughly dry 3 × 8 oz (225 g) baked bean tins. Grease and line the base and sides of the tins with greased greaseproof paper.

Measure the almonds, lemon rind, flour, mixed spice, ground almonds, sugar, margarine, treacle and egg into another large bowl and mix together. Beat thoroughly for about 2 minutes until the mixture is smooth. Add the soaked fruit and any liquid to the bowl and stir to mix in thoroughly. Spoon the mixture into the prepared tins, spreading it evenly. Level the surfaces and then sprinkle with flaked almonds.

Bake in the pre-heated oven for about 1–1¼ hours or until a fine skewer inserted into the centre comes out clean. Allow the cakes to cool in the tins.

Pierce the top of the cakes in several places with a skewer and spoon in a little brandy, rum or sherry. Remove the cakes from the tins but do not remove the lining paper as this helps to keep the cakes moist. Wrap in more greaseproof paper and then foil and store in a cool place for a week.

Sieve the apricot jam and warm it slightly then brush it over the surface of the cake. Cover with almond paste and icing in the usual way. Decorate as liked.

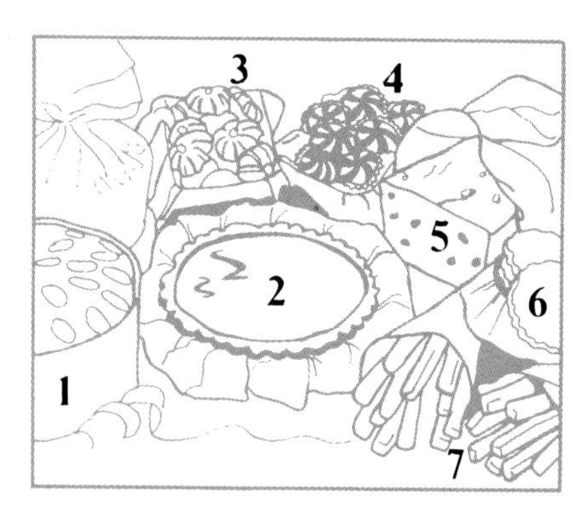

Cakes and Biscuits for Presents

1 *Special Fruit Cake (page 268)*

2 *Deep Treacle Tart (page 278)*

3 *Petits Fours aux Amandes (page 280)*

4 *Chocolate Ganache Petits Fours (page 281)*

5 *Pineapple and Cherry Loaf Cake (page 267)*

6 *Special Shortbread Biscuits (page 272)*

7 *Cheese Straws (page 279)*

Special Shortbread Biscuits

Makes about 30 Biscuits

Buy a pretty tin – a variety are available in shops run by organizations like the National Trust – and fill with a variety of home-made biscuits. Vary the recipe by using caster sugar in place of the light muscovado sugar, if liked. (See photograph on pages 270–71.)

6 oz (175 g) plain flour
3 oz (75 g) light muscovado sugar
4 oz (100 g) butter
demerara sugar for sprinkling

Pre-heat the oven to 160°C/325°F/Gas 3. Lightly grease 2 baking trays.

Measure the flour and sugar into a large bowl and rub in the butter with the fingertips. Knead gently to bring together to form a dough. (Alternatively, process the ingredients in a food processor.)

Roll out the dough on a lightly floured work surface to a thickness of about ¼ in (5 mm). Cut into circles using a 2 in (5 cm) fluted cutter and transfer the biscuits to the prepared baking trays. Prick the biscuits all over with a fork and sprinkle with demerara sugar.

Bake in the pre-heated oven for about 15–20 minutes or until pale golden. Lift on to a wire rack and leave to cool.

Cherry Shortbreads

Makes about 30 Biscuits

Glacé cherries and other fruits can be added to a shortbread dough, but the biscuits don't then keep so long because of the moisture in the fruit. Putting the chopped cherries on top of the biscuits is better, and also looks very attractive.

6 oz (175 g) plain flour
3 oz (75 g) light muscovado sugar
4 oz (100 g) butter
1 oz (25 g) red and/or green glacé cherries, chopped

Pre-heat the oven to 160°C/325°F/Gas 3. Lightly grease 2 baking trays.

Measure the flour and sugar into a large bowl and rub in the butter with the fingertips. Knead gently to bring together to form a dough. (Alternatively, process the ingredients in a food processor.)

Roll out the dough on a lightly floured work surface to a thickness of about $\frac{1}{4}$ in (5 mm). Cut into circles using a 2 in (5 cm) fluted cutter and transfer the biscuits to the prepared baking trays. Prick the biscuits all over with a fork and press the cherries into the top of the biscuits.

Bake in a pre-heated oven for about 15–20 minutes or until pale golden. Lift on to a wire rack and leave to cool.

Walnut Shortbreads

MAKES ABOUT 30 BISCUITS

WALNUTS ARE DELICIOUS IN *this recipe, or you can use hazelnuts or Brazil nuts for a change.*

6 oz (175 g) plain flour

3 oz (75 g) light muscovado sugar

4 oz (100 g) butter

2 oz (50 g) walnuts, roughly chopped

icing sugar for sprinkling

Pre-heat the oven to 160°C/325°F/Gas 3. Lightly grease 2 baking trays.

Measure the flour and sugar into a large bowl and rub in the butter with the fingertips. Mix in the walnuts. Knead gently to bring together to form a dough. (Alternatively, process the ingredients in a food processor.)

Roll out the dough on a lightly floured work surface to a thickness of about $\frac{1}{4}$ in (5 mm). Cut into circles using a 2 in (5 cm) fluted cutter and transfer the biscuits to the prepared baking trays. Prick the biscuits all over with a fork.

Bake in the pre-heated oven for about 15–20 minutes or until pale golden. Lift on to a wire rack and leave to cool then dredge with icing sugar.

Jane's Fruit Cake

Makes 1 × 9 in (23 cm) Cake

This is a good family cake. It goes quite dark when baked because of the wholemeal flour.

7 oz (200 g) soft margarine
12 oz (350 g) light muscovado sugar
3 eggs
1 lb (450 g) wholemeal self-raising flour
5 fl oz (150 ml) buttermilk
12 oz (350 g) sultanas
12 oz (350 g) currants
about 2 oz (50 g) flaked almonds for sprinkling

Pre-heat the oven to 140°C/275°F/Gas 1. Line the base and sides of a 9 in (23 cm) deep round cake tin with a double layer of greased greaseproof paper.

Measure all the cake ingredients, except the flaked almonds, into a large bowl and mix thoroughly. Beat the mixture for 2–3 minutes until smooth and glossy. Spoon into the prepared tin and level the surface. Sprinkle with the flaked almonds.

Bake in the pre-heated oven for about 3–3½ hours or until a skewer inserted into the centre comes out clean. Allow to cool in the tin, then remove from the tin but leave the lining paper on as this helps to keep the cake moist.

To store, wrap the cake in more greaseproof paper and then foil and keep in a cool place.

Jane's Fruit Cake

Sugared Pretzels

Makes about 16 Pretzels

You can make up this pastry in the classic way, or by the quick method as here.

$4\frac{1}{2}$ oz (115 g) plain flour

$2\frac{1}{2}$ oz (65 g) butter

1 oz (25 g) caster sugar

1 egg, beaten

a few drops of vanilla essence

To Finish

icing sugar for dredging

Pre-heat the oven to 200°C/400°F/Gas 6. Lightly grease 2 baking trays.

Measure the flour into a large bowl, add the butter and rub in with the fingertips until the mixture resembles fine breadcrumbs. Stir in the sugar and then the egg and vanilla essence and mix until the pastry comes together. Knead very gently on a lightly floured work surface until smooth, then wrap in cling film and chill for about 30 minutes, or until firm enough to roll.

Divide the dough into pieces about the size of a walnut. Roll each piece into a thin sausage shape and then twist into the traditional pretzel shape, like a loose knot (see *figure 44*). Place on the prepared baking trays.

Bake in the pre-heated oven for about 8 minutes or until barely changing colour. Lift on to a wire rack and dredge thickly with icing sugar while still hot.

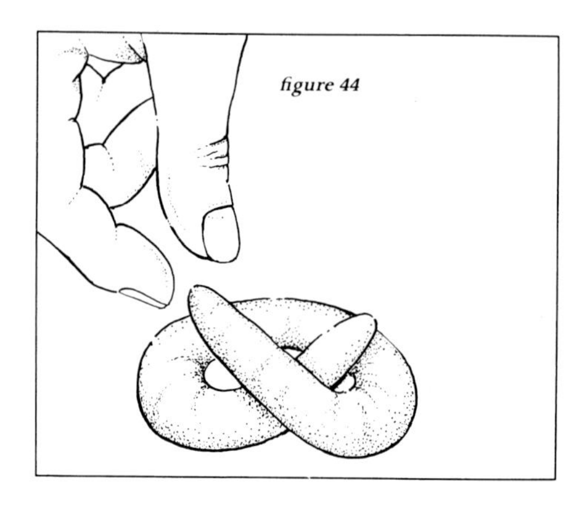

figure 44

MAKES ABOUT 50 BISCUITS

VERY QUICK TO MAKE and deliciously crunchy, these look nice in an attractive glass jar.

- ***4 oz (100 g) margarine***
- ***1 generous tablespoon golden syrup***
- ***12 oz (350 g) self-raising flour***
- ***4 oz (100 g) demerara sugar***
- ***4 oz (100 g) light muscovado sugar***
- ***1 teaspoon bicarbonate of soda***
- ***1 tablespoon ground ginger***
- ***1 egg, beaten***

Pre-heat the oven to 160°C/325°F/Gas 3. Lightly grease 3 baking trays.

Measure the margarine and golden syrup into a small pan and gently heat together until the margarine has melted.

Mix all the dry ingredients together in a large bowl then add the melted margarine mixture and the egg. Mix together thoroughly then roll into balls about the size of a walnut. Place on the prepared baking trays, allowing room for the biscuits to spread.

Bake in the pre-heated oven for about 15–20 minutes or until golden. Lift off the baking trays and leave to cool on a wire rack.

Lime Lattice Cookies

MAKES ABOUT 16 COOKIES

USE THE JUICE OF the limes in drinks, or to add sharpness to whipped cream.

- ***4 oz (100 g) butter, softened***
- ***2 oz (50 g) caster sugar***
- ***5 oz (150 g) self-raising flour***
- ***grated rind of 2 limes***

Pre-heat the oven to 180°C/350°F/Gas 4. Lightly grease 2 baking trays.

Measure the butter and sugar into a bowl and cream together until soft. Add the flour and grated lime rind and bring the mixture together to form a dough.

Roll the mixture into balls the size of a walnut and place on the prepared baking trays. Use a skewer to form a lattice pattern in the top of the biscuits.

Bake in the pre-heated oven for about 10–15 minutes or until just beginning to colour. Lift on to a wire rack and leave to cool.

Deep Treacle Tart

Serves 6

A good present for a man because it is such a masculine favourite; for some reason, all golf clubs seem to serve it for lunch! The lard makes the pastry very short; if you prefer use all butter. (See photograph on pages 270–71.)

For the Pastry

6 oz (175 g) plain flour

1½ oz (40 g) lard

1½ oz (40 g) butter

about 2 tablespoons cold water

For the Filling

12 oz (350 g) golden syrup

about 7 oz (200 g) fresh white or brown breadcrumbs

grated rind and juice of 2 large lemons

First make the pastry. Measure the flour into a large bowl and rub in the fats with the fingertips until the mixture resembles fine breadcrumbs. Add enough water to mix to a firm dough, wrap in cling film and chill for about 30 minutes.

Pre-heat the oven to 200°C/400°F/Gas 6.

Roll the pastry out thinly on a lightly floured work surface and use to line a 6½ in (16.5 cm) base diameter, 2 in (5 cm) deep, fluted, loose-bottomed flan tin.

Heat the syrup in a large pan and stir in the breadcrumbs, lemon rind and juice. If the mixture looks runny, add a few more breadcrumbs (it depends whether you use white or brown bread). Pour the syrup mixture into the pastry case and level the surface.

Bake in the pre-heated oven for 10 minutes then reduce the oven temperature to 180°C/350°F/Gas 4 and bake for a further 25–30 minutes until the pastry is golden and the filling set. Leave to cool in the tin. Serve warm or cold in wedges.

MAKES ABOUT 30 STRAWS

A PERFECT GIFT FOR a gentleman, beautifully presented in a tiny box. They can be made in advance, but do not keep them in the box in the larder; they can quickly go rancid. Freeze them once cold, and in fact they taste good even when freezer-hard! (See photograph on pages 270–71.)

4 oz (100 g) plain flour

3 oz (75 g) butter, at room temperature

2 oz (50 g) mature Cheddar, grated

1 extra large egg yolk

finely grated Parmesan for sprinkling

Lightly grease 2 baking trays.

Measure the flour into a bowl and rub in the butter until the mixture resembles fine breadcrumbs. Stir in the grated Cheddar. Reserve a tiny bit of the egg yolk for glazing and stir in the remainder. Bring the mixture together to form a pastry. Wrap in cling film and chill in the fridge for about 30 minutes.

Pre-heat the oven to 190°C/375°F/Gas 5.

Roll the chilled dough out on a lightly floured work surface to a thickness of about $\frac{1}{4}$ in (5 mm). Cut into neat strips about $\frac{1}{4}$ in (5 mm) wide and about 4 in (10 cm) long. Place on the prepared baking trays, brush with the remaining egg yolk and sprinkle generously with grated Parmesan.

Bake in the pre-heated oven for about 10–15 minutes or until golden. Lift off the baking trays and allow to cool completely on a wire rack.

Pack carefully in a gift box and give as fresh as possible (or freeze as above).

Petits Fours aux Amandes

MAKES ABOUT 24 *PETITS FOURS*

THESE MAKE A VERY special present – petits fours *tend to be rather fiddly to make for oneself! Look out for a pretty or unusual plate in an antique shop or car boot sale, and arrange the* petits fours *on this. Cover with clear cellophane and decorate with a ribbon. The milk and sugar glaze is optional for these* petits fours, *but it does give a nice shine.* *(See photograph on pages 270–71.)*

2 egg whites
4 oz (100 g) ground almonds
3 oz (75 g) caster sugar
a little almond essence

TO DECORATE

glacé cherries and angelica

TO FINISH (OPTIONAL)

1 tablespoon caster sugar
2 tablespoons milk

Pre-heat the oven to 180°C/350°F/Gas 4. Line 2 baking trays with non-stick baking paper.

Whisk the egg whites until stiff. Fold in the ground almonds, sugar and almond essence. Spoon the mixture into a piping bag fitted with a large star nozzle, and pipe the mixture into small rosettes. Decorate each rosette with a small piece of glacé cherry or angelica.

Bake in the pre-heated oven for about 15 minutes or until golden. Lift on to a wire rack.

To finish, mix the caster sugar and milk together and lightly brush over the cooked *petits fours.*

Chocolate Ganache Petits Fours

Makes about 25 *petits fours*

These are irresistible, but keep them in a cool place or they'll become very soft. You could make half plain chocolate ganache and half milk chocolate ganache to fill the chocolate cases, and present a mixture as a gift. *(See photograph on pages 270–71.)*

For the Casing

6 oz (175 g) plain chocolate, broken into pieces

1 teaspoon sunflower oil

For the Chocolate Ganache

5 fl oz (150 ml) double cream

4 oz (100 g) plain or milk chocolate broken into pieces

a little rum or brandy to flavour

To Decorate

shredded pistachio nuts

edible gold leaf

First make the chocolate casings. Melt the chocolate slowly in a bowl with the oil over a pan of hot water. Allow to cool slightly then brush the inside of about 25 *petits fours* cases with a thin layer of chocolate. (You can use a fine brush to do this, or even just the ball of one finger.) Leave to set in a cool place. Give the cases a second coat of chocolate and leave to set in the same way.

For the ganache, place the cream into a small saucepan and bring to the boil. Remove from the heat and add the chocolate pieces and a little rum or brandy. Stir until the chocolate has melted. Return the pan to the heat, bring to the boil and then take off the heat and allow to cool. When firm, spoon the chocolate ganache into a piping bag fitted with a medium star nozzle and pipe rosettes of the ganache into the chocolate cases.

Carefully peel off the *petits fours* cases. Decorate the top of each with a shred of pistachio nut or a touch of gold leaf, and chill until required.

Chapter 14

Healthy Cakes and Biscuits

Firstly, there's absolutely nothing healthy about cakes! But if health equates with a good, well-balanced diet, then why shouldn't we include some cake? I've interpreted healthy here as using less refined flours, and a little less sugar and fat in some of the recipes. I've also included vegetables in some cakes, both sweet *and* savoury, and used many ingredients which add texture, flavour and fibre.

I believe home-made cakes and biscuits are healthier anyway, as you know exactly what has gone into them – there are no oxidants or emulsifiers, no E numbers or additives of any sort. You can still be an enthusiastic cake-maker and be healthy: simply eat less of your own wares and encourage the rest of the family to do the same. One way of achieving this is to freeze cakes in slices, then you can only enjoy a little at a time! (Divide with bits of foil or non-stick baking paper.)

A lot of recipes in the other chapters could be regarded as comparatively healthy as well – scones, for instance, contain very little sugar or fat. To make a 'healthier' Victoria sponge sandwich cake, you could use whole-wheat self-raising flour. You could always slightly alter the ingredients of cakes to make them healthier: use a little more, or different, dried fruits or nuts, for instance; simply brush the top of a cake with warm honey instead of a sugary icing; or fill a cake with a lower-fat cream or yoghurt or a bought low-sugar jam.

If you want to use any of the new low-sugar products in baking, do write to individual manufacturers for their own instructions. Certain makes are formulated differently and you need to find out which products are suitable for baking and which are not. This way you'll avoid any baking accidents and the disappointment of the hungry members of your family or friends!

Date and Cherry Butter Bars

Makes 24 Bars

Use soft margarine if preferred, but I like the buttery flavour! (See photograph on page 287.)

8 oz (225 g) self-raising flour

½ teaspoon baking powder

3 oz (75 g) butter

4 oz (100 g) caster sugar

3 oz (75 g) dates, chopped

1 oz (25 g) glacé cherries, chopped

1 egg, beaten

Pre-heat the oven to 190°C/375°F/Gas 5. Grease a 12 × 9 in (30 × 23 cm) roasting tin.

Measure the flour and baking powder into a bowl and rub in the butter using the fingertips until the mixture resembles fine breadcrumbs. Stir in the sugar, chopped dates and chopped cherries. Add the beaten egg and bring the mixture together to form a dough. Knead lightly until smooth, then press into the prepared tin.

Bake in the pre-heated oven for about 10 minutes then take out of the oven and cut into 24 bars. Return to the oven for about another 10 minutes until beginning to tinge a golden colour. Re-cut into bars and leave to cool in the tin. Ease the bars out of the tin and store in an airtight container.

Oat Rounds

MAKES ABOUT 16 BISCUITS

THESE BISCUITS ARE FIRST cousin to the digestive biscuit, with added oats. They are good with cheese or eaten by themselves with morning coffee. Since I started writing this book, this recipe has become a firm favourite in our house. The biscuits can also be frozen. *(See photograph on page 287.)*

2 oz (50 g) caster sugar
4 oz (100 g) soft margarine
4 oz (100 g) rolled oats
2 oz (50 g) plain flour

Pre-heat the oven to 160°C/325°F/Gas 3. Lightly grease 2 baking trays.

Measure the sugar and margarine into a bowl and cream together. Add the oats and flour and work them into the mixture. Lightly knead the mixture until smooth and then roll out to a thickness of ¼ in (5 mm) on a lightly floured work surface. Cut into rounds using a 2½ in (6 cm) plain cutter and place on the prepared baking trays.

Bake in the pre-heated oven for about 20 minutes or until beginning to colour. Lift on to a wire rack to cool.

Muesli Cookies

Makes about 28 Cookies

The flavour and consistency will depend, as always, on the muesli used. These are good for a lunchbox, for a snack at school or work, or to take on a picnic. *(See photograph on page 287.)*

6 oz (175 g) soft margarine

4 oz (100 g) caster sugar

1 egg

6 oz (175 g) self-raising flour

6 oz (175 g) muesli

demerara sugar for sprinkling

Pre-heat the oven to 180°C/350°F/Gas 4. Lightly grease 3 baking trays.

Measure all the ingredients, except the muesli and the demerara sugar, into a large bowl and mix together until well blended and smooth. Stir in the muesli. Spoon teaspoonfuls of the mixture on to the prepared baking trays, allowing room between each biscuit for expansion. Sprinkle the top of each with a little extra muesli and a little demerara sugar.

Bake in the pre-heated oven for about 10–15 minutes or until golden brown at the edges. Lift on to a wire rack to cool.

Dorchester Biscuits

Makes about 30 Biscuits

These are lovely cheesy, nutty biscuits which are delicious served with drinks. Children like to roll these little balls, and they could give them as a present to an uncle or grandfather. The biscuits freeze well, too. (See photograph opposite.)

4 oz (100 g) mature Cheddar, grated

4 oz (100 g) plain flour

a pinch of salt

4 oz (100 g) butter, softened

$\frac{1}{4}$ teaspoon cayenne pepper

2 oz (50 g) chopped mixed nuts, plus a few more for sprinkling

Pre-heat the oven to 180°C/350°F/Gas 4. Lightly grease 2 baking trays.

Measure all the ingredients, except the nuts for sprinkling, into a bowl and work together with a knife and then your hand to form a dough. Form into balls about the size of a walnut and place on the prepared baking trays. Sprinkle with chopped mixed nuts and then just lightly flatten the balls with your hand.

Bake in the pre-heated oven for about 15–20 minutes or until golden brown. Lift on to a wire rack to cool. Serve warm or cold.

Secrets of Success

For the topping, instead of the chopped nuts, you could use whole or half cashew nuts or similar.

Healthy Cakes and Biscuits

1 Date and Cherry Butter Bars (page 283)

2 Muesli Cookies (page 285)

3 Dorchester Biscuits (above)

4 Oat Rounds (page 284)

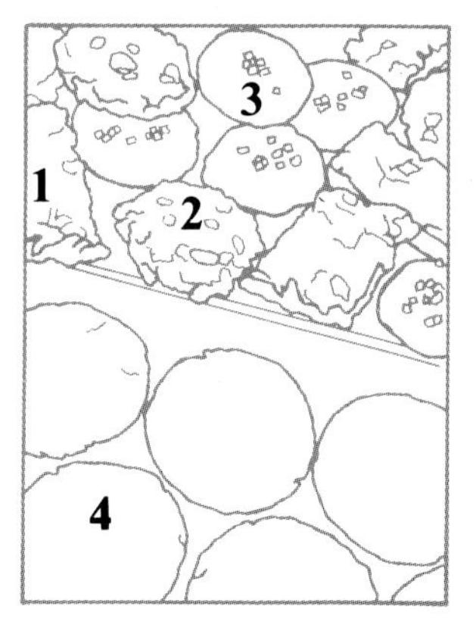

Sultana Streusel Buns

Makes about 18 Buns

These are fairly plain buns which are best eaten when freshly baked.

8 oz (225 g) self-raising flour
1 teaspoon baking powder
3 oz (75 g) butter
3 oz (75 g) caster sugar
2 oz (50 g) sultanas
1 egg
5 fl oz (150 ml) milk

For the Streusel Topping

1 oz (25 g) self-raising flour
2 oz (50 g) light muscovado sugar
1 oz (25 g) butter, melted

To Finish

icing sugar

Pre-heat the oven to 190°C/375°F/Gas 5. Place about 18 paper cake cases in bun tins.

Measure the flour and baking power into a large bowl. Add the butter and rub into the flour until the mixture resembles fine breadcrumbs. Stir in the sugar and sultanas. Lightly mix the egg and milk and add all at once to the dry mixture. Beat well to give a smooth mixture. Spoon into the bun cases.

For the streusel topping, mix together the flour and sugar and add the melted butter. Use a fork to mix until crumbly. Sprinkle this mixture over the tops of the cakes.

Bake in the pre-heated oven for about 15 minutes until well risen and firm to the touch. Lift the paper cake cases out of the bun tins and leave to cool on a wire rack. Dust with sifted icing sugar to serve.

Apricot and Walnut Sandwich Bars

Makes 8 Bars

These bars are very moist, so are not the easiest to handle. They are similar to those you can buy in health-food shops and are quite substantial for a healthy lunchbox.

For the Oat Mixture

2 oz (50 g) rolled oats

2 oz (50 g) light muscovado sugar

1½ oz (40 g) walnuts, chopped

7 oz (200 g) wholemeal self-raising flour

6 oz (175 g) margarine, melted

For the Filling

6 oz (175 g) ready-to-eat dried apricots, snipped into pieces

2 fl oz (50 ml) water

2 tablespoons caster sugar

grated rind of 1 lemon

Pre-heat the oven to 150°C/300°F/Gas 2. Grease and base line a 7 in (18 cm) shallow square tin with greased greaseproof paper.

First prepare the filling. Place the snipped apricots in a small pan with the water, caster sugar and lemon rind. Bring to the boil and then simmer very gently until the apricots are really soft and the liquid has evaporated. Leave to cool.

While the apricot filling is cooling, make the oat mixture. Measure the oats, sugar, walnuts and flour into a bowl and add the melted margarine. Stir to mix. Divide the oat mixture in half and spread one half into the base of the prepared tin. Spoon the cooled apricot mixture on top and carefully spread it to form an even layer. Cover evenly with the remaining oat mixture.

Bake in the pre-heated oven for about 45 minutes or until firm and a golden brown. Cut into bars while still warm.

Wholewheat Sultana and Apricot Rock Cakes

MAKES 12 CAKES

WHOLEWHEAT FLOURS VARY A little in the amount of liquid they absorb, so be prepared to add a little more milk if necessary. Wholewheat rock cakes tend to be a little drier than normal ones, and they are best eaten on the day of making.

4 oz (100 g) white self-raising flour

4 oz (100 g) wholemeal self-raising flour

2 teaspoons baking powder

4 oz (100 g) soft margarine

2 oz (50 g) light muscovado sugar

2 oz (50 g) sultanas

2 oz (50 g) ready-to-eat dried apricots, snipped into small pieces

1 egg

about 2 tablespoons milk

a little demerara sugar for sprinkling

Pre-heat the oven to 200°C/400°F/Gas 6. Lightly grease 2 baking trays.

Measure the flours and baking powder into a large bowl, add the margarine and rub into the flour with the fingertips until the mixture resembles fine breadcrumbs. Stir in the sugar, sultanas and snipped apricots. Beat the egg and milk together, add and mix to a stiff mixture. If too dry add a little more milk.

Using 2 teaspoons, shape the mixture into about 12 rough mounds on the baking trays and sprinkle each mound generously with demerara sugar.

Bake in the pre-heated oven for about 15 minutes until beginning to tinge with brown at the edges. Cool on a wire rack.

Wholewheat Sultana and Apricot Rock Cakes

Carrot Cake

Makes 1 × 8 in (20 cm) Cake

This really is a good recipe. At a recent charity event this is the cake which sold most quickly. I'm afraid, though, that it sounds rather more healthy than it is! (See photograph on page 294.)

8 oz (225 g) self-raising flour
2 teaspoons baking powder
5 oz (150 g) light muscovado sugar
2 oz (50 g) walnuts, chopped
4 oz (100 g) carrots, grated
2 ripe bananas, mashed
2 eggs
5 fl oz (150 ml) sunflower oil

For the Topping

6 oz (175 g) full-fat soft cheese
2 oz (50 g) soft margarine
4 oz (100 g) icing sugar, sifted
a few drops of vanilla essence
walnut halves to decorate

Pre-heat the oven to 180°C/350°F/Gas 4. Grease and base line an 8 in (20 cm) deep round cake tin with greased greaseproof paper.

Measure all the ingredients for the cake into a large bowl and mix well until thoroughly blended and smooth. Turn into the prepared tin and level the surface.

Bake in the pre-heated oven for about 50–60 minutes until the cake is well risen and shrinking away from the sides of the tin. Allow to cool in the tin for a few minutes before turning out and leaving to cool completely on a wire rack.

For the topping, measure all the ingredients, except the walnuts, into a bowl, or into a food processor, and mix well until smooth. Spread over the top of the cake, swirling the top with a spatula for a decorative effect. Decorate the top with the walnut halves. Chill a little before serving, and store in the fridge as the topping is soft.

Courgette Loaf

MAKES 2 × 2 LB (900 G) LOAVES

EXPECT THIS CAKE TO have a sugary top, which is quite normal. This recipe makes two loaves. Freeze one and store the second one in the fridge. Serve sliced and buttered, or spread with low-fat soft cheese. (See photograph on page 295.)

3 eggs

9 fl oz (275 ml) sunflower oil

12 oz (350 g) caster sugar

12 oz (350 g) courgettes (or small marrow), grated

5½ oz (165 g) plain flour

5½ oz (165 g) buckwheat flour

1 teaspoon baking powder

2 teaspoons bicarbonate of soda

1 tablespoon ground cinnamon

6 oz (175 g) raisins

5 oz (150 g) walnuts, chopped

Pre-heat the oven to 180°C/350°F/Gas 4. Grease and base line two 2 lb (900 g) loaf tins with greased greaseproof paper.

Measure all the ingredients into a large bowl and mix well to make a thick batter. Pour into the prepared tins.

Bake in the pre-heated oven for about 1 hour or until the loaves are firm and a fine skewer inserted into the centre comes out clean. Cool the cakes a little before turning out and leaving to cool completely on a wire rack. Store in the fridge and use within 3 weeks.

Carrot Cake (page 292)

(page 292)

Courgette Loaf (page 293)

Lemon Yoghurt Cake

MAKES 1 × 8 IN (20 CM) CAKE

ALTHOUGH IT DOESN'T look spectacular, this is a lovely moist cake. Keep in the fridge and eat within a week.

11 oz (300 g) caster sugar
2 oz (50 g) butter, softened
3 eggs, separated
8 oz (225 g) Greek yoghurt
grated rind of 1 lemon
6 oz (175 g) self-raising flour

FOR THE ICING

4 oz (100 g) icing sugar, sifted
about 1½ tablespoons lemon juice

Pre-heat the oven to 180°C/350°F/Gas 4. Grease and base line an 8 in (20 cm) deep round cake tin with greased greaseproof paper.

Mix the sugar, butter and egg yolks in a bowl. Add the yoghurt and lemon rind and stir until smooth. Gently fold in the flour. Whisk the egg whites to a soft peak and carefully fold into the mixture. Turn into the prepared tin.

Bake in the pre-heated oven for 1–1¼ hours or until the cake is well risen and firm to the touch. Allow to cool in the tin for a few minutes before turning out and leaving to cool completely on a wire rack.

For the icing, mix together the sifted icing sugar and the lemon juice and pour over the cold cake. Smooth over with a palette knife and leave to set.

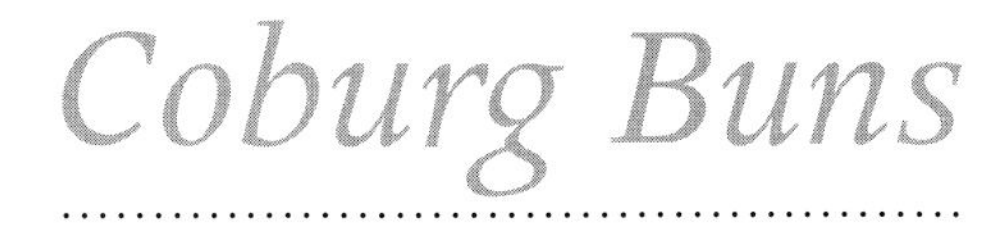

Coburg Buns

Makes about 12 Buns

These 'upside-down' buns should be eaten very fresh, on the day of making. You really need a fluted or fancy bun tray to give them their pretty shape, but you can make them plain if you like. *(See photograph on pages 6–7.)*

about 2 oz (50 g) flaked almonds

5 oz (150 g) self-raising flour

1 teaspoon baking powder

½ teaspoon mixed spice

½ teaspoon ground ginger

½ teaspoon ground cinnamon

2 oz (50 g) soft margarine

2 oz (50 g) caster sugar

1 egg

1 tablespoon golden syrup

4 tablespoons milk

Pre-heat the oven to 180°C/350°F/Gas 4. Lightly grease a tray of 12 fluted bun tins.

Place a few flaked almonds in the base of each bun tin. Measure the flour, baking powder and spices into a large bowl and then add the remaining ingredients. Beat for about 2 minutes until the mixture is well blended and smooth.

Divide the mixture between the tins and bake in the pre-heated oven for about 15 minutes, until well risen, golden and firm to the touch. Allow to cool in the tins for a few minutes then lift out, turn upside-down and leave to cool completely on a wire rack.

Questions and Answers

Q ***WHY DO CAKES SINK?***

A Too much baking powder.
Oven door opened too soon.
Under baking.

Q ***WHY DO CAKES BURN ON THE TOP, WITHOUT COOKING IN THE MIDDLE?***

A Oven too hot, or in oven too long.

Q ***WHY DO CAKES CRACK WHEN BAKING?***

A Oven too hot or cake placed too high in oven; the crust is formed too soon, the cake continues to rise, therefore the crust cracks.

Q ***HOW DO YOU TELL IF A CAKE IS COOKED?***

A *Sponge cake* – springy to the touch, shrinking slightly from the sides of the tin. Pale golden brown in colour.
Fruit cake – fine skewer inserted into the centre should come out clean and the cake should look the expected colour, light brown for a light fruit cake, darker brown for a traditional rich fruit cake.

Q ***WHY DO SOME BAKED CAKES HAVE A SPECKLY TOP?***

A Granulated sugar used instead of caster sugar.
Mixture not mixed sufficiently, sugar therefore not dissolved.

Q ***WHY DO MY CAKES ALWAYS SEEM TOO DRY?***

A Too much baking powder.
In oven for too long.
Not packed as soon as cool.

Q ***WHY DO MERINGUES WEEP ON BAKING?***

A Sugar added too quickly or too much sugar added at once.

Q ***WHY DO MERINGUES STICK TO THE PAPER?***

A Oven too hot.
Whites not whisked sufficiently.
Oiled greaseproof paper used, which is not so effective as non-stick baking paper or 'magic paper' (see *page 21*).

Q ***HOW DO YOU AVOID GETTING A CAKE RACK MARK ON TOP OF CAKES?***

A Cover the cake rack with a clean tea towel or cloth before inverting the cake on to the rack.

Q ***WHY DOES FRUIT SINK TO THE BOTTOM OF THE CAKE?***

A Cake mixture too slack.
Fruit too large and/or syrupy e.g. glacé cherries (see next question).

Q ***WHY DO CHERRIES SINK TO THE BOTTOM?***

A They contain a lot of moisture and syrup.
Need to quarter, wash and dry thoroughly before adding to the cake mixture. Addition of ground almonds to the cake mixture helps as well.

Q ***WHY DO CAKES NOT RISE?***

A No or insufficient raising agent.
Mixture too stiff.
Mixture overbeaten and air knocked out, or insufficient whisking (whisked sponge).
Too cool an oven.

Q ***HOW DO YOU PREVENT A CAKE FROM STICKING TO THE TIN ONCE BAKED?***

A Line tin properly (see *pages 26–7*).
Make sure cake is cooked through before removing from oven.
Measure ingredients carefully.
Mix thoroughly.

Q ***WHY ARE THERE WHITE LUMPS OF FLOUR IN A WHISKED SPONGE MIXTURE?***

A Eggs and sugar whisked until too thick, therefore difficult to fold in flour.
Flour not folded in adequately – flour must be sieved before it is folded into the mixture.

Q ***WHY DOES GELATINE GO LUMPY WHEN ADDED TO MIXTURE?***

A Gelatine not dissolved properly.
Hot gelatine added to a very cold mixture – see *page 110* for best method.

Q ***WHY DO MY FROZEN CAKES ALWAYS SEEM TO BE DRY?***

A Inadequate wrapping or packing.
Not frozen as soon as cool.

Q ***WHY DO BISCUITS GO SOGGY ON STORING?***

A Not cold before storing in tin.
Stored in same tin as cake – the biscuits absorb moisture from the cake.
Stored in a moist environment.
If biscuits contain glacé cherries, apricots etc., the moisture from these seeps into the biscuit.

Q ***ICING RUNNING OFF TOP OF CAKE?***

A Too much liquid – much better to have icing too thick, then it can be let down with more liquid very carefully and slowly.

Q ***ICING TOO THICK?***

A Let down with a little water.
Warm through, e.g. chocolate fudge icing.

Q ***CRUMBS IN THE ICING?***

A Brush the cake with warmed apricot jam first to seal.

American Chocolate Wedding Cake

THE AMERICAN CHOCOLATE WEDDING CAKE recipe (page 100) serves about 100 people. If you want a practice run you can use the separate quantities below to make the layers of the cake individually.

MAKES 1 × 6 IN (15 CM) CAKE

3 eggs, separated
1 whole egg
5 oz (150 g) caster sugar
6 oz (175 g) good quality plain chocolate, broken into pieces and melted
3 oz (75 g) ground almonds
½ teaspoon black coffee
2 tablespoons apricot jam, sieved

FOR THE ICING

8 oz (225 g) plain chocolate, broken into pieces
3 oz (75 g) unsalted butter

Bake for about 45 minutes.

MAKES 1 × 9 IN (23 CM) CAKE

10 eggs, separated
2 whole eggs
15 oz (425 g) caster sugar
1 lb 3 oz (525 g) good quality plain chocolate, broken into pieces and melted
10 oz (275 g) ground almonds
2½ teaspoons black coffee
3 oz (75 g) apricot jam, sieved

FOR THE ICING

12 oz (350 g) plain chocolate, broken into pieces
5 oz (150 g) unsalted butter

Bake for about 1 hour.

MAKES 1 × 12 IN (30 CM) CAKE

17 eggs, separated
5 whole eggs
1 lb 9 oz (700 g) caster sugar
2 lb (900 g) good quality plain chocolate, broken into pieces and melted
1 lb 1 oz (475 g) ground almonds
4½ teaspoons black coffee
4 oz (100 g) apricot jam, sieved

FOR THE ICING

1¼ lb (550 g) plain chocolate, broken into pieces
8 oz (225 g) unsalted butter

Bake for about 1½ hours.
(Cover loosely after 1 hour.)

Index

Page numbers in *italic* refer to the illustrations

Specialist Suppliers

Most equipment for making cakes can be bought from ordinary hardware stores or cake shops. However, if you do have a problem getting equipment, the companies below have very good catalogues and everything, from almond paste to cake tins, can be obtained by mail order.

SQUIRES KITCHEN SUGARCRAFT
Squires House
3A Waverley Lane
Farnham
Surrey GU9 8BB
Tel: 01252 711749

DAVID MELLOR
4 Sloane Square
London SW1W 8EE
Tel: 020 7730 4259

DIVERTIMENTI
45–47 Wigmore Street
London W1U 1PS
Tel: 020 7935 0689

LAKELAND LTD
Alexandra Buildings
Windermere
Cumbria LA23 1BQ
Tel: 015394 88100

NISBETS
1110 Aztec West
Bristol BS32 4HR
Tel: 01454 855655

NKS
Dogcraig House
Peebles
Scotland EH45 9HS
Tel: 0172 172 9824